Pock **~~et Rough Guide~~**

BARCELONA

written and researched by
JULES BROWN

Contents

<< CAMP NOU FOOTBALL STADIUM
< FONT MÀGICA

INTRODUCTION TO

Barcelona

It's tempting to say that there's nowhere quite like Barcelona – there's certainly not another city in Spain to touch it for sheer style, looks or energy. The glossy mags and travel press dwell enthusiastically on its outrageous architecture, designer shopping, cool bars and vibrant cultural scene, but Barcelona is more than just this year's fad. It's a confident, progressive city, one that is tirelessly self-renewing while preserving all that's best about its past. As old neighbourhoods bloom, and landmark museums and sights are restored with panache, there's still an enduring embrace of the good things in life, from the daily market to the late-night café.

ON THE BEACH

Best places for a Barcelona picnic

Parc de la Ciutadella is the city centre's favourite green space, while the gardens of Montjuïc offer some fantastic views. Any time the sun shines, the beach between Barceloneta and Port Olímpic makes for a great alfresco lunch, though for a real in-the-know experience stock up at the market and head for the Collserola hills.

The province of Catalunya (Catalonia in English), of which Barcelona is the capital, has a historical identity going back as far as the ninth century, and through the long period of domination by outside powers, as well as during the Franco dictatorship, it proved impossible to stifle the Catalan spirit. The city reflects this independence, being at the forefront of Spanish political activism, radical design and architecture, and commercial dynamism.

This is seen most perfectly in the glorious *modernista* (Art Nouveau) buildings that stud the city's streets and avenues. Antoni Gaudí is the most famous of those who have left their mark on Barcelona in this way: his Sagrada Família church is rightly revered, but just as fascinating are the (literally) fantastic houses, public buildings and parks that he and his contemporaries designed.

The city also boasts an extensive medieval Old Town – full of pivotal buildings from an earlier age of expansion – and a stupendous artistic legacy, from national (ie, Catalan) collections of Romanesque, Gothic and contemporary art to major galleries containing the life's work of the Catalan artists Joan Miró and Antoni Tàpies (not to mention a celebrated showcase of the work of Pablo Picasso).

Barcelona is equally proud of its cutting-edge restaurants – featuring some of the best chefs in Europe – its late-night bars, even its football team, the mercurial, incomparable FC Barcelona. Add a spruced-up waterfront, five kilometres of resort-standard sandy beach, and Olympic-rated sports and leisure facilities, and you have a city that entertains and cossets locals and visitors alike.

Despite its size, Spain's second city is a surprisingly easy place to find your way around. In effect, it's a series of self-contained neighbourhoods stretching out from the harbour, flanked by parks, hills and woodland. Much of what there is to see in the centre – Gothic cathedral, Picasso museum,

CARVED DOOR AT CASA BATLLÓ

markets, Gaudí buildings and art galleries – can be reached on foot, while a fast, cheap, integrated public transport system takes you directly to the peripheral attractions and suburbs. Meanwhile, bike tours, sightseeing buses and cruise boats all offer a different way of seeing the city.

True, for all its go-ahead feel, Barcelona has its problems, not least a petty crime rate that occasionally makes the international news. But there's no need to be unduly paranoid, and it would be a shame to stick solely to the main tourist sights since you'll miss so much. Tapas bars hidden down decrepit alleys, designer boutiques in gentrified Old Town quarters, street opera singers belting out an aria, bargain lunches in workers' taverns, neighbourhood funicular rides, unmarked gourmet restaurants, craft workshops, restored medieval palaces and specialist galleries – all are just as much Barcelona as the Ramblas or Gaudí's Sagrada Família.

When to visit

Barcelona is an established city-break destination with a year-round tourist, business and convention trade. Different seasons have different attractions, from spring dance festivals to Christmas markets, but there's always something going on. As far as the weather is concerned, the best times to go are spring and autumn, when the temperatures are comfortably warm and walking the streets isn't a chore. In summer, the city can be very hot and humid while August sees many shops, bars and restaurants close as the locals head out of the city in droves. It's worth considering a winter break, as long as you don't mind the prospect of occasional rain. It's generally still warm enough to sit out at a café, for example, even in December or January.

BARCELONA AT A GLANCE

>>EATING

In the popular Old Town areas food and service can be indifferent and expensive. There are some great bars and restaurants in tourist-heavy **La Ribera** and the **Barri Gòtic**, but you really need to explore the up-and-coming neighbourhoods of **Sant Pere**, **El Raval** and **Poble Sec** for the best local finds, from traditional taverns to chic contemporary tapas bars. Michelin stars and big bills are mostly found in the **Eixample**, while for the best fish and seafood head for harbourside **Barceloneta** or the **Port Olímpic**. The suburb of **Gràcia** is also a nice, village-like place to spend the evening, with plenty of good mid-range restaurants.

>>DRINKING

It should probably be called Bar-Celona – whatever you're looking for, you'll find it here, from bohemian boozer to cocktail bar. **Passeig del Born** (La Ribera) is one of the hottest destinations, with Sant Pere close on its heels, while there's an edgier scene in **El Raval** and around **Carrer de Blai** (Poble Sec). The main concentration of designer bars (as well as the city's gay scene) is in the **Esquerra de l'Eixample**, while the theme bars of **Port Olímpic** are mainstream summer-night playgrounds for locals and visitors. Bars usually stay open till any time between 11pm and 2 or 3am.

>>SHOPPING

Designer and high-street fashion can be found in the Eixample along **Passeig de Gràcia** and **Rambla de Catalunya**, though for new names and boutiques the best hunting ground is in the Old Town streets around **Passeig del Born** (La Ribera). Secondhand and vintage clothing stores line **c/de la Riera Baixa** (El Raval), there's music and streetwear along nearby **c/dels Tallers**, and for antiques and curios it's best in the streets near **c/Banys Nous** (Barri Gòtic). The markets, meanwhile, are king, from the heavyweight **Boqueria** to lesser-known gems like the **Mercat Santa Caterina** in trendy Sant Pere or Gràcia's **Mercat de la Llibertat**.

>>NIGHTLIFE

Clubs in Barcelona start late and go on until 5 or 6am, and while Thursday to Sunday sees the most action, there are **DJs** on the decks every night. The big name venues tend to be found out in the old industrial zones like **Poble Nou**; downtown music clubs are often jazz-orientated, though local rock, pop, indie and even flamenco get regular airings in venues across the **Barri Gòtic** and **El Raval**. For typically Catalan surroundings, a concert at Sant Pere's **Palau de la Música Catalana** can't be beaten, while the principal venue up in the Eixample is the contemporary city concert hall, **L'Auditori**.

OUR RECOMMENDATIONS ON WHERE TO EAT, DRINK AND SHOP ARE LISTED AT THE END OF EACH PLACES CHAPTER.

Day One in Barcelona

1 The Ramblas > p.34. Everyone starts with a stroll down Barcelona's most emblematic street.

2 Mercat de la Boqueria > p.36. Wander through the stalls of one of Europe's best markets and soak up the vibrant atmosphere.

3 La Seu > p.42. The calm cloister of Barcelona's cathedral is a haven amid the bustle of the Gothic Quarter.

4 Museu d'Història de Barcelona > p.46. This place holds the archeological history of Roman Barcelona – right under your feet.

🍴 **Lunch** > p.53. Stop near the church of Santa María del Pi for alfresco drinks and a market-fresh meal at *Taller de Tapas*.

5 Museu Picasso > p.78. Walk through the tight-knit medieval streets of La Ribera to the must-see museum, housed in the city where Picasso developed his inimitable style.

6 Parc de la Ciutadella > p.86. Take time out in the museums, palm-houses and gardens of the city's favourite park.

7 Port Olímpic > p.100. The beach, boardwalk and seafront promenade set the scene for a sundowner drink.

🍴 **Dinner** > p.70. Some of the city's coolest places to eat and drink are in El Raval; try the creative cuisine at stylish *Biblioteca*'s open kitchen.

Day Two in Barcelona

1 Sagrada Família > p.114. To avoid the worst of the bustling crowds, arrive at Gaudí's masterpiece at opening time.

2 Passeig de Gràcia > p.104. Europe's most extraordinary urban architecture decorates the modern city's main avenue.

3 Palau Montaner > p.108. Don't miss the weekend guided tours of this unique private *modernista* mansion.

4 Vinçon > p.110. Design, style and shopping opportunities, all under one roof.

Lunch > p.113. There's fabulous food at *TapaÇ24*, a classy uptown bar-diner.

5 Museu Nacional d'Art de Catalunya > p.93. The triumphant landscaped approach to Montjuïc culminates in the extraordinary Catalan National Art Gallery.

6 Fundació Joan Miró > p.96. The modernist building on the hill houses the life's work of Catalan artist Joan Miró.

7 Ride the Trasbordador Aeri > p.59. A thrilling cable car sweeps you across the inner harbour from Montjuïc to Port Vell.

8 Barceloneta > p.58. For marina or beach views, grab a table at an outdoor café in the old fishermen's quarter.

Dinner > p.84. After cold beer and tapas in up-and-coming Sant Pere, dine in Catalan style at La Ribera's *Senyor Parellada*.

Modernista Barcelona

Visionary *modernista* architects, like Antoni Gaudí, changed the way people looked at buildings. Their style, a sort of Catalan Art Nouveau, left Barcelona with an extraordinary architectural legacy that goes far beyond the famous sights of the Sagrada Família church and Parc Güell.

1 Hospital de la Santa Creu i de Sant Pau > p.115. Don't miss Lluís Domènech i Montaner's innovative public hospital, near the Sagrada Família.

2 La Pedrera > p.109. Inventive design permeates every aspect of Gaudí's fantastical "stone quarry" apartment building.

3 Casa Amatller > p.106. Catch a guided tour of this stunning house belonging to a nineteenth-century chocolate manufacturer.

Lunch > p.112. Take a lunch stop at *Casa Calvet*, an early Gaudí townhouse, now a classy Catalan restaurant.

4 Palau de la Música Catalana > p.74. Book in advance for a tour of this dramatic concert hall, or buy a ticket for an evening performance.

5 Arc de Triomf > p.86. Gateway to the Ciutadella park is this giant red-brick arch.

6 Museu de Zoologia > p.87. The park's eye-catching "castle" is a *modernista* showcase for the city's natural science museum.

Dinner > p.132. In summer, Parc Güell is open until well into the evening – and the bars and restaurants of fashionable Gràcia are close at hand.

Budget Barcelona

Barcelona may be one of Europe's most fashionable cities, but it remains remarkably good value as far as most visitors are concerned. You certainly don't need to spend a fortune to eat well, see the major sights and enjoy yourself.

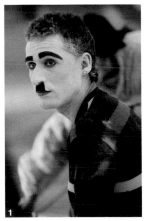

1 The Ramblas > p.34. Barcelona's greatest show – a stroll down the Ramblas – is a free spectacle around the clock.

2 MNAC > p.93. The ticket for the showpiece National Art Gallery is valid for two full days, and there's free entry on the first Sunday of every month.

Lunch > p.52. Virtually every restaurant offers a weekday *menú del día*, so lunch is a bargain at places like *Café de l'Acadèmia* where dinner might cost three times as much.

3 Relax at the beach > p.101. Enjoy five miles of sand, boardwalks and promenades.

4 Parc Güell > p.130. There's no charge to visit Gaudí's extraordinarily fanciful city park.

5 Caixa Forum > p.91. Dazzling arts and cultural centre with excellent free exhibitions.

6 Palau Reial > p.140. Three museums on one ticket – the city's fabulous applied art collections.

Dinner > p.77. Many of Barcelona's markets also have stylish restaurants attached – like *Cuines Santa Caterina* in Sant Pere's dramatic Mercat Santa Caterina.

Big sights

1 La Seu Pride of the Gothic era, the city's majestic medieval cathedral anchors the Old Town. > **p.42**

3 Sagrada Família The most famous unfinished church in the world — the "Sacred Family" temple is the essential visit for Gaudí fans. > **p.114**

2 Parc Güell A public park without compare, where contorted stone pavilions, gingerbread buildings and surreal ceramics combine unforgettably. > **p.130**

4 Museu Nacional d'Art de Catalunya (MNAC) The National Museum of Art celebrates the glories of a thousand years of Catalan painting and sculpture. > **p.93**

5 The Ramblas The city's iconic central thoroughfare, where buskers, hawkers, stall-holders, eccentrics and tourists collide to gleeful effect. > **p.34**

Shopping

1 Mercat de la Boqueria The city's finest food market is a show in its own right, busy with locals and tourists from dawn to dusk. > **p.36**

2 Jamonísimo Food fetishists make a beeline for the best hams and cured meats in Barcelona. > **p.124**

3 Vinçon The most eminent showcase in town for Catalan household style, design and furnishings. > **p.110**

4 Custo Barcelona Barcelona's brightest designer brand injects colour and fun into shop windows across the city. > **p.82**

5 L'Arca del Avia Vintage heaven in the Gothic Quarter. > **p.50**

Restaurants

1 Biblioteca Creative, market-led Catalan cuisine is on the menu at fashionable *Biblioteca*. > **p.70**

2 Flash, Flash A fun retro Gràcia landmark that specializes in tortillas of all tastes, savoury to sweet. > **p.132**

4 Gaig For Michelin-starred dining, Barcelona style, *Gaig* leads the pack. > **p.125**

3 La Tomaquera Food cooked on the chargrill (*a la brasa*) is the speciality at this bustling tavern. > **p.98**

5 Senyor Parellada To eat home-style food with the locals, make time for this ravishingly handsome Old Town restaurant. > **p.84**

Museums

1 Museu Marítim Engaging maritime museum, housed in the great medieval shipyards that underpinned Barcelona's early prosperity. > **p.56**

3 Museu Frederic Marès Don't miss the museum dedicated to the "mad collector" to beat them all. > **p.43**

2 Museu Egipci Break off from your uptown shopping to view this select showing of fascinating Egyptian antiquities. > **p.107**

4 CosmoCaixa A science museum complete with its own rainforest. > **p.147**

5 Camp Nou and FC Barcelona Tour one of Europe's most magnificent stadiums, home to the local football heroes. > **p.137**

Art galleries

1 Fundació Joan Miró There's no more beautiful gallery in the city than the house on the hill presenting the life's work of Joan Miró. > **p.96**

2 Caixa Forum There's always an exhibition worth seeing in the city's best arts and cultural centre — not to mention concerts, films and other events. > **p.91**

3 Fundació Antoni Tàpies Acquaint yourself with the work of the master Catalan abstract artist, contained within a striking Eixample mansion. > **p.107**

4 Museu d'Art Contemporani de Barcelona (MACBA) Post-war contemporary art (Spanish, Catalan and international) has a home in a stunning building in El Raval. > **p.62**

5 Museu Picasso The city's most visited art collection traces Picasso's career in its entirety. > **p.78**

Tapas bars

1 El Xampanayet Long the stop in La Ribera for a glass of Catalan fizz and a bite or two before dinner. > **p.85**

2 **Bodega La Plata** Stand-up snacks and wine from the barrel are the staples at this famous Old Town bar. > **p.52**

3 **Ginger** Retro style meets contemporary tapas at 1970s-influenced *Ginger*. > **p.52**

5 **Bar Pinotxo** The best tapas bar in the best market — the Boqueria's *Pinotxo*, no contest. > **p.41**

4 **Inopia** Join the cool crowd at one of Barcelona's most stylish tapas bars. > **p.98**

Bars and clubs

1 Club Catwalk The swish dancing-and-dining Port Olímpic club is the favoured hangout for local celebs and ritzy visitors alike. > **p.103**

3 Almirall In a city where even the bars are works of art, Almirall sports a dramatic *modernista* flourish. > **p.72**

2 Moog The city's techno club of choice for aficionados, open from midnight for nonstop dancing. > **p.73**

4 Resolis Resolis is the signature boho bar in the thriving El Raval neighbourhood. > **p.72**

5 Milk Mixology at its finest in the Barri Gòtic's most welcoming bar and bistro. > **p.54**

Music, dance and theatre

1 Sidecar This rootsy Plaça Reial rock club presents a varied roster of gigs and club nights, with indie and global sounds to the fore. > **p.55**

2 Palau de la Música Catalana
The city's finest concert hall, a
modernista classic encased in a
contemporary shell. > **p.74**

3 Tarantos The best place for
flamenco sessions — the after-show
dancing carries on into the small
hours. > **p.55**

5 Gran Teatre del Liceu Book
ahead for opera tickets at this
renowned city landmark, though the
guided tours are open to all. > **p.38**

4 Café Teatre Llantiol It's mime,
magic and much, much more at
Barcelona's long-established cabaret
venue. > **p.73**

Outdoor
Barcelona

1 Parc Zoològic Barcelona's zoo packs the world's fauna into the rolling grounds of the Ciutadella park. > **p.89**

2 City beaches The great urban escape is to the city's 5km of sand-fringed ocean, dotted with parks and playgrounds. > **p.101**

3 Jardi Botànic de Barcelona The impressive botanical gardens spread across a hillside above the Olympic Stadium. > **p.97**

4 Parc de la Ciutadella Whatever the season, the city's nicest park always springs a surprise. > **p.86**

5 Port Olímpic Twin towers and the landmark Frank Gehry fish dominate Barcelona's liveliest resort area. > **p.100**

Along the Ramblas

No day in the city seems complete without a stroll along the Ramblas, Spain's most famous thoroughfare. Cutting through Barcelona's Old Town areas, and connecting Plaça de Catalunya with the harbour, it's at the heart of the city's self-image – lined with cafés, restaurants, souvenir shops, flower stalls and newspaper kiosks. The name (from the Arabic *ramla* or "sand") refers to a seasonal stream bed that was paved over in medieval times. Since the nineteenth century it's been a fashionable promenade, and today the show goes on, day or night, as human statues, portrait painters, buskers and card sharps add to the vibrancy of Barcelona's most enthralling street. There are metro stops at Catalunya (top of the Ramblas), Liceu (middle) and Drassanes (bottom), or you can walk the entire length in about twenty minutes.

PLAÇA DE CATALUNYA

Ⓜ Catalunya. MAP P.35, POCKET MAP D18

The huge formal square at the top of the Ramblas stands right at the heart of the city. It's not only the focal point of events and demonstrations – notably a mass party on New Year's Eve – but also the site of prominent landmarks like the main city tourist office, the white-faced El Corte Inglés department store and El Triangle shopping centre (with the popular *Zurich* outdoor café beneath it).

The Ramblas itself actually comprises five separate named sections, starting with the northern stretch, Rambla Canaletes, nearest Plaça de Catalunya, which is marked by an iron fountain – a drink from this supposedly means you'll never leave Barcelona. Further down is the bird market on Rambla Estudis and the sudden profusion of flower stalls on Rambla Sant Josep, near the Boqueria market.

PLAÇA DE CATALUNYA

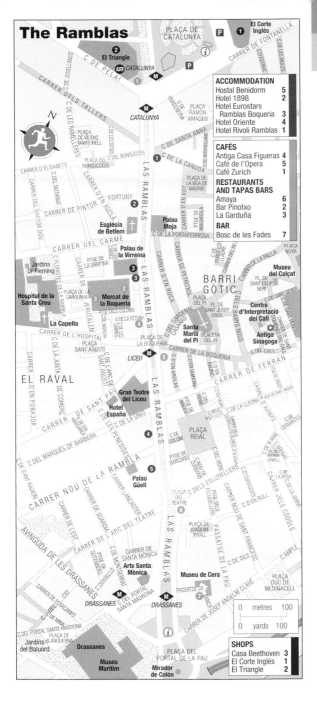

The Ramblas

ACCOMMODATION
Hostal Benidorm	5
Hotel 1898	2
Hotel Eurostars Ramblas Boqueria	3
Hotel Oriente	4
Hotel Rivoli Ramblas	1

CAFÉS
Antiga Casa Figueras	4
Café de l'Opera	5
Café Zurich	1

RESTAURANTS AND TAPAS BARS
Amaya	6
Bar Pinotxo	2
La Garduña	3

BAR
Bosc de les Fades	7

SHOPS
Casa Beethoven	3
El Corte Inglés	1
El Triangle	2

ESGLÉSIA DE BETLEM

Ramblas 107 ⓜ Liceu. Daily 8am–6pm.
MAP P.35, POCKET MAP C11

It seems hard to believe, but the Ramblas was a war zone during the Spanish Civil War as the city erupted into factionalism in 1937. George Orwell was caught in the crossfire (an episode recorded in his *Homage to Catalonia*) and, with anarchists sacking the city's churches at will, the rich interior of the Baroque Església de Betlem was completely destroyed. However, the main facade on c/del Carme still sports a fine sculpted portal.

PALAU MOJA

Ramblas 188 ⓜ Liceu ☏ 933 162 740.
Bookshop Mon–Fri 9am–8pm, Sat 9am–2pm & 4–8pm; Sala Palau Moja Tues–Sat 11am–8pm, Sun & hols 11am–3pm. Gallery admission usually free. MAP P.35, POCKET MAP D11

The ground floor of the elegant Palau Moja is now a cultural bookshop, while the palace's gallery, the Sala Palau Moja, is open for art and other exhibitions relating to all things Catalan – the gallery entrance is around the corner in c/Portaferrissa. Take a look at the illustrated tiles above

the fountain at the start of c/Portaferrissa, which show the medieval gate (the *Porta Ferriça*) and market that once stood here.

PALAU DE LA VIRREINA

Ramblas 99 ⓜ Liceu ☏ 933 161 000, ⓦ www .bcn.cat/cultura. Galleries Tues–Fri 11am–2pm & 4–8pm, Sat 11am–8pm, Sun 11am–3pm; for current exhibitions see ⓦ www.bcn.cat /virreinacentredelaimatge; information office daily 10am–8pm. MAP P.35, POCKET MAP C12

Graceful eighteenth-century Palau de la Virreina is the HQ of the cultural department of the Ajuntament (city council), and there's a ground-floor information centre where you can find out about upcoming events and buy tickets. Two galleries house changing exhibitions of contemporary art (Espai 2; admission sometimes charged) and photography (Espai Xavier Miserachs; free), while at the back of the palace courtyard you can usually see the city's enormous Carnival giants (*gegants*), representing the thirteenth-century Catalan king Jaume I and his wife Violant. The origin of these ornate, five-metre-high figures is unclear, though they probably first enlivened medieval travelling fairs and are now an integral part of Barcelona's festival parades.

MERCAT DE LA BOQUERIA

Ramblas 91 ⓜ Liceu ☏ 933 182 584, ⓦ www .boqueria.info. Mon–Sat 8am–8.30pm.
MAP P.35, POCKET MAP C12

Other markets might protest, but the city's glorious main food market really can claim to be the best in Spain. It's officially called the Mercat Sant Josep, though everyone knows it as La Boqueria. A riot of noise and colour, it's as popular with locals who come here to shop daily as with snap-happy

SCULPTED PORTAL OF THE ESGLÉSIA DE BETLEM

An insider's guide to the Ramblas

There are pavement cafés and restaurants all the way down the Ramblas, but the food can be indifferent and the prices high, so be warned. (For better value, go into the Boqueria market, where the traders eat.) The strolling crowds, too, provide perfect cover for pickpockets – keep a wary eye on your possessions at all times, especially when watching the buskers or shopping at the kiosks. And – however easy it looks to win – if you're going to play cards or dice with a man on a street, you've only yourself to blame if you get ripped off.

tourists. Everything radiates out from the central fish and seafood stalls – bunches of herbs, pots of spices, mounds of cheese and sausage, racks of bread and overloaded meat counters. It's easy to get waylaid at the entrance by the fruit cartons and squeezed juices, but the flagship fruit and veg stalls here are pricey. It's better value further in, in particular in the small outdoor square just beyond the north side of the market where the local allotment holders and market-gardeners gather. Everyone has a favourite market stall, but don't miss Petras, the wild mushroom and dried insect stall (it's at the back, by the restaurant *Garduña*). If you really don't fancy chilli worms, ant candy and crunchy beetles, there are also some excellent stand-up

tapas bars in the market, open from dawn onwards for the traders.

PLAÇA DE LA BOQUERIA

Ⓜ Liceu. MAP P.35, POCKET MAP C12

The halfway point of the Ramblas is marked by Plaça de la Boqueria, with its large round pavement **mosaic by Joan Miró**. It's become something of a symbol for the city and is one of a number of public works in Barcelona by the artist, who was born just a couple of minutes' away in the Barri Gòtic. Over at Ramblas 82, **Casa Bruno Quadros** – the lower floor is now the Caixa Sabadell – was built in the 1890s to house an umbrella store, which explains its delightful facade, decorated with Oriental designs, dragons and parasols.

MERCAT DE LA BOQUERIA

GRAN TEATRE DEL LICEU

Ramblas 51–59 ⓂLiceu Ⓦwww
.liceubarcelona.com. Box office ☎934 859
913; tours ☎934 859 914, daily at 10am,
11.30am, noon, 12.30pm & 1pm. €4.10/8.80.
MAP P.35, POCKET MAP C13

Barcelona's celebrated opera
house was first founded in 1847
and rebuilt after a fire in 1861
to become Spain's grandest
theatre. Regarded as a bastion
of the city's late nineteenth-
century commercial and
intellectual classes, the Liceu
was devastated again in 1893
when an anarchist threw two
bombs into the stalls during a
production of *William Tell* –
twenty people died. The
unfortunate Liceu then burned
down for the third time in
1994, when a workman's
blowtorch set fire to the
scenery of an opera set. The
latest restoration of the lavishly
decorated interior took five
years, and the opera house
opened again in 1999. Tours
depart from the modern
extension, the Espai Liceu,
which also houses a music and
gift shop and a café. You'll see
and learn most on the more
expensive, hour-long 10am
guided tour (the other, shorter,
cheaper tours are self-guided).
Highlights include the Salon of
Mirrors and the impressive
gilded auditorium containing
almost 2300 seats, making it
one of the world's largest opera
houses. Some tours also include
the option of visiting the
glorious *modernista*-styled
rooms of the Cercle del Liceu,
the opera house's private
members' club.

For Liceu performances,
check the website for details
and make bookings well in
advance. The traditional
meeting place for audience and
performers alike, meanwhile, is
the famous *Café de l'Opera*, just
across the Ramblas.

ARTS SANTA MÒNICA

Ramblas 7 ⓂDrassanes ☎935 671 110,
Ⓦwww.artsantamonica.cat. Tues–Sun
11am–9pm. Free. MAP P.35, POCKET MAP C14

Down from the Liceu, the
bottom part of the Ramblas
(Rambla de Santa Mònica) was
historically a theatre and

The Ramblas statues

You can't move for human statues on the Ramblas, standing on their little home-made plinths or posing for photos. Classical figures and movie characters have always formed part of the parade, but there's also some real wit and invention on display, like "Fruit Lady", a one-woman mobile market stall, or the twin "Bicycling Skeletons". Many are actors (or at least waiters who say they're actors), and others make a claim to art – how else to begin to explain the various men without heads or the kennel-dwelling "Human Dog"? Then there's just the plain weird, like "Lady Under Rock", crushed under a boulder, issuing plaintive shrieks at passers-by. And quite what demons drive "Man Sitting on Toilet", only he can say.

red-light district, and it still has a rough edge or two. Flagship building is the Augustinian convent of Santa Mònica, which dates originally from 1626, making it the oldest building on the Ramblas. It was remodelled in the 1980s as a contemporary arts centre, and hosts regularly changing exhibitions – it's an unusual gallery space dedicated to "artistic creation, science, thought and communication" so there's usually something worth seeing, from an offbeat art installation to a show of archive photographs. Meanwhile, pavement artists and palm readers set up stalls outside on the Ramblas, augmented on weekend afternoons by a street market selling jewellery, beads, bags and ornaments.

MUSEU DE CERA

Ramblas 4–6, entrance on Ptge. de Banca ⓂDrassanes ☎933 172 649, Ⓦwww .museocerabcn.com. July–Sept daily 10am–10pm; Oct–June Mon–Fri 10am–1.30pm & 4–7.30pm, Sat & Sun 11am–2pm & 4.30–8.30pm. €12.
MAP P.35, POCKET MAP C14

You'd have to be hard-hearted indeed not to derive some pleasure from the city's wax museum. Located in a

nineteenth-century bank building, it presents an ever more ludicrous series of tableaux in cavernous salons and gloomy corridors, depicting recitals, meetings and parlour gatherings attended by an anachronistic – not to say perverse – collection of characters, from Hitler to Princess Diana. Needless to say, it's enormously amusing, culminating in cheesy underwater tunnels and space capsules and an unpleasant "Terror Room". Even if this doesn't appeal it is definitely worth poking your head into the museum's extraordinary grotto bar, the *Bosc de les Fades*.

STREET PERFORMER, RAMBLAS

Shops

CASA BEETHOVEN

Ramblas 97 Ⓜ Liceu Ⓦ www
.casabeethoven.com. Mon–Fri 9am–2pm &
4–8pm, Sat 9am–2pm & 5–8pm; closed Aug.
MAP P.35, POCKET MAP C12

Wonderful old shop selling
sheet music from wooden
library stacks, plus CDs and
music reference books – not
just classical, but also rock, jazz
and flamenco.

EL CORTE INGLÉS

Pl. de Catalunya 14 Ⓜ Catalunya Ⓦ www
.elcorteingles.es. Mon–Sat 10am–10pm.
MAP P.35, POCKET MAP E10

The city's biggest department
store has nine retail floors
(fashion, cosmetics, household
goods, toys), a good basement
supermarket and – best of all –
a top-floor café with terrific
views. For music, books,
computers and sports gear,
head for the nearby branch at
Av. Portal de l'Angel 19.

EL TRIANGLE

Pl. de Catalunya 4 Ⓜ Catalunya Ⓦ www
.eltriangle.es. Mon–Sat 10am–10pm.
MAP P.35, POCKET MAP D10

Shopping centre dominated by
the flagship FNAC store, which
specializes in books (good
English-language selection),
music, film and computer stuff.
Also a Camper (for shoes),
Habitat (homeware) and
Sephora (cosmetics), plus lots
of boutiques, and a café on the
ground floor next to the
extensive newspaper and
magazine section.

Cafés

ANTIGA CASA FIGUERAS

Ramblas 83 Ⓜ Liceu ☎ 933 016 027, Ⓦ www
.escriba.es. Mon–Sat 9am–3pm & 5–8.30pm.
MAP P.35, POCKET MAP C12

Wonderful pastries and cakes
from the renowned Escribà
family business in a classy Art
Nouveau shop. Many rate this
as the best bakery in Barcelona.

CAFÉ DE L'OPERA

Ramblas 74. Ⓜ Liceu ☎ 933 177 585,
Ⓦ www.cafeoperabcn.com. Daily 8.30am–2am.
MAP P.35, POCKET MAP C12

If you're going to pay through
the nose for a seat on the
Ramblas, it may as well be at
this famous old café-bar
opposite the opera house,
which retains a *fin-de-siècle*
feel. Surprisingly, it's not a
complete tourist-fest and locals
pop in day and night for
drinks, cakes and tapas.

CAFÉ ZURICH

Pl. Catalunya 1 Ⓜ Catalunya
☎ 933 179 153. Mon–Fri 8am–11pm, Sat &
Sun 10am–11pm, June–Sept open until 1am.
MAP P.35, POCKET MAP D10

The most famous
meet-and-greet café in town,
right at the top of the Ramblas
and underneath El Triangle
shopping centre. It's good for
croissants and breakfast
sandwiches and there's a huge
pavement terrace, but sit inside
if you don't want to be
bothered by endless rounds of
buskers and beggars.

ANTIGA CASA FIGUERAS

BAR PINOTXO

Mercat de la Boqueria, Ramblas 91 Ⓜ Liceu
☎ 933 171 731. Mon–Sat 6am–5pm; closed
Aug. MAP P.35, POCKET MAP C12

The market's most renowned refuelling stop – just inside the main entrance on the right – attracts traders, chefs, tourists and celebs, who stand three deep at busy times. A coffee, a grilled sandwich and a glass of *cava* is the local breakfast of choice, or let the cheery staff steer you towards the tapas and daily specials (€5–15), anything from a slice of tortilla to fried baby squid.

LA GARDUÑA

Mercat de la Boqueria, c/Jerusalem 18
Ⓜ Liceu ☎ 933 024 323. Mon–Sat 1–4pm
& 8pm–midnight. MAP P.35, POCKET MAP C12

Tucked away at the back of the frenetic Boqueria market, this is an especially enticing place for lunch when there's a good-value *menú del dia* – basically, you'll be offered the best of the day's produce at pretty reasonable prices, and if you're lucky you'll get an outdoor seat with market views. At dinner, most mains are €9–20.

Restaurants and tapas bars

AMAYA

Ramblas 20–24 Ⓜ Drassanes ☎ 933 026 138
(bar), ☎ 933 021 037 (restaurant), Ⓦ www.
restauranteamaya.com. Bar daily
10am–12.30am; restaurant daily 1.30 4pm &
8.30pm–midnight. MAP P.35, POCKET MAP C14

There aren't too many reliable places on the Ramblas itself, but the *Amaya* – a fixture since 1941 – fits the bill for a snack or a meal. It's restaurant on one side, tapas bar on the other, both serving Basque seafood specialities, including octopus, squid, mussels, anchovies and prawns. The bar offers the cheapest and most enjoyable introduction to the cuisine; otherwise, main dishes in the restaurant cost €14–20.

Bar

BOSC DE LES FADES

Ptge. de Banca 5 Ⓜ Drassanes ☎ 933 172
649. Mon–Thurs & Sun 10am–1am, Fri & Sat
10am–2am. MAP P.35, POCKET MAP C14

Down an alley by the wax museum, the "Forest of the Fairies" is festooned with gnarled plaster tree trunks, hanging branches, fountains and stalactites. It's a bit cheesy, which is perhaps why it's a huge hit with the twenty-something crowd who huddle in the grottoes with a cocktail or two.

Barri Gòtic

The Barri Gòtic, or Gothic Quarter, on the east side of the Ramblas forms the heart of Barcelona's Old Town. Its buildings date principally from the fourteenth and fifteenth centuries, and culminate in the extraordinary Gothic cathedral known as La Seu. Around here are hidden squares, some fascinating museums, the city's old Jewish quarter and the remains of the Roman walls. It takes the best part of a day to see everything – longer if you factor in the abundant cafés, antique shops, boutiques and galleries. Note that the southern area, en route to the harbour, is rather less gentrified than the cathedral district – take care at night in the poorly lit streets. Metros Liceu (west), Jaume I (east) and Drassanes (south) provide access to the neighbourhood.

LA SEU

Pl. de la Seu ⓜ Jaume I. Daily 8am–12.45pm & 5.15–7.30pm, cathedral and cloister free; otherwise Mon–Sat 1–5pm, Sun & hols 2–5pm; €5, includes entrance to all sections, including roof terrace and museum.
MAP P.44–45, POCKET MAP E12

Barcelona's cathedral is one of the great Gothic buildings of Spain, dedicated to Santa Eulàlia, who was martyred by the Romans for daring to prefer Christianity – her ornate tomb rests in a crypt beneath the high altar. A magnificent fourteenth-century **cloister** looks over a lush tropical garden complete with soaring palm trees and honking white geese. Don't leave without ascending to the **roof** (€2.50) for intimate views of the surrounding buildings.

Performances of the Catalan national dance, the *sardana*, take place in front of the cathedral (usually Sun at noon, plus Easter–Nov Sat at 6pm), while the pedestrianized Avinguda de la Catedral hosts an antiques market every Thursday, and a Christmas craft fair in December.

LA SEU

MUSEU DIOCESÀ

Av. Catedral 4 ⓜ Jaume I ☎ 933 152 213. Tues–Sat 10am–2pm & 5–8pm, Sun & hols 11am–2pm. €6. MAP P.44–45, POCKET MAP E12

Stand back to look at the cathedral buildings and it's easy to see the line of Roman towers that originally stood on this spot incorporated into the later medieval structures. One such tower formed part of the cathedral almshouse, now the Museu Diocesà, whose soaring

spaces have been beautifully adapted to show an impressive collection of religious art and church treasures. The ticket also includes entrance into the temporary art and architecture exhibitions held here.

DALÍ BARCELONA

Real Cercle Artístic, c/Arcs 5 Ⓜ Jaume I ☎ 933 181 774, Ⓦ www.dalibarcelona.com. Daily 10am–10pm. €8. MAP P.44–45, POCKET MAP D12

The handsome Gothic palace housing the Royal Art Circle hosts various free exhibitions and concerts, though the big draw is the collection of 44 original sculptures by Salvador Dalí, completed in the 1970s. A lovely terrace restaurant above the Gothic streets also offers a pricey lunch, while on your way to or from the cathedral spare a glance for the graffiti-like frieze surmounting the nearby **Collegi d'Arquitectes** on Plaça Nova – designed by that other inimitable master, Pablo Picasso.

PLAÇA DEL REI

Ⓜ Jaume I. MAP P.44–45, POCKET MAP E12

The harmonious enclosed square of Plaça del Rei was once the palace courtyard of the Counts of Barcelona. Stairs climb from here to the palace's main hall, the fourteenth-century **Saló del Tinell**. It was here that Ferdinand and Isabella received Christopher Columbus on his triumphant return from his famous voyage of 1492. At one time the Spanish Inquisition met in the hall, taking full advantage of the popular belief that the walls would move if a lie was spoken. Nowadays it hosts temporary exhibitions, while concerts are occasionally held in the hall or outside in the square. The palace buildings include the beautiful fourteenth-century **Capella de Santa Agata**, and the romantic Renaissance **Torre del Rei Martí**. There's no public access to the tower, but the interiors of the hall and chapel can usually be seen during a visit to the adjacent Museu d'Història de Barcelona.

MUSEU FREDERIC MARÈS

Pl. de Sant Iu 5–6 Ⓜ Jaume I ☎ 932 563 500, Ⓦ www.museumares.bcn.cat. Tues–Sat 10am–7pm, Sun 10am–8pm, hols 10am–3pm. €4.20. MAP P.44–45, POCKET MAP E12

One of the Old Town's most fascinating museums, Museu Frederic Marès, was undergoing a remodelling at the time of writing – admission details may change when it reopens in 2011. It celebrates the diverse passions of sculptor, painter and restorer Frederic Marès (1893–1991), whose beautifully presented collection of ancient and medieval sculpture does little to prepare visitors for Marès's true obsession, namely a kaleidoscopic array of curios and collectibles. Entire rooms are devoted to keys and locks, cigarette cards and snuffboxes, fans, gloves and brooches, walking sticks, dolls' houses, old gramophones and archaic bicycles – to list just a sample of what's in the collection.

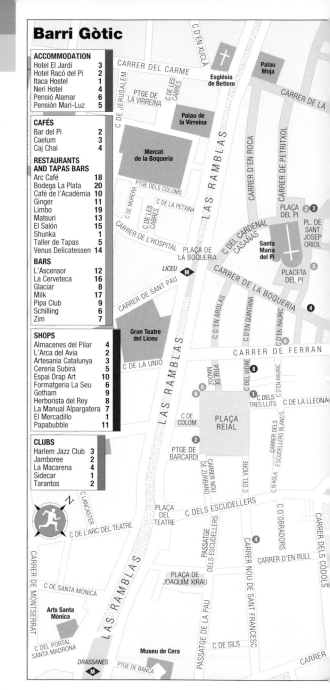

Barri Gòtic

ACCOMMODATION
Hotel El Jardí	3
Hotel Racó del Pi	2
Itaca Hostel	1
Neri Hotel	4
Pensió Alamar	6
Pensión Mari-Luz	5

CAFÉS
Bar del Pi	2
Caelum	3
Caj Chai	4

RESTAURANTS AND TAPAS BARS
Arc Café	18
Bodega La Plata	20
Café de l'Acadèmia	10
Ginger	11
Limbo	19
Matsuri	13
El Salón	15
Shunka	1
Taller de Tapas	5
Venus Delicatessen	14

BARS
L'Ascensor	12
La Cerveteca	16
Glaciar	8
Milk	17
Pipa Club	9
Schilling	6
Zim	7

SHOPS
Almacenes del Pilar	4
L'Arca del Avia	2
Artesania Catalunya	3
Cereria Subirà	5
Espai Drap Art	10
Formatgeria La Seu	6
Gotham	9
Herborista del Rey	8
La Manual Alpargatera	7
El Mercadillo	1
Papabubble	11

CLUBS
Harlem Jazz Club	3
Jamboree	2
La Macarena	4
Sidecar	1
Tarantos	2

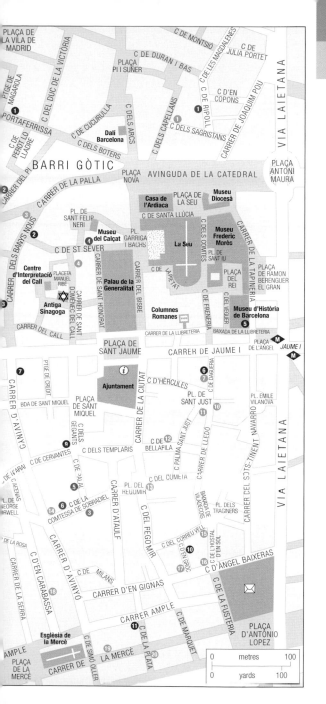

MUSEU D'HISTÒRIA DE BARCELONA (MUHBA)

Pl. del Rei, entrance on c/del Veguer
Ⓜ Jaume I ☎ 932 562 100, ⓦ www
.museuhistoria.bcn.cat. Tues–Sat 10am–8pm
(Oct–March 10am–2pm & 4–7pm), Sun
10am–8pm, hols 10am–3pm. €7.
MAP P.44–45, POCKET MAP E12

The Barcelona History Museum comprises half a dozen sites across the city, though its principal hub is what's known as the "Conjunt Monumental" (or monumental ensemble) of Plaça del Rei, whose crucial draw is an amazing underground archeological section – nothing less than the remains of the Roman city of Barcino (first century BC to the sixth century AD), which stretch under the surrounding streets as far as the cathedral. Excavations and explanatory diagrams show the full extent of the streets and buildings – from lookout towers to laundries – while models, mosaics, murals and finds help flesh out the reality of daily life in Barcino.

There's a well-stocked book and gift shop on site (entrance on c/Llibreteria), while the museum ticket also allows entry to the other MUHBA sites, notably the Poble Sec air-raid shelter and Pedralbes monastery. Roman fans should also take the opportunity to see the four remarkable Roman columns ("columnes Romanes") in the courtyard of the nearby Centre Excursionista de Catalunya (c/Paradis 10; closed Mon).

ESGLÉSIA DE SANTA MARÍA DEL PI

Pl. Sant Josep Oriol Ⓜ Liceu. Mon–Fri
9.30am–1pm & 5–8.30pm, Sat 9.30am–1pm
& 4–8.30pm, Sun 9.30am–2pm & 5–8.30pm.
MAP P.44–45, POCKET MAP D12

The fourteenth-century church of Santa María is known for its marvellous stained glass, particularly a 10m-wide rose window (often claimed, rather boldly, to be the largest in the world). The church flanks Plaça Sant Josep Oriol, the prettiest of three delightful adjacent squares and an ideal place for an outdoor coffee and a browse around the weekend **artists' market** (Sat 11am–8pm, Sun 10am–3pm).

The church is named – like the squares on either side, Plaça del Pi and Plaçeta del Pi – after the pine tree that once stood here. A **farmers' market**

EXHIBIT AT THE MUSEU D'HISTÒRIA DE BARCELONA

spills across Plaça del Pi on the last Saturday and Sunday of the month (Oct to May only), while the characteristic cafés of narrow **Carrer de Petritxol** (off Plaça del Pi) are the places to head to for a cup of hot chocolate – *Dulcinea* at no. 2 is the traditional choice – and a browse around the street's commercial art galleries. The most famous is **Sala Pares** at c/Petritxol 5, well known as the site of Picasso's first solo exhibition.

MUSEU DEL CALÇAT

Pl. Sant Felip Neri 5 ⓜ Liceu ☎ 933 014 533. Tues–Sun & hols 11am–2pm. €2.50. MAP P.44–45, POCKET MAP D12

The former headquarters of the shoemakers' guild (founded in 1202) houses a one-room footwear museum, containing originals dating back to the 1600s as well as oddities like the world's biggest shoe, made for the city's Columbus statue. The museum flanks one side of pretty Plaça Sant Felip Neri, where in summer you can eat outside at the restaurant of the boutique *Neri Hotel*, which sets

out candlelit tables in the square.

ANTIGA SINAGOGA

C/Marlet 5, corner with c/Sant Domènec del Call ⓜ Liceu ☎ 933 170 790, ⓦ www .calldebarcelona.org. Mon–Fri 11am–6pm, Sat & Sun 11am–3pm. €2. MAP P.44–45, POCKET MAP D12

Barcelona's medieval Jewish quarter was centred on c/Sant Domènec del Call, where a synagogue existed from as early as the third century AD until the pogrom of 1391, but even after that date the building survived in various guises and has since been sympathetically restored. The city authorities have signposted a few other points of interest in what's known as "El Call Major", including the **Centre d'Interpretació del Call** in nearby Plaçeta Manuel Ribé (Wed–Fri 10am–2pm, Sat 11am–6pm, Sun & hols 11am–3pm; free), whose informative storyboards (in English) shed more light on Barcelona's fascinating Jewish heritage

PLAÇA DE SANT JAUME

Ⓜ Jaume I. MAP P.44–45, POCKET MAP D13

The spacious square at the end of the main c/de Ferran was once the site of Barcelona's Roman forum; now it's at the heart of city and regional government business, as well as being the traditional place for demonstrations and local festivals. Whistle-happy local police try to keep things moving, while taxis and bike-tour groups weave between the pedestrians.

AJUNTAMENT DE BARCELONA

Pl. de Sant Jaume Ⓜ Jaume I ☎ 934 027 000. Public admitted Sun 10am–2pm, entrance on c/Font de Sant Miquel. Free. MAP P.44–45, POCKET MAP D13

On the south side of Plaça de Sant Jaume stands Barcelona's city hall, parts of which date from as early as 1373, though the Neoclassical façade was added in the nineteenth century. On Sundays you're allowed into the building for a self-guided tour around the splendid marble halls, galleries and staircases. The high-lights are the magnificent fourteenth-century council chamber, known as the **Saló de Cent**, and the dramatic

PALAU DE LA GENERALITAT

historical murals in the **Saló de les Cròniques** (Hall of Chronicles).

PALAU DE LA GENERALITAT

Pl. de Sant Jaume Ⓜ Jaume I ☎ 934 024 600. Tours on 2nd and 4th Sun of the month (not Aug), every 30–60min, 10am–2pm; also on April 23, and Sept 11 & 24. Passport or ID required. Free. MAP P.44–45, POCKET MAP D12/13

The home of the Catalan government presents its oldest aspect around the side, where the fifteenth-century c/del Bisbe facade contains a medallion portraying Sant Jordi (St George, patron saint of Catalunya as well as England). Incidentally, the enclosed Gothic bridge across this narrow street – subject of countless photographs and postcards – is an anachronism, added in 1928. Inside the palace there's a beautiful first-floor cloister, while opening off this are the intricately worked chapel and salon of Sant Jordi as well as an upper courtyard planted with orange trees. You can visit the interior on a one-hour guided tour on alternate Sundays (note only one or two tours each day are in English), while the Generalitat is also open on public holidays, particularly April 23 – the **Dia de Sant Jordi** (St George's Day). Celebrated as a nationalist holiday in Catalunya, this is also a local Valentine's Day, when it's traditional to exchange books and roses.

PLAÇA REIAL

Ⓜ Liceu. MAP P.44–45, POCKET MAP C13

The elegant Plaça Reial – hidden behind an archway off the Ramblas – is studded with palm trees and decorated iron lamps (designed by the young Antoni Gaudí), and bordered by pastel-coloured arcaded

buildings. Sitting in the square certainly puts you in mixed company – punks, buskers, eccentrics, tramps and bemused visitors. However, most of the really unsavoury characters have been driven off over the years and predatory, menu-toting waiters are usually the biggest nuisance these days. Don't expect to see too many locals until night falls, when the surrounding bars come into their own. Passing through on a Sunday morning, look in on the **coin and stamp market** (10am–2pm).

CARRER D'AVINYÓ

Ⓜ Liceu. MAP P.44–45, POCKET MAP D13/14

Carrer d'Avinyó, running south from c/de Ferran towards the harbour, cuts through the most atmospheric part of the southern Barri Gòtic. It used to be a red-light district and was frequented by the young Picasso, whose family moved into the area in 1895. It still looks the part – lined with dark overhanging buildings – but the funky cafés, streetwear shops and boutiques tell the story of its creeping gentrification. A few rough edges still show, particularly around **Plaça George Orwell**, a favoured hangout for city

skate-kids with its cheap cafés and grunge bars, such as *Oviso*.

LA MERCÈ

Ⓜ Drassanes. MAP P.44–45, POCKET MAP D14

In the eighteenth century, the harbourside neighbourhood known as La Mercè was home to the nobles and merchants enriched by Barcelona's maritime trade. Most moved north to the more fashionable Eixample later in the nineteenth century, and since then Carrer de la Mercè and surrounding streets (particularly Ample, d'en Gignàs and Regomir) have been home to a series of old-style taverns known as *tascas* or *bodegas* – a glass of wine from the barrel and a plate of tapas here is one of the Old Town's more authentic experiences.

At Plaça de la Mercè, the **Església de la Mercè** is the focus of the city's biggest annual bash, the Festes de la Mercè every September, dedicated to the co-patroness of Barcelona, whose image is paraded from the church. It's an excuse for a week of partying, parades, special events and concerts, culminating in spectacular pyrotechnics along the seafront.

Shops

ALMACENES DEL PILAR

C/Boqueria 43 Ⓜ Liceu ⓦ www
.almacenesdelpilar.com. Mon–Sat 10am–2pm
& 4.30–8pm; closed Aug. MAP P.44–45,
POCKET MAP D13

A world of frills, lace, cloth and
material used in the making of
Spain's traditional regional
costumes. You can pick up a
decorated fan for just a few
euros, though quality items go
for a lot more.

L'ARCA DEL AVIA

C/Banys Nous 20 Ⓜ Liceu ⓦ www
.larcadelavia.com. Mon–Fri 10am–2pm &
5–8pm, Sat 11am–2pm; closed Aug.
MAP P.44–45, POCKET MAP D12

Catalan brides used to fill up
their nuptial trunk (*l'arca*) with
embroidered linen and lace,
and this shop is a treasure-trove
of vintage and antique textiles.
Period costumes can be hired
or purchased as well – one of
Kate Winslet's *Titanic* costumes
came from here.

ARTESANIA CATALUNYA

C/Banys Nous 11 Ⓜ Liceu ⓦ www
.artesania-catalunya.com. Mon–Fri
10am–7pm, Sat 10am–2pm & 3–7pm, Sun &
hols 10am–2pm. MAP P.44–45, POCKET MAP D12

L'ARCA DEL AVIA

It's always worth a look in the
showroom of the arts and crafts
promotion board. Exhibitions
change but most of the work is
contemporary in style, from
basketwork to glassware,
though traditional methods are
still very much encouraged.

CERERÍA SUBIRÀ

Bxda. Llibreteria 7 Ⓜ Jaume I. Mon–Fri
9am–1.30pm & 4–7.30pm, Sat 9am–1.30pm.
MAP P.44–45, POCKET MAP E13

Barcelona's oldest shop (it's
been here since 1760) boasts a
beautiful interior, selling
unique handcrafted candles.

ESPAI DRAP ART

C/Groc 1 Ⓜ Jaume I ⓦ www.drapart.org.
Tues–Fri 11am–2pm & 5–8pm, Sat 6–9pm.
MAP P.44–45, POCKET MAP E14

The Drap Art creative recycling
organisation has a shop and
exhibition space for artists to
show their wildly inventive
wares, from trash bangles to
tin bags.

FORMATGERIA LA SEU

C/Dagueria 16 Ⓜ Jaume I ⓦ www
.formatgerialaseu.com. Tues–Thurs 10am–2pm
& 5–8pm, Fri & Sat 10am–3.30pm & 5–8pm;
closed Aug. MAP P.44–45, POCKET MAP E13

Sells the best farmhouse cheeses
from independent producers all
over Spain. Chatty Scottish
owner Katherine is usually on
hand to advise, and you can try
before you buy with a €2.50
tasting plate – ask about the
"formatgelat", a cheese-ice cream
fusion that's unique to the shop.

GOTHAM

C/Cervantes 7 Ⓜ Jaume I ⓦ www
.gotham-bcn.com. Mon–Fri 10.30am–2pm
& 5–8.30pm, Sat 10.30am–2pm; closed Sat
in Aug. MAP P.44–45, POCKET MAP D13

The place to come for retro
(1930s to 1970s) furniture,
lighting, homeware and
accessories, plus original
designs.

CAELUM

PAPABUBBLE

C/Ample 28 Ⓜ Jaume I Ⓦ www.papabubble.com. Tues–Fri 10am–2pm & 4–8.30pm, Sat 10am–8.30pm, Sun 11am–7.30pm; closed Aug. MAP P.44–45, POCKET MAP D14

Groovy young things roll out home-made candy to a chill-out soundtrack. Come and watch them at work, sample a sweet, and take home a gorgeously wrapped gift.

Cafés

BAR DEL PI

Pl. Sant Josep Oriol 1 Ⓜ Liceu ☎ 933 022 123. Mon–Sat 9am–11pm, Sun 10am–10pm; closed 2 weeks in Jan & Aug. MAP P.44–45, POCKET MAP D12

Best known for its terrace tables on one of Barcelona's prettiest squares. Linger over drinks and sandwiches as the Old Town reveals its charms, especially during the weekend artists' market.

CAELUM

C/Palla 8 Ⓜ Liceu ☎ 933 026 993. Mon noon–8.30pm, Tues–Sun 10.30am–8.30pm; closed 2 weeks in Aug. MAP P.44–45, POCKET MAP D12

The lovingly packaged confections in this upscale café deli (the name is Latin for "heaven") are made in convents and monasteries across Spain. Choose from marzipan sweets from Seville, Benedictine preserves or Cistercian cookies.

CAJ CHAI

C/Sant Domènec del Call 12 Ⓜ Liceu ☎ 933 019 592, Ⓦ www.cajchai.com. Mon 3–10pm, Tues–Sun 10.30am–10pm. MAP P.44–45, POCKET MAP D12

This refined back-street boudoir offers a menu of painstakingly prepared teas, from Moroccan mint to organic Nepalese *oolong*, plus brownies, *baklava* and sandwiches.

HERBORISTA DEL REY

C/del Vidre 1 Ⓜ Liceu. Tues–Fri 4–8pm, Sat 10am–8pm. MAP P.44–45, POCKET MAP D13

A renowned early nineteenth-century herbalist's shop, tucked off Plaça Reial, which stocks more than 250 medicinal herbs.

LA MANUAL ALPARGATERA

C/d'Avinyó 7 Ⓜ Liceu Ⓦ www.lamanualalpargatera.com. Mon–Fri 9.30am–1.30pm & 4.30–8pm, Sat 10am–1.30pm & 4.30–8pm. MAP P.44–45, POCKET MAP D13

In this traditional workshop they make and sell *alpargatas* (espadrilles) to order, as well as producing other straw, rope and basket work.

EL MERCADILLO

C/Portaferrissa 17 Ⓜ Liceu. Mon–Sat 10am–8.30pm. MAP P.44–45, POCKET MAP D12

The camel at the entrance marks this hippy-dippy indoor street market of shops and stalls selling T-shirts, skate-wear, vintage gear and jewellery. There's a café upstairs with a patio garden.

BARRI GÒTIC

51

Restaurants and tapas bars

ARC CAFÉ

C/Carabassa 19 ⓜ Drassanes ☎ 933 025 204, ⓦ www.arccafe.com. Daily 10.30am–1am (Fri & Sat until 2am). MAP P.44–45, POCKET MAP D14

Chilled-out bistro-bar that's a real neighbourhood stalwart. The kitchen's open all day, and the seasonally changing menu is good value (most mains around €10), offering things like hearty soups, Mediterranean salads, spring rolls, pastas and Thai curries (with Thurs & Fri nights designated Thai food nights).

BODEGA LA PLATA

C/de la Mercè 28 ⓜ Drassanes ☎ 933 151 009. Daily 10am–4pm & 8–11pm. MAP P.44–45, POCKET MAP E14

A classic taste of the Old Town, with a marble tapas counter open to the street (anchovies are the speciality) and dirt-cheap wine straight from the barrel.

DRINKER AT BODEGA LA PLATA

CAFÉ DE L'ACADÈMIA

C/Lledó 1 ⓜ Jaume I ☎ 933 198 253. Mon–Fri 1.30–4pm & 8.45–11.30pm; closed 2 weeks in Aug. MAP P.44–45, POCKET MAP E13

Great for a date or a lazy lunch, with creative Catalan dishes served in a romantic stone-flagged restaurant or outside in the medieval square. Expect classy grills, fresh fish, rice dishes, seasonal game and a taste of local favourites like salt cod, wild mushrooms or grilled veg. Prices are pretty reasonable (mains €11–18) and it's always busy, so dinner reservations are essential. A no-choice *menú del dia* is a bargain for the quality (and it's even cheaper eaten at the bar).

GINGER

C/Palma Sant Just 1 ⓜ Jaume I ☎ 933 105 309. Tues–Sat 7pm–3am; closed 2 weeks in Aug. MAP P.44–45, POCKET MAP E13

Cocktails and fancy tapas in a slickly updated 1970s-style setting. It's a world away from *patatas bravas* and battered squid – think roast duck vinaigrette, stuffed aubergine rolls, tuna tartare and vegetarian satay for around €6.50–9 a pop.

LIMBO

C/de la Mercè 13 ⓜ Drassanes ☎ 933 107 699. Mon 8.30pm–midnight, Tues–Sat 1.30–4pm & 8.30pm–midnight (Fri & Sat until 1am). MAP P.44–45, POCKET MAP D14

Designer restaurant with a warehouse-style interior of exposed brick and wooden beams. The market-led menu reflects Asian and Mediterranean influences, so there's fresh pasta made daily or things like swordfish tartare with red onion marmalade and wasabi (most dishes cost between €7 and €18). The weekday lunch is a really good deal.

MATSURI

Pl. Regomir 1 ⓜ Jaume I ☎ 932 681 535,
ⓦ www.matsuri-restaurante.com. Daily 8pm–
midnight. MAP P.44–45, POCKET MAP E13

A soothing place for creative Southeast-Asian cuisine, with a large menu concentrating on Thai-style noodles, salads and curries, as well as sushi, sashimi and tempura dishes. A daily specials list has some more unusual choices, and staff offer friendly advice. Around €30 a head.

EL SALÓN

C/l'Hostal d'en Sol 6–8 ⓜ Jaume I ☎ 933 152 159, ⓦ www.elsalon.es. Tues–Sun 8.30pm–midnight; closed 2 weeks in Aug. MAP P.44–45, POCKET MAP E14

It's easy to fall for the cosy charms of *El Salón*, with its candlelit tables in a Gothic dining room and summer terrace in the nearby square. The contemporary Mediterranean menu changes every few months, with inventive salads giving way to things like grilled aubergine, pepper and onion served with goat's cheese, or lamb with mustard and honey sauce. Salads and starters are from €8, with most mains in the range of €10 to €16.

SHUNKA

C/Sagristans 5 ⓜ Jaume I ☎ 934 124 991. Tues–Fri 1.30–3.30pm & 8.30–11.30pm, Sat & Sun 2–4pm & 8.30–11.30pm; closed 2 weeks in Aug. MAP P.44–45, POCKET MAP E12

Locals think this is the best Japanese restaurant in the Old Town – it's certainly always busy, so advance reservations are essential, though you might strike lucky if you're prepared to eat early or late. The open kitchen and bustling staff are half the show, while the food – sushi to udon noodles – is really good. Around €35.

GINGER

TALLER DE TAPAS

Pl. Sant Josep Oriol 9 ⓜ Liceu ☎ 933 018 020, ⓦ www.tallerdetapas.com. Daily noon–midnight (Fri & Sat until 1am). MAP P.44–45, POCKET MAP D12

The fashionable "tapas workshop" sucks in tourists with its pretty location by the church of Santa María del Pi. There's a year-round outdoor terrace, while the open kitchen turns out reliable, market-fresh dishes, with fish a speciality at dinner, from grilled langoustine to seared tuna (most tapas €4–12). There are other branches around town, (including one at c/Argenteria 51 in the Born), though this was the first.

VENUS DELICATESSEN

C/d'Avinyó 25 ⓜ Liceu ☎ 933 011 585. Daily noon–midnight. MAP P.44–45, POCKET MAP D13

Not a deli, despite the name, but it's a handy place serving Mediterranean bistro cuisine throughout the day and night. It's also good for vegetarians, with things like lasagne, couscous, moussaka and salads, mostly meat-free and costing around €7–10.

Bars

L'ASCENSOR

C/Bellafila 3 ⓜ Jaume I ☎ 933 185 347.
Daily 7pm–3am. MAP P.44-45, POCKET MAP E13
Sliding antique wooden
elevator doors signal the
entrance to "The Lift", but it's
no theme bar – just an
easy-going local hangout, great
for a late-night drink.

LA CERVETECA

C/d'en Gignàs 25 ⓜ Jaume I ☎ 933 150 407,
ⓦ www.lacerveteca.com. Mon–Thurs 4–10pm,
Fri–Sun 1–11pm. MAP P.44-45, POCKET MAP E14
Is it a bar, or the coolest drinks
shop in town? Either way, *La
Cerveteca* offers the city's best
world beer selection, available
to drink in or take out. Brews
are taken seriously here, but it's
not a beard-and-sandals
beer-fest, more a modern art,
Muddy Waters, Latino-beat
kind of place for ale enthusiasts
of all kinds.

GLACIAR

Pl. Reial 3 ⓜ Liceu ☎ 933 021 163. Mon–Sat
4pm–2am (Fri & Sat until 3am), Sun
9am–2am. MAP P.44-45, POCKET MAP C13
At this traditional Barcelona
meeting point the terrace
seating is packed most sunny
evenings and at weekends, and
the comings and goings in the
Old Town's funkiest square are
half the entertainment.

MILK

C/d'en Gignàs 21 ⓜ Jaume I ☎ 932 680 922,
ⓦ www.milkbarcelona.com. Mon–Wed
6pm–3am, Thurs–Sun 11am–3am.
MAP P.44-45, POCKET MAP E14
Irish-owned bar and bistro
that's carved a real niche as a
welcoming neighbourhood
hangout. Decor, they say, is that
of a "millionaire's drawing
room", with its sofas, cushions
and antique chandeliers. Get
there early for the famously

relaxed brunch (Thurs–Sun
11am–4pm), or there's dinner
and cocktails every night to a
funky soundtrack.

PIPA CLUB

Pl. Reial 3 ⓜ Liceu ☎ 933 024 732, ⓦ www
.bpipaclub.com. Daily 10pm–3am.
MAP P.44-45, POCKET MAP C13
Historically a pipe-smoker's
haunt, it's a wood-panelled,
jazzy, late-night kind of place –
ring the bell to be let in and
make your way up the stairs.

SCHILLING

C/de Ferran 23 ⓜ Liceu ☎ 933 176 787,
ⓦ www.cafeschilling.com. Mon–Sat 10am–3am,
Sun noon–3am. MAP P.44-45, POCKET MAP D13
Something of a haven on this
heavily touristed drag, *Schilling*
has a certain European
"grand-café" style, with its high
ceilings, big windows and
upmarket feel. It has a loyal gay
following, but it's a mixed,
chilled place to meet friends,
grab a *copa* and move on.

ZIM

C/Daguería 20 ⓜ Jaume I. Mon–Fri
noon–4pm & 6pm–midnight.
MAP P.44-45, POCKET MAP E13
The owner of the adjacent
Formatgeria La Seu (cheese

L'ASCENSOR

shop) offers up this tiny, hole-in-the-wall tasting bar for selected wines from boutique producers. It can be a real squeeze, and hours are somewhat flexible, but for a reviving glass or two accompanied by farmhouse cheese, cured meat and artisan-made bread, you can't beat it.

Clubs

HARLEM JAZZ CLUB

C/Comtessa de Sobradiel 8 ⓜ Jaume I
☎ 933 100 755, ⓦ www.harlemjazzclub.es.
Closed Aug. MAP P.44–45, POCKET MAP D13

For many years *the* hot place for jazz, where every style gets an airing, from African and Gypsy to flamenco and fusion. Live music nightly at 10.30pm and midnight (weekends 11.30pm & 1am). Entry €5–10, depending on the night and the act.

JAMBOREE

Pl. Reial 17 ⓜ Liceu ☎ 933 191 789, ⓦ www
.masimas.com. MAP P.44–45, POCKET MAP C13

They don't get the big jazz names here that they used to, but the nightly gigs (at 9pm & 11pm; from €10) still pull in the crowds, while the wild Monday night WTF jazz, funk and hip-hop jam session (from 9pm; €5) is a city fixture. Stay on for the club, which kicks in after midnight (entry €10) and you get funky sounds and retro pop, rock and disco until 5am.

LA MACARENA

C/Nou de Sant Francesc 5 ⓜ Drassanes
ⓦ www.macarenaclub.com. Mon–Thurs & Sun
midnight–4.30am, Fri & Sat midnight–5am.
MAP P.44–45, POCKET MAP D14

Once a place where flamenco tunes were offered up to La Macarena, the Virgin of Seville – now, a heaving temple to all

PERFORMER AT TARANTOS

things electro. Entry free until around 1am, then €5.

SIDECAR

Pl. Reial 7 ⓜ Liceu ☎ 933 021 586, ⓦ www
.sidecarfactoryclub.com. Tues–Sun
8pm–4.30am. MAP P.44–45, POCKET MAP C13

Hip music club – pronounced "See-day-car" – with gigs (usually at 10.30pm) and DJs (from 12.30am) that champion rock, indie, roots and fusion acts, so a good place to check out the latest Catalan hip-hop, rumba and flamenco sounds. Entry €7–10, though some gigs up to €20.

TARANTOS

Pl. Reial 17 ⓜ Liceu ☎ 933 191 789, ⓦ www
.masimas.com. MAP P.44–45, POCKET MAP C13

Jamboree's sister club is the place for short, exuberant flamenco tasters, where young singers, dancers and guitarists perform nightly at 8.30pm, 9.30pm & 10.30pm. Purists are a bit sniffy, but it's a great introduction to the scene. Entry €7.

Port Vell and Barceloneta

Barcelona has an urban waterfront that merges seamlessly with the Old Town, providing an easy escape from the claustrophobic medieval streets. The harbour at the bottom of the Ramblas has been thoroughly overhauled in recent years and Port Vell (Old Port), as it's now known, presents a series of heavyweight tourist attractions, from sightseeing boats and maritime museum to aquarium and IMAX cinema. By way of contrast, Barceloneta – the wedge of land to the east, backing the marina – retains its eighteenth-century character, and the former fishing quarter is still the most popular place to come and eat paella, fish and seafood. Metro Drassanes, at the bottom of the Ramblas, is the best starting point for Port Vell; Barceloneta has its own metro station.

MIRADOR DE COLÓN

Pl. Portal de la Pau ⓜ Drassanes ☎ 933 025 224. May–Oct daily 9am–8.30pm; Nov–April daily 10am–6.30pm. €3. MAP P.58–59, POCKET MAP C15

The monument at the foot of the Ramblas commemorates the visit made by Christopher Columbus in June 1493, when the navigator received a royal welcome in Barcelona. Columbus tops a grandiose iron column, 52m high, guarded by lions, and you can ride the lift up to the panoramic viewing platform at Columbus's feet. Meanwhile, from the quayside in front of the Columbus monument, Las Golondrinas sightseeing boats depart on regular trips throughout the year around the inner harbour.

MUSEU MARÍTIM

Av. de les Drassanes ⓜ Drassanes ☎ 933 429 920, ⓦ www.mmb.cat. Daily 10am–8pm. MAP P.58–59, POCKET MAP B14/15

Barcelona's medieval shipyards, or Drassanes, were in continuous use – fitting and arming Catalunya's war fleet or trading vessels – until well into the eighteenth century. The stone-vaulted buildings make a fitting home for the city's excellent Maritime Museum, though a large-scale renovation project (due for completion in 2012) means access is restricted. In the meantime, there's cut-price admission (free on Sun after 3pm) to

some parts of the complex as well as to temporary exhibitions, and continued access to museum activities, shop and café. The ticket also includes a short tour of the *Santa Eulàlia*, a vintage three-masted schooner moored down on the Moll de la Fusta harbourside (closed Mon, check hours at the museum).

L'AQUÀRIUM

Moll d'Espanya Ⓜ Drassanes ☎ 932 217 474, ⓦ www.aquariumbcn.com. Daily: July & Aug 9.30am–11pm; Sept–June 9.30am–9pm, until 9.30pm at weekends. €17.50. MAP P.58–59, POCKET MAP G8–H8

Port Vell's high-profile aquarium drags in families and school parties throughout the year to see "a magical world, full of mystery". Or, to be more precise, to see 11,000 fish and sea creatures in 35 themed tanks representing underwater caves, tropical reefs and other maritime habitats. It's vastly overpriced, and despite the claims of excellence it offers few new experiences, save perhaps the 80-metre-long walk-through underwater tunnel, which brings you face to face with gliding rays and cruising sharks.

MAREMÀGNUM

Moll d'Espanya Ⓜ Drassanes. Daily 10am–10pm. MAP P.58–59, POCKET MAP G8

From near the Columbus statue, the wooden Rambla de Mar swing bridge strides across the harbour to the Maremàgnum mall and leisure centre on Moll d'Espanya. It's a typically bold piece of Catalan design, its soaring glass lines tempered by the undulating wooden walkways that provide scintillating views back across the harbour to the city. Inside are two floors of gift shops and boutiques, plus a range of cafés and tapas bars.

IMAX PORT VELL

Moll d'Espanya Ⓜ Drassanes ☎ 932 251 111, ⓦ www.imaxportvell.com. Screenings 11am–10pm, later at weekends. Tickets €8.50 or €12.50 depending on the film. MAP P.58–59, POCKET MAP G8–H8

Barcelona's IMAX theatre has three screens showing films virtually hourly in 3D or giant-screen format. The themes are familiar – forces of nature, heroic exploration, alien adventure, etc, and some Hollywood 3D blockbusters are shown, but films are in Spanish or Catalan only.

THE CROSS-HARBOUR CABLE CAR

MUSEU D'HISTÒRIA DE CATALUNYA

Palau de Mar, Pl. de Pau Vila 3 ⓜ Barceloneta
☎ 932 254 700, ⓦ www.mhcat.net. Tues–Sat
10am–7pm (Wed until 8pm), Sun & public hols
10am–2.30pm. €4; first Sun of month free.
MAP P.58–59, POCKET MAP F15

A dramatic harbourside warehouse conversion contains a museum tracing the history of Catalunya from the Stone Age to the present day. Poke around the interior of a Roman grain ship or compare the rival nineteenth-century architectural plans for the Eixample. The top-floor café-bar boasts a glorious view of the city from its terrace – no museum ticket needed – while the flash restaurants in the **Palau de Mar** arcade below overlook the busy marina.

BARCELONETA

ⓜ Barceloneta. MAP P.58–59, POCKET MAP H8–J7
There's no finer place for lunch on a sunny day than Barceloneta, an eighteenth-century neighbourhood of tightly packed gridded streets with bustling harbour on one side and sandy beach on the other. There's a local market, the **Mercat de la Barceloneta** (open

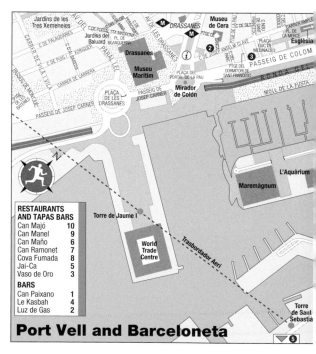

RESTAURANTS AND TAPAS BARS	
Can Majó	10
Can Manel	9
Can Maño	6
Can Ramonet	7
Cova Fumada	8
Jai-Ca	5
Vaso de Oro	3
BARS	
Can Paixano	1
Le Kasbah	4
Luz de Gas	2

Port Vell and Barceloneta

The cross-harbour cable car

The most thrilling ride in the city is across the harbour on the Trasbordador Aeri, or cable car, which sweeps from the Sant Sebastià tower at the foot of Barceloneta to Montjuïc. Departures are every 15min (daily 10.30am–6pm, June–Sept until 8pm; €9 one-way, €12.50 return), but expect queues in summer and at weekends as the cars only carry about twenty people at a time.

from 7am, closed Mon & Sat afternoons), with a couple of excellent bars and restaurants, while Barceloneta's famous seafood restaurants are found across the neighbourhood, but most characteristically lined along the harbourside Passeig Joan de Borbó.

PLATJA DE SANT SEBASTIÀ

Ⓜ Barceloneta. MAP P.58–59, POCKET MAP G9–K8

Barceloneta's beach – the first in a series of sandy city beaches – curves from the

flanks of the neighbourhood, past the swimming pools of the Club Natació and out to the landmark sail-shaped *W Barcelona* hotel. Closer to the Barceloneta end there are beach bars, outdoor cafés and sculptures, while a double row of palms backs the esplanade that runs above the sands as far as the Port Olímpic (a 15min walk). Bladers, skaters, joggers and cyclists have one of the Med's best views for company.

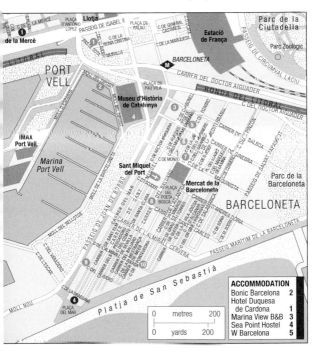

ACCOMMODATION	
Bonic Barcelona	2
Hotel Duquesa de Cardona	1
Marina View B&B	3
Sea Point Hostel	4
W Barcelona	5

Restaurants and tapas bars

CAN MAJÓ

C/Almirall Aixada 23 Ⓜ Barceloneta ☎ 932 215 818, Ⓦ www.canmajo.es. Tues–Sat 1–3.30pm & 8–11.30pm, Sun 1–3.30pm. MAP P.58–59, POCKET MAP H8

This ticks all the boxes for a quality seafood meal, with a bonus of a lovely summer *terrassa* by the beach promenade where you can tuck into wonderful rice dishes, *fideuà* (noodles with seafood), *suquet* (fish stew) or grilled fish. The menu changes daily according to what's off the boat; expect to spend €40–50 a head.

CAN MANEL

Pg. Joan de Borbó 60 Ⓜ Barceloneta ☎ 932 215 013. Daily 1–4pm & 8pm–midnight. MAP P.58–59, POCKET MAP H8

An institution since 1870, with reliably good food and moderate prices. If you want lunch outside on the terrace, get there by 1.30pm. Paella and other seafood rice and noodle dishes are staples – from around €14 per person – while the catch of the day ranges from cuttlefish to sole, bream or hake (up to €23).

CAN MAÑO

C/Baluard 12 Ⓜ Barceloneta ☎ 933 193 082. Mon–Fri 8am–5.30pm & 8–11pm, Sat noon–5pm; closed Aug. MAP P.58–59, POCKET MAP F15

There's rarely a tourist in sight in this classic old-fashioned diner, packed with noisy locals around formica tables. Basically, your choice is fried or grilled fish, supplemented by a few daily seafood specials and basic meat dishes. It's an authentic, no-frills experience that's likely to cost you less than €15 a head.

SEAFOOD TAPAS

CAN RAMONET

C/Maquinista 17 Ⓜ Barceloneta ☎ 933 193 064, Ⓦ www.elnouramonet.com. Daily noon–midnight (meals from 1pm & 8pm), closed Sun dinner, 2 weeks in Jan, & Aug. MAP P.58–59, POCKET MAP J8

Reputedly the oldest restaurant in the port area, and boasting a shady *terrassa* in front of the neighbourhood market. There's pricey tapas, splendid paella, plus whatever's fresh from the stalls that day, though with mains running at €17–25 the bill soon adds up.

COVA FUMADA

C/Baluard 56 Ⓜ Barceloneta ☎ 932 214 061. Mon–Wed & Sat 9am–3pm, Thurs & Fri 9am–3pm & 6–8pm; closed Aug. MAP P.58–59, POCKET MAP H8

Behind brown wooden doors on the market square (there's no sign) is this rough-and-ready tavern with battered marble tables and antique barrels. That it's always packed is a testament to the quality of the market-fresh tapas (€2–10), from griddled prawns and fried artichokes to the house speciality, the *bomba* (spicy potato meatball).

It takes two

You want a seafood paella or an *arròs negre* (black rice, with squid ink), or maybe a garlicky *fideuà* (noodles with seafood) – of course you do. Problem is, you're on your own and virtually every restaurant that offers these classic Barcelona dishes does so for a minimum of two people (often you don't find out until you examine the menu's small print). Solution? Ask the waiter upfront, as sometimes the kitchen will oblige single diners, or look for the dishes on a *menú del dia* (especially on Thurs, traditionally rice day), when there should be no minimum. Probably best not to grab a stranger off the street to share a paella, however desperate you are.

JAI-CA

C/Ginebra 13 Ⓜ Barceloneta ☎ 932 683 265. Daily 10am–11pm. MAP P.58–59, POCKET MAP F15
A great choice for tapas (dishes up to €10), with bundles of stuffed mussels, crisp baby squid and other seafood platters.

VASO DE ORO

C/Balboa 6 Ⓜ Barceloneta ☎ 933 193 098. Daily 9am–midnight. MAP P.58–59, POCKET MAP F15
An old favourite for stand-up tapas (€3–10) – there's no menu, but order the *patatas bravas*, some thick slices of fried sausage and a dollop of tuna salad and you've touched all the bases. Unusually, they also brew their own beer, light and dark.

Bars

CAN PAIXANO

C/de la Reina Cristina 7 Ⓜ Barceloneta ☎ 933 100 839, Ⓦ www.canpaixano.com. Daily 9am–10.30pm; closed 2 weeks in Aug. MAP P.58–59, POCKET MAP E14
A must on everyone's itinerary is this counter-only joint where the drink of choice – all right, the only drink – is *cava* (Catalan champagne) by the glass or bottle, served with little sandwiches. It's very popular, so you'll probably have to fight your way in.

LE KASBAH

Pl. Pau Vila, behind Palau de Mar Ⓜ Barceloneta ☎ 932 380 722, Ⓦ www .ottozutz.com. Tues–Sun 10pm–3am. MAP P.58–59, POCKET MAP F15
The *terrassa* is the big summer draw, when nothing but a reviving cocktail and a breath of fresh air will do, though the funky, sort-of-Oriental interior has a chilled-out charm.

LUZ DE GAS

Moll del Diposit, in front of Palau de Mar Ⓜ Barceloneta ☎ 932 097 711. March–Oct daily noon–3am. MAP P.58–59, POCKET MAP E15
Sip a chilled drink on the deck of the boat, and soak up some great marina and harbour views. It's especially nice at dusk as the city lights begin to twinkle.

CAN PAIXANO

El Raval

The Old Town area west of the Ramblas is known as El Raval (from the Arabic word for suburb), and has always formed a world apart from the nobler Gothic quarter. Traditionally a red-light area, and once notorious for its sleazy Barri Xinès (China Town), it still has some very seedy corners (particularly south of Carrer de Sant Pau), though it's changing rapidly, notably in the "upper Raval" around Barcelona's contemporary art museum, MACBA. Cutting-edge galleries, designer restaurants and fashionable bars are all part of the scene these days, while an arty, affluent crowd rubs shoulders with the area's Asian and North African immigrants and the older, traditional residents. Metros Catalunya, Liceu, Drassanes and Paral.lel serve the neighbourhood.

MUSEU D'ART CONTEMPORANI DE BARCELONA (MACBA)

Pl. dels Àngels 1 ⓂCatalunya ☎934 120 810, ⓌWww.macba.cat. Mon & Wed 11am–8pm, Thurs & Fri 11am–midnight (mid-Sept to mid-June closes weekdays at 7.30pm), Sat 10am–8pm, Sun & hols 10am–3pm; closed Tues all year. €7.50.
MAP P.64–65, POCKET MAP B10/11–C10/11

The iconic contemporary art museum – with a stark main facade constructed entirely of glass – anchors the regenerated upper Raval. The collection represents the main movements in art since 1945, mainly (but not exclusively) in Catalunya and Spain, and depending on the changing exhibitions you may catch works by major names such as Joan Miró or Antoni Tàpies. There are free guided tours of the permanent collection (in English on Mon at 6pm, otherwise in Catalan/Spanish Wed–Sat at 6pm, plus weekends at 1pm), and a good museum shop.

MUSEU D'ART CONTEMPORANI DE BARCELONA

FOMENT DE LES ARTES DÉCORATIVES (FAD)

Pl. dels Àngels 5–6 ⓜ Catalunya ☎ 934 437 520, ⓦ www.fad.cat. Tues–Fri 11am–8pm, Sun 11am–4pm. Free. MAP P.64–65, POCKET MAP B11–C11

A section of the former Convent dels Àngels now houses the FAD arts and design organisation, whose various exhibition spaces are dedicated to industrial and graphic design, crafts, architecture, contemporary jewellery and fashion. FAD also coordinates the annual **Tallers Oberts** (or "Open Workshops"; usually over two weekends in May), when visitors can tour craft outlets in the Old Town and join workshops.

CENTRE DE CULTURA CONTEMPORÀNIA DE BARCELONA (CCCB)

C/Montalegre 5 ⓜ Catalunya ☎ 933 064 100, ⓦ www.cccb.org. Tues–Sun 11am–8pm, Thurs until 10pm. €4.50 or €6 depending on exhibitions visited, free on 1st Wed of month & Sun after 3pm. MAP P.64–65, POCKET MAP B10–C10

There's a wide range of city-related exhibitions on show at the contemporary culture centre (photography to architecture), as well as a varied cinema, concert and festival programme. The imaginatively restored building was once an infamous workhouse and asylum, and the main courtyard still retains its old tile panels and presiding statue of patron saint, Sant Jordi. At

the back, the C3 café-bar makes the most of its *terrassa* overlooking the modern square joining the CCCB to MACBA.

PLAÇA DE VICENÇ MARTORELL

ⓜ Catalunya. MAP P.64–65, POCKET MAP C11

The Raval's nicest traffic-free square lies just a few minutes' walk from MACBA. The small playground here is well used by local families, and the arcaded square features a first-rate café, the *Kasparo* – a real find if you're looking for a break from sightseeing. Meanwhile, around the corner are several other cafés, while the narrow **Carrer del Bonsuccés**, **Carrer Sitges** and **Carrer dels Tallers** house a concentrated selection of the city's best independent music stores and urban and streetwear shops.

The beat from the street

The Barcelona sound – *mestiza* – is a cross-cultural musical fusion whose heartland is the immigrant melting-pot of the Raval. Parisian-born Barcelona resident Manu Chao kick-started the whole genre, but check out the Carrer dels Tallers music stores for the other flag-bearers – Cheb Balowski (Algerian–Catalan fusion), Ojos de Brujo (Catalan flamenco and rumba), GoLem System (dub/reggae) and Macaco (rumba, raga, hip-hop).

El Raval

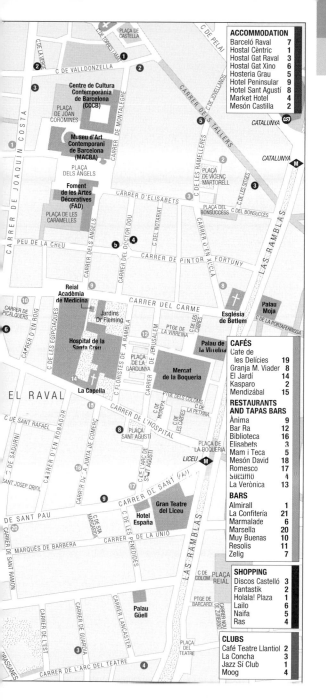

HOSPITAL DE LA SANTA CREU

Entrances on c/del Carme and c/de l'Hospital ⓂLiceu. Daily 10am–dusk. Free. La Capella exhibition information available on ⓦwww.bcn.cat/lacapella. MAP P.64–65, POCKET MAP B12–C12

The neighbourhood's most historic relic is the Gothic hospital complex founded in 1402. After the hospital shifted location in 1930, the buildings were subsequently converted to cultural and educational use (including the Catalan national library), and visitors and students now wander freely through the charming medieval cloistered garden. Inside the c/del Carme entrance (on the right) you can see some superb seventeenth-century decorative tiles, while opposite is a remarkable eighteenth-century anatomical theatre inside the **Reial Acadèmia de Medicina** (open Wed only 10am–noon; free; ring the bell). There's also the rather nice open-air *El Jardí* café at the c/de l'Hospital side, while the hospital's former chapel, **La Capella** (entered separately from c/de l'Hospital), is an exhibition space for new contemporary artists.

RAMBLA DE RAVAL

ⓂLiceu. MAP P.64–65, POCKET MAP B12/13

The most obvious manifestation of the changing character of El Raval is the palm-lined boulevard that was gouged through former tenements and alleys, providing a huge pedestrianized space between c/de l'Hospital and c/de Sant Pau. The *rambla* has a distinct character that's all its own, mixing kebab joints, phone shops and grocery stores with an increasing number of fashionable cafés and bars. Signature building, halfway down, is the glow-in-the-dark, designer *Barceló Raval* hotel, while kids find it hard to resist a clamber on the bulbous cat sculpture. A Saturday street market (selling everything from samosas to hammocks) adds a bit more character.

Just off the top of the *rambla*, **Carrer de la Riera Baixa** is at the centre of the city's secondhand/vintage clothing scene. A dozen funky little independent clothes shops provide the scope for an hour's browsing.

PALAU GÜELL

C/Nou de la Rambla 3–5 ⓂLiceu ☎933 173 974, ⓦwww.palauguell.cat. Tues–Sat 10am–2.30pm. Free. MAP P.64–65, POCKET MAP C13

El Raval's outstanding building is the extraordinary townhouse designed (1886–90) by the young Antoni Gaudí for a wealthy industrialist. At a time when other architects sought to conceal the iron supports within buildings, Gaudí displayed them instead as decorative features. Columns, arches and ceilings are all shaped and twisted in an elaborate style that was to become the hallmark of Gaudí's later works, while the roof terrace culminates in a

CAT SCULPTURE ON THE RAMBLA DE RAVAL

High society hotel

Some of the most influential names in Catalan *modernista* design came together to transform the dowdy nineteenth-century **Hotel España** (c/de Sant Pau 9–11, www.hotelespanya.com; map p.64–65, pocket map C13) into one of the city's most lavish addresses. With a gloriously tiled dining room, an amazing marble fireplace and a mural-clad ballroom, the hotel was the fashionable sensation of its day. A contemporary restoration under way at the time of writing should bring the hotel up to scratch while retaining its original appeal – a meal here has long been a Raval highlight.

fantastical series of tiled chimneys. The building is under long-term restoration, though partial visits are currently available – expect admission details to change.

ESGLÉSIA DE SANT PAU DEL CAMP

C/de Sant Pau 101 Paral.lel. Mon 5–8pm, Tues–Fri 10am–1.30pm & 5–8pm, Sat 10am–1.30pm. Admission to cloister €2. MAP P.64–65, POCKET MAP A13

The unusual name of the church of Sant Pau del Camp (St Paul of the Field) is a graphic reminder that it once stood in open countryside beyond the city walls. Sant Pau was a Benedictine foundation of the tenth century, and above the main entrance are primitive thirteenth-century carvings of fish, birds and faces, while others adorn the charming cloister.

MERCAT DE SANT ANTONI

C/del Comte d'Urgell 1 Sant Antoni 934 234 287, www.mercatsbcn.cat. Mon–Thurs 7am–2.30pm & 5–8.30pm, Fri & Sat 7am–8.30pm. MAP P.64–65, POCKET MAP E5

The neighbourhood's impressive nineteenth-century market is another that's being entirely remodelled (for completion in 2012) but a provisional market building continues in operation in the meantime (on Ronda Sant Antoni). Come on Sunday and there's a **book and coin market** (9am–2pm) instead, with collectors and enthusiasts arriving early to pick through the best bargains. The traditional bolt hole is *Els Tres Tombs*, the restaurant-bar on the corner of Ronda de Sant Antoni, open from 6am until late for a good-natured mix of locals, market traders and tourists.

PALAU GÜELL

Shops

DISCOS CASTELLÓ

C/del Tallers 3; and Tallers 7 Ⓜ Catalunya.
Mon–Sat 10am–8pm. MAP P.64–65, POCKET MAP C11

You can track down pretty much anything you want from the c/Tallers music stores, including classical recordings at no. 3, and rock, *mestiza*, hardcore and Spanish and Catalan sounds at no. 9. If these are no good, other nearby specialists like Revolver (c/Tallers 11; rock, indie and alternative) or Etnomusic (c/del Bonsuccés 6; world music) should do the job.

FANTASTIK

C/Joaquin Costa 62 Ⓜ Universitat Ⓦ www
.fantastik.es. Mon–Thurs 11am–2pm &
4–9pm, Fri & Sat 11am–9pm.
MAP P.64–65, POCKET MAP B10

Beguiling gifts, crafts and covetable objects from four continents. You'll never know how you lived without them, whether it's Chinese robots, African baskets, Russian domino sets or Vietnamese kitchen scales.

HOLALA! PLAZA

Pl. Castella 2 Ⓜ Universitat Ⓦ www
.holala-ibiza.com. Mon–Sat 11am–9pm.
MAP P.64–65, POCKET MAP C10

Vintage heaven in a warehouse setting (up past CCCB), for denim, flying jackets, Hawaiian shirts, baseball gear and much, much more. Also check out the other Raval stores at c/Riera Baixa 11 and c/Tallers 73.

LAILO

C/de la Riera Baixa 20 Ⓜ Liceu. Mon–Sat
11am–2pm & 5–8.30pm. MAP P.64–65,
POCKET MAP B12

Secondhand and vintage clothes shop with a massively wide-ranging stock. If you're serious about the vintage scene, this is your first stop – and if you don't find what you want just move on down the street to the neighbouring stores and outlets.

NAIFA

C/Dr. Joaquim Dou 11 Ⓜ Catalunya Ⓦ www
.naifa-bcn.com. Mon–Sat 11.30am–3pm &
4.30–9pm. MAP P.64–65, POCKET MAP C11

Original, colourful and informal men's and women's collections by Argentinian designer Paula Guillaumin. There's another Naifa outlet in the Barri Gòtic at c/de les Magdalenes 10 (near Via Laietana).

RAS

C/Dr. Joaquim Dou 10 Ⓜ Catalunya Ⓦ www
.rasbcn.com. Tues–Sat 1–9pm.
MAP P.64–65, POCKET MAP C11

Specializes in books and magazines on graphic design, architecture, photography and contemporary art. It's a cutting-edge gallery space too, so the exhibitions here are always worth a look.

Cafés

CAFÉ DE LES DELÍCIES

Rambla de Raval 47 ⓜ Liceu ☎ 934 415 714.
Mon–Wed 8.30am–11pm, Thurs–Sun
8.30am–2am. MAP P.64–65, POCKET MAP B13

One of the first off the blocks
in this revamped part of the
neighbourhood, and still
perhaps the best, plonking
thrift-shop chairs and tables
beneath exposed pipes and
girders and coming up with
something cute, cosy, mellow
and arty. Locals love to linger
here, meeting for breakfast
breakfast, sandwiches and tapas
to share.

GRANJA M. VIADER

C/Xuclà 4–6 ⓜ Catalunya ☎ 933 183 486.
Mon 5–8.45pm, Tues–Sat 9am–1.45pm &
5–8.45pm; closed 2 weeks in Aug.
MAP P.64–65, POCKET MAP C11

The oldest traditional *granja*
(milk bar) in town is a real
historical survivor – it even has
a pavement plaque outside for
services to the city. The original
owner was the inventor of
"Cacaolat" (a popular chocolate
drink), but for a taste of the old
days you could also try *mel i
mató* (curd cheese and honey)
or *llet Mallorquina* (fresh
milk with cinnamon and
lemon rind).

EL JARDÍ

C/de l'Hospital 56 ⓜ Liceu ☎ 933 291 550,
ⓦ www.eljardibarcelona.es. Mon–Sat
8am–11pm. MAP P.64–65, POCKET MAP B12

The "garden bar", hidden in the
elegant courtyard of the Gothic
Hospital de la Santa Creu, is a
real away-from-the-bustle find
– a year-round covered deck
offering drinks, snacks, salads
and sandwiches during the day,
plus a decent lunch menu and a
changing list of market-fresh
tapas.

KASPARO

Pl. Vicenç Martorell 4 ⓜ Catalunya ☎ 933
022 072. Daily 9am–10pm, until midnight in
summer; closed Jan. MAP P.64–65, POCKET MAP C11

A place to relax, in the arcaded
corner of a quiet square, with
outdoor seating year-round.
There's muesli, Greek yoghurt
and toast and jam for early
birds. Later, sandwiches, tapas
and assorted *platos del dia*
(dishes of the day) are on offer
– things like hummus and
bread, vegetable quiche,
couscous or pasta.

MENDIZÁBAL

C/Junta de Comerç 2 ⓜ Liceu. Daily 10am–
midnight, June–Sept until 1am.
MAP P.64–65, POCKET MAP C12

Don't look for a café because
there isn't one. Instead, this
cheery stand-up counter across
from the Hospital de la Santa
Creu dispenses juices, shakes,
beer and sandwiches to passing
punters. The lucky ones grab a
table over the road in the shady
little square.

GRANJA M. VIADER

Restaurants and tapas bars

ÀNIMA

C/dels Àngels 6 Ⓜ Liceu ☎ 933 424 912.
Mon–Sat 1–4pm & 9pm–midnight; Aug open
lunch only. MAP P.64–65, POCKET MAP C11

Sleek, arty joint attracting a young crowd who come for the seasonally influenced fusion cooking – courgette flowers and mussels *tempura* is a typical summer dish, or there might be braised oregano pork in autumn, with mains €10–16. The weekday lunch is the best deal, and if you're lucky you'll get a table outside.

BAR RA

Pl. de la Garduña 3 Ⓜ Liceu ☎ 615 959 872.
Ⓦ www.ratown.com. Daily 9am–1am; closed
Sun Nov–March. MAP P.64–65, POCKET MAP C12

Hip place behind the Boqueria market, with a funky feel and a sunny *terrassa*. "It's not a restaurant," they proclaim, but who are they kidding? Breakfast runs from 9am, there's a *menú del dia* served every day (weekends as well) from 1.30pm, with dinner from

8.30pm. The menu is eclectic to say the least – veggie lasagne to tuna with wasabi and avocado – but with the market on the doorstep it's all good stuff. Around €25.

BIBLIOTECA

C/Junta del Comerç 28 Ⓜ Liceu ☎ 934 126
261. Ⓦ www.bibliotecarestaurant
.cat. Mon–Sat 8pm–midnight; closed 2 weeks
in Aug. MAP P.64–65, POCKET MAP B12

One of the finest places to sample what Barcelona tends to call "creative cuisine". It's a stylish operation, with an open kitchen turning out fish dishes that might be cooked Japanese- or Basque-style, lamb given the local treatment (with parsnip and turnip), or the signature dish of venison pie served with a zippy veg purée of the day. Meals cost from around €40, and clued-up English-speaking staff make it a hassle-free dining experience. Reservations advisable.

ELISABETS

C/d'Elisabets 2 Ⓜ Catalunya ☎ 933 175 826.
Mon–Sat 8am–11pm; closed Aug.
MAP P.64–65, POCKET MAP C11

Reliable Catalan home cooking served at cramped tables in a jovial brick-walled dining room. Everyone piles in early for breakfast, the hearty lunch (1–4pm) is hard to beat for price, or you can just have tapas, sandwiches and drinks at the bar.

MAM I TECA

C/de la Lluna 4 Ⓜ Sant Antoni ☎ 934 413
335. Mon, Wed–Fri & Sun 1–4pm & 8.30pm–
midnight, Sat 8.30pm–midnight.
MAP P.64–65, POCKET MAP B11

An intimate (code for very small) place for superior tapas and fine wines, run by a wine-loving gourmet. All the meat is organic, the regional cheeses are well chosen, and

BAR RA

ROMESCO

C/de l'Arc de Sant Agusti s/n ⓜ Liceu ☎ 934
189 381. Mon–Sat 1–11.30pm; closed Aug.
MAP P.64–65, POCKET MAP C13

Old Barcelona hands talk
lovingly of the *Romesco*, and as
long as you accept its
limitations (dining under
strip-lights, gruff waiters) you
can hardly go wrong, as the
most expensive thing on the
menu is a €9 grilled sirloin and
most dishes go for €6 or less.
It's basic but good, with big
salads, country broths and
grilled veg to start, followed by
tuna steak, lamb chops or
grilled prawns from the
market, scattered with parsley
and chopped garlic. If you
spend more than €15, you've
probably eaten someone else's
dinner as well.

market-fresh ingredients go to
make up things like daily pasta
dishes, a platter of grilled
vegetables or a serving of lamb
cutlets (most dishes €6–12,
though some up to €20). Finish
with chocolate truffles or
home-made ice cream. There
are only three or four tables, or
you can perch at the bar.

MESÓN DAVID

C/de les Carretes 63 ⓜ Paral.lel ☎ 934 415
934, ⓦ www.mesondavid.com Tues–Sun
1–4pm & 8.30pm–1am. MAP P.64–65,
POCKET MAP A13

This down-to-earth Galician
bar-restaurant is a firm
favourite with neighbourhood
families, who bring their kids
before they can even walk. The
weekday *menú del dia* is a steal
– maybe lentil broth followed
by grilled trout – while
traditional Galician dishes like
octopus or the *combinado
Gallego* ("ham, salmi, ear") go
down well with the regulars.
Lunch is around €12, otherwise
most dishes €7–15, and there's
a good-natured bang on the
clog gong for anyone who
leaves a tip.

SESAMO

C/Sant Antoni Abat 52 ⓜ Sant Antoni ☎ 934
416 411. Tues–Sun 7.30pm–2.30am.
MAP P.64–65, POCKET MAP A11

A classy fusion tapas place
offering up a heavily vegetarian-
orientated chalkboard menu of
innovative dishes. Small and
not-so-small plates roll out of
the open kitchen –
veggie-stuffed courgette rolls (a
sort of Catalan sushi),
slow-roast tomato tart, coconut
curry or a daily risotto and
pasta dish, all in the €7–15
range. The Catalan wines and
cheeses are a high point too.

LA VERÒNICA

Rambla de Raval 2–4 ⓜ Liceu ☎ 933 293
303. Daily noon–1am; closed 2 weeks in Aug.
MAP P.64–65, POCKET MAP B12

Funky, retro pizzeria *La
Verònica* fits right into the
new-look Rambla de Raval.
Loads of crispy pizzas (mostly
vegetarian, between €10 and
€15) and inventive salads,
enjoyed by a young crowd.

Bars

ALMIRALL

C/de Joaquin Costa 33 ⓂUniversitat ☎ 933 189 917. Daily 6pm–2am (Fri & Sat until 3am). MAP P.64–65, POCKET MAP B11

Dating from 1860, Barcelona's oldest bar is a *modernista* classic – check out the ornate doors, counter and stupendous, glittering bar. It's long been a venerated leftist hangout and because it's not too young and not too loud, it's always good for a late-night drink away from the party crowd.

LA CONFITERÍA

C/de Sant Pau 128 ⓂParal.lel ☎ 934 430 458. Mon–Sat 8pm–3am, Sun 7pm–2am. MAP P.64–65, POCKET MAP A13

This old bakery and confectioner's – carved wood bar, faded tile floor, murals, antique chandeliers – is now a popular bar and meeting point. It's out on a limb in the Raval, but the glorious interior is certainly worth a detour, and it's a handy stop-off in any case on the way to a night out in Poble Sec.

MARMALADE

C/de Riera Alta 4–6 ⓂSant Antoni ☎ 934 423 966, ⓌWwww.marmaladebarcelona.com. Mon–Sat 7pm–3am, Sun 11am–3am. MAP P.64–65, POCKET MAP B11

A hugely glam facelift for the old Muebles Navarro furniture store goes for big, church-like spaces and a back-lit Art Deco bar that resembles a high altar. Drinks and eats are the familiar lounge-bar staples of cocktails and fancy tapas, and there's a restaurant menu served daily from 7.30pm (and brunch on Sunday). If you like the style, give the more informal Barri Gòtic sister bar, *Milk*, a whirl too.

MARSELLA

C/de Sant Pau 65 ⓂLiceu ☎ 934 427 263. Mon–Sat 10pm–3am; closed 2 weeks in Aug. MAP P.64–65, POCKET MAP B13

Authentic, atmospheric, sleaze-period bar – named after the French port of Marseilles – where absinthe is the drink of choice. It's frequented by a spirited mix of oddball locals and young trendies, all looking for a slice of the old Barri Xines.

MUY BUENAS

C/del Carme 63 ⓂLiceu ☎ 934 425 053. Tues–Sat 9am–3am. MAP P.64–65, POCKET MAP B11

Arguably the Raval's nicest traditional watering hole, with a restored *modernista* interior and eager-to-please staff. A long marble trough does duty as the bar, and the beer's pulled from antique beer taps.

RESOLIS

C/Riera Baixa 22 ⓂSant Antoni ☎ 934 412 948. Mon–Wed 1pm–1am, Thurs–Sat 1pm–2.30am. MAP P.64–65, POCKET MAP B11

The team behind *Ànima* restaurant rescued this decayed, century-old bar and turned it into a cool hangout with decent tapas, from veggie bruschetta to steamed mussels. They didn't do much – a lick of paint, polish the panelling, patch up the brickwork – but now

LA CONFITERÍA

punters spill out of the door onto "secondhand clothes street" and a good time is had by all.

ZELIG

C/del Carme 116 Ⓜ Sant Antoni ☎ 934 415 622. Tues–Sun 7pm–2am (Fri & Sat until 3am). MAP P.64–65, POCKET MAP A11

The photo-frieze on granite walls and a fully stocked cocktail bar make it very much of its *barri*, but *Zelig* stands out from the crowd. It offers a chatty welcome, a tendency towards 1980s sounds and a slight whiff of camp.

Clubs

CAFÉ TEATRE LLANTIOL

C/Riereta 7 Ⓜ Sant Antoni ☎ 933 299 009, Ⓦ www.llantiol.com. Closed Mon. MAP P.64–65, POCKET MAP A12

Local-language theatre isn't accessible to non-speakers, but you might give this idiosyncratic café-cabaret a try – the shows feature a mix of mime, song, clowning, magic and dance, and sometimes there's English-language stand-up comedy by local and visiting acts. Shows (€10–15) normally begin at 9pm and 11pm (6pm & 9pm on Sun), with an additional late-night Saturday special.

LA CONCHA

C/Guardia 14 Ⓜ Drassanes ☎ 933 024 118. Daily 5pm–3am. MAP P.64–65, POCKET MAP B13

The Arab-flamenco fusion creates a great atmosphere, worth braving the slightly dodgy area for. It's a kitsch, gay-friendly joint, dedicated to the "incandescent presence" of Sara Montiel, Queen of Song and Cinema, with uninhibited dancing by tourists and locals alike. Admission free.

RESOLIS

JAZZ SÍ CLUB

C/Requesens 2 Ⓜ Sant Antoni ☎ 933 290 020, Ⓦ www.tallerdemusics.com. MAP P.64–65, POCKET MAP A11

This is a great place for inexpensive (€6–8) gigs in a tiny sweat-box of a club associated with the Taller de Musics (music school). Every night from around 8.30 or 9pm there's something different, from exuberant rock, blues, jazz and jam sessions to the popular weekly Cuban (Thursday) and flamenco (Friday) nights. There are usually a couple of sessions a night, with an interval in between – your first drink is included in the price, and the bar is as cheap as chips.

MOOG

C/Arc del Teatre 3 Ⓜ Drassanes ☎ 933 017 282, Ⓦ www.masimas.com. Daily midnight–5am. MAP P.64–65, POCKET MAP C14

Influential club with a minimalist look, playing techno, electro, drum 'n' bass, house, funk and soul to a cool but up-for-it crowd. Admission €10.

Sant Pere

Perhaps the least visited part of the Old Town is the medieval *barri* of Sant Pere, the area that lies immediately north of the Barri Gòtic and across Carrer de la Princesa from La Ribera. It has two remarkable buildings – the *modernista* concert hall, known as the Palau de la Música Catalana, and the stylishly designed neighbourhood market, Mercat Santa Caterina. There's been much regeneration in the *barri* over recent years, and it's well worth an afternoon's stroll or a night out, with new boulevards and community projects alongside DJ bars and designer shops. To walk through the neighbourhood, you can start at Metro Urquinaona, close to the Palau de la Música Catalana, with Metro Jaume I marking the southern end of Sant Pere.

PALAU DE LA MÚSICA CATALANA

C/Sant Pere Més Alt ⓂUrquinaona ☎ 902 475 485, ⓌWwww.palaumusica.org. Guided tours daily 10am–3.30pm, plus Easter week & Aug 10am–6pm, in English on the hour. €12. MAP P.75, POCKET MAP E11

Barcelona's most extraordinary concert hall was built in 1908, to a design by visionary *modernista* architect Lluís Domènech i Montaner. The elaborate exterior is simply smothered in tiles and mosaics, while a mighty bulbous stained-glass skylight caps the second-storey auditorium (which contemporary critics claimed to be an engineering impossibility). The more recent Petit Palau offers a smaller auditorium space, while to the side a contemporary glass facade and courtyard provide the main public access. Concerts here (Oct–June)

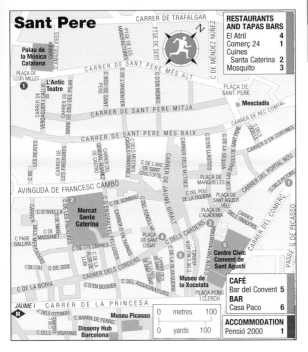

Orfeo Català choral group and
the Barcelona city orchestra,
though you can also catch
anything from flamenco to
world music. Numbers are
limited on the very popular
fifty-minute guided tours, so it's
best to buy a ticket a day or two
in advance (by phone, online or
at the box office).

L'ANTIC TEATRE

C/Verdaguer i Callis 12 ⓜ Urquinaona
ⓣ 933 152 354, ⓦ www.lanticteatre.com.
MAP P.75, POCKET MAP E11

An independent theatre with a
wildly original programme,
from video shows and offbeat
cabaret to modern dance and
left-field music. The best bit
may just be the magical,
light-strung garden-bar (daily
4–11pm), a real insiders' place
but open to all.

PLAÇA DE SANT PERE

ⓜ Arc de Triomf. MAP P.75, POCKET MAP G11
The neighbourhood extends
around three parallel medieval
streets, carrers de Sant Pere
Més Alt (upper), Mitja
(middle) and Baix (lower),
which contain the bulk of the
finest buildings and shops – a
mixture of boutiques, textile
shops, groceries and old family
businesses. The streets all
converge on the original
neighbourhood square, Plaça
de Sant Pere, whose foursquare
church flanks one side,
overlooking a flamboyant iron
drinking fountain. Look in on
Mescladis (Pl. de Sant Pere 5,
ⓦ www.mescladis.org), a
community project and
cookery school – the café
(closed Mon) has a great world
menu, especially the weekend
Mexican brunch.

MERCAT SANTA CATERINA

Av. Francesc Cambò 16 ⓂJaume I ☎933 195 740, ⓦwww.mercatsantacaterina.net. Mon 7.30am–2pm, Tues, Wed & Sat 7.30am–3.30pm, Thurs & Fri 7.30am–8.30pm; Aug open mornings only. MAP P.75, POCKET MAP F12

An eye-catching renovation of the neighbourhood market retained its original walls but added slatted wooden doors and windows and a dramatic multicoloured wave roof. It's one of the best places in the city to shop for food, and its market restaurant and bar are definitely worth a visit in any case. During renovation work, the foundations of a medieval convent were discovered here and the excavations are visible in the **Espai Santa Caterina** (Mon–Wed & Sat 8.30am–2pm, Thurs & Fri 8.30am–8pm; free) at the rear of the market.

PLAÇA DE SANT AGUSTI VELL

ⓂJaume I. MAP P.75, POCKET MAP G12

The pretty, tree-shaded Plaça de Sant Agusti Vell sits in the middle of an ambitious urban regeneration project, which has transformed previously crowded alleys. To the north, locals tend organic allotments in the middle of the landscaped Pou de la Figuera *rambla*, while south down **Carrer d'Allada Vermell** are

overarching trees, a children's playground and a series of outdoor cafés and bars. Meanwhile, running down from Plaça de Sant Agusti Vell, **Carrer dels Carders** – once "ropemakers' street" – is now a funky retail quarter mixing grocery stores, cafés, boutiques and craft shops.

CENTRE CÍVIC CONVENT DE SANT AGUSTI

C/del Comerç 36 ⓂJaume I ☎932 103 732, ⓦwww.bcn.cat/centrecivicsantagusti. Mon–Fri 9am–10pm, Sat 10am–2pm & 4–9pm. Admission charges vary, some events free. MAP P.75, POCKET MAP F12–G12

Driving many of the neighbourhood improvements is the community centre installed inside the revamped Convent de Sant Agusti, whose thirteenth-century cloister provides a unique performance space. There's a full cultural programme here, from workshops to concerts, with a particular emphasis on electronic and experimental music and art, and don't miss the excellent convent café.

MUSEU DE LA XOCOLATA

C/del Comerç 36 ⓂJaume I ☎932 687 878, ⓦwww.pastisseria.com. Mon & Wed–Sat 10am–7pm, Sun 10am–3pm. €4.30, first Mon of month free. MAP P.75, POCKET MAP F12–G13

Part of the Convent de Sant Agusti contains Barcelona's chocolate museum, which is a rather uninspiring plod through the history of the stuff. Whether you go in or not depends on how keen you are to see models of Gaudí buildings or religious icons sculpted in chocolate. There are some very nice chocs to buy in the shop though (free to enter), while at the adjacent Escola de Pastisseria, glass windows look onto the students learning their craft in the kitchens.

MERCAT SANTA CATERINA

Café

BAR DEL CONVENT

Pl. de l'Acadèmia, C/del Comerç 36
Ⓜ Jaume I | ☎ 932 103 732. Mon–Thurs
10am–9pm, Fri & Sat noon–11pm.
MAP P.75, POCKET MAP G12

The cloister café-bar is a
bargain for lunch and light
meals, with soups, stir-fries,
lasagne and couscous for €4–7.
At night it's more of a bar,
with a range of live shows, DJs
and concerts.

Restaurants and tapas bars

EL ATRIL

C/dels Carders 23 Ⓜ Jaume I | ☎ 933 101
220, Ⓦ www.atrilbarcelona.com. Tues–Sun
noon–midnight. MAP P.75, POCKET MAP F12

The "Music Stand" is a cosy
bar-restaurant complete with
summer *terrassa* and an
international menu, from
kangaroo fillet to *moules frites*
(mains €10–15). There's a
good-value lunch, and dinner
from 7pm, otherwise it's
modern tapas, drinks and a
decent Sunday brunch.

COMERÇ 24

C/Comerç 24 Ⓜ Jaume I | ☎ 933 192 102,
Ⓦ www.comerc24.com. Tues–Sat 1.30–3.30pm
& 8.30–11pm; closed 2 weeks in Aug. MAP P.75,
POCKET MAP G12

Carles Abellan calls his cuisine
"glocal" (ie global + local) and
in the oh-so-cool interior
you're presented with
tapas-style dishes mixing
flavours and textures to
calculated effect (foie gras and
truffle hamburger, tuna sashimi
on pizza). This is cutting-edge
Barcelona dining – prices are
high (€70–80 a head), and
reservations advised.

CASA PACO

CUINES SANTA CATERINA

Mercat Santa Caterina, Av. Francesc Cambó
16 Ⓜ Jaume I | ☎ 932 689 918, Ⓦ www
.cuinessantacaterina.com. Bar daily
9am–11.30pm, restaurant 1–4pm &
8–11.30pm (Thurs–Sat until 12.30am).
MAP P.75, POCKET MAP F12

A ravishing open-plan tapas
bar and market restaurant
with tables under soaring
rafters. Food touches all bases
– pasta to sushi, Catalan rice
to Thai curry – with most
things costing €9–12.

MOSQUITO

C/dels Carders 46 Ⓜ Jaume I | ☎ 932 687
569, Ⓦ www.mosquitotapas.com. Mon &
Wed–Sun 7.30pm–12.30am (Fri & Sat until
2am). MAP P.75, POCKET MAP F12

Asian tapas bar with paper
lanterns, artisan beers and an
authentic, made-to-order dim
sum menu (dishes €3–5), from
shrimp dumplings to tofu rolls.

Bar

CASA PACO

C/d'Allada Vermell 10 Ⓜ Jaume I | ☎ 935 073
719. Daily 9am–2am (Fri & Sat until 3am),
Oct–March opens 6pm. MAP P.75, POCKET MAP F12

This cool music joint is a hit on
the weekend DJ scene. There's a
great *terrassa* under the trees,
but if you can't get a table here
try one of several other alfresco
bars down the boulevard.

La Ribera

The traditional highlights of the old artisans' quarter of La Ribera are the Museu Picasso (Barcelona's single biggest tourist attraction) and the graceful church of Santa María del Mar. The cramped streets between the two were at the heart of medieval industry and commerce, and it's still the neighbourhood of choice for local designers, craftspeople and artists, whose boutiques and workshops lend La Ribera an air of creativity. Galleries and applied art museums occupy the medieval mansions of Carrer de Montcada – the neighbourhood's most handsome street – while the *barri* is at its most hip in the area around the Passeig del Born, whose cafés, restaurants and bars make it one of the city's premier nightlife centres. The most direct access point for La Ribera is Metro Jaume I.

MUSEU PICASSO

C/de Montcada 15–23 ⓂJaume I ☎932 563 000, ⓦwww.museupicasso.bcn.cat. Tues–Sun & hols 10am–8pm. General admission €9, exhibitions €5.80, Sun after 3pm & first Sun of the month free. MAP P.80, POCKET MAP F13

The celebrated Museu Picasso is one of the most important collections of Picasso's work in the world, but even so some visitors are disappointed, since the museum contains none of his best-known pictures and few in the Cubist style. But there are almost 4000 works in the permanent collection – housed in five adjoining medieval palaces – which provide a fascinating opportunity to trace Picasso's development from his drawings as a young boy to the mature works of later years. Paintings

from his art-school days in Barcelona (1895–97) show tantalizing glimpses of the city that the young Picasso was beginning to explore, while works in the style of Toulouse-Lautrec reflect his interest in Parisian art. Other selected works are from the famous Blue Period (1901–04) and Pink Period (1904–06), and from his Cubist (1907–20) and Neoclassical (1920–25) stages. The large gaps in the main collection only underline Picasso's extraordinary changes of style and mood, best illustrated by the jump to 1957, a year represented by his interpretations of Velázquez's masterpiece *Las Meninas*.

As well as showing changing selections of sketches, prints and drawings, the museum addresses Picasso's work as a ceramicist, highlighting the vibrantly decorated dishes and jugs donated by his wife Jacqueline.

A free guided tour is the best way to get to grips with the collection – in English currently on Tuesdays and Thursdays at 4pm (book in advance by phone or via the website). There's a courtyard café, and, of course, a shop full of Picasso-related gifts.

Picasso in Barcelona

Although born in Málaga, **Pablo Picasso** (1881–1973) spent much of his youth – from the age of 14 to 23 – in Barcelona. This time encompassed the whole of his Blue Period (1901–04) and provided many of the formative influences on his art. Not far from the Museu Picasso you can see many of the buildings in which Picasso lived and worked, notably the Escola de Belles Arts de Llotja (c/Consolat del Mar, near Estació de França), where his father taught drawing and where Picasso himself absorbed an academic training. The apartments where the family lived when they first arrived in Barcelona were at Pg. d'Isabel II 4 and c/Reina Cristina 3, both near the Escola, while Picasso's first real studio (in 1896) was located over on c/de la Plata at no. 4. A few years later, many of his Blue Period works were finished at a studio at c/del Comerç 28. His first public exhibition was in 1901 at the extravagantly decorated *Els Quatre Gats* tavern (c/Montsió 3, Barri Gòtic; ⊚www.4gats.com); you can still have a meal there today.

DISSENY HUB BARCELONA

DHUB, c/de Montcada 12 🚇 Jaume I ☎ 932 562 300, 🌐 www.dhub-bcn.cat. Tues–Sat 11am–7pm, Sun 11am–8pm, hols 11am–3pm. Some exhibitions free, otherwise €5, Sun after 3pm & first Sun of the month free.
MAP P.80, POCKET MAP F13

The city's unparalleled design (*disseny*) and applied art collections are on display at the Palau Reial at Pedralbes pending the construction of a Design Centre at Glòries. In the meantime, the umbrella organisation hosts a range of interesting contemporary exhibitions – from photography to design industry developments – at DHUB Montcada (in what was the old Textile Museum building), and the ticket is valid for entry to the Palau Reial collections. There's also a good café-restaurant on site.

MUSEU BARBIER-MUELLER

C/de Montcada 14 🚇 Jaume I ☎ 933 104 516, 🌐 www.barbier-mueller.ch. Tues–Fri 11am–7pm, Sat 10am–7pm, Sun 10am–3pm. €3.50, first Sun of the month free.
MAP P.80, POCKET MAP F13

The sixteenth-century Palau Nadal houses a fascinating collection of Pre-Columbian art at the Museu Barbier-Mueller. Temporary exhibitions highlight wide-ranging themes, and draw on a peerless collection of sculpture, pottery, jewellery and textiles as well as everyday items, from decorated Mongolian belt-buckles to carved African furniture. Afterwards, have a browse in the museum shop, which has a wide range of artefacts, including wall hangings, jewellery, terracotta pots and figurines.

RESTAURANTS & TAPAS BARS		CAFÉS	
Cal Pep	12	La Bascula	1
Casa Delfin	8	Café del Born	9
Euskal Etxea	6	**BARS**	
Salero	13	Espai Barroc	4
Senyor		La Fianna	7
Parellada	2	Mudanzas	11
Wushu	14	El Nus	3
El Xampanyet	5	La Vinya del Senyor	10

ACCOMMODATION	
Chic & Basic	1
Gothic Point Hostel	2
Hostal Nuevo Colón	4
Hotel Banys Orientals	3

SHOPS	
Almacen Marabi	3
La Botifarreria de Santa Maria	6
Bubó	7
La Campana	1
Casa Gispert	4
Custo Barcelona	9
Iriarte Iriarte	2
Old Curiosity Shop	5
U-Casas	8
Vila Viniteca	10

ESGLÉSIA DE SANTA MARÍA DEL MAR

Pl. de Santa Maria ⓜ Jaume I. Mon–Sat 9am–1.30pm & 4.30–8.30pm, Sun 9.30am–1.45pm & 4.30–8.45pm.
MAP P.80, POCKET MAP F13

The Ribera's flagship church was begun on the order of King Jaume II in 1324, and finished in only five years. Built on what was the seashore in the fourteenth century, Santa María was at the centre of the medieval city's trading district (nearby c/Argentería, for example, is named after the silversmiths who once worked there), and it came to embody the commercial supremacy of the Crown of Aragon, of which Barcelona was capital. It's an exquisite example of Catalan-Gothic architecture – as all the later Baroque trappings were destroyed during the Civil War, eyes instead are concentrated on the simple spaces of the interior, especially the beautiful stained glass.

PASSEIG DEL BORN

ⓜ Jaume I. MAP P.80, POCKET MAP F13

Fronting the church of Santa María del Mar is the fashionable Passeig del Born, once the site of medieval fairs and entertainments ("born" means tournament) and now an avenue lined with a parade of plane trees shading a host of classy bars, delis and shops. At night the Born becomes one of Barcelona's biggest bar zones, as spirited locals frequent a panoply of drinking haunts – from old-style cocktail lounges to thumping music bars. Shoppers and browsers, meanwhile, scour the narrow medieval alleys on either side of the *passeig* for boutiques and craft workshops – carrers Flassaders, Vidriera and Rec, in particular, are noted for clothes, shoes, jewellery and design galleries.

ANTIC MERCAT DEL BORN

Pg. del Born ⓜ Barceloneta.
MAP P.80, POCKET MAP G13

The old Mercat del Born (1873–76) was the biggest of Barcelona's nineteenth-century market halls. It was the city's main wholesale fruit and veg market until 1971, and was then due to be demolished, but was saved by local protest. It lay empty for decades, but work is under way to turn the building into a neighbourhood cultural centre (by 2012), which will also showcase the extensive archeological remains found on site of eighteenth-century shops, factories, houses and taverns.

Shops

ALMACEN MARABI

C/Flassaders 30 Ⓜ Jaume I Ⓦ www
.almacenmarabi.blogspot.com. Tues–Fri
noon–2.30pm & 5–8.30pm, Sat 5–8.30pm.
MAP P.80, POCKET MAP F13

Mariela Marabi, originally from
Argentina, makes handmade
felt finger dolls, mobiles,
puppets and animals of
extraordinary invention. She's
often at work at the back, while
her eye-popping showroom
also has limited-edition pieces
by other selected artists and
designers.

LA BOTIFARRERIA DE SANTA MARIA

C/Santa Maria 4 Ⓜ Jaume I. Mon–Fri
8.30am–2.30pm & 5–8.30pm, Sat
8.30am–2.30pm. MAP P.80, POCKET MAP F14

If you ever doubted the power
of the humble Catalan pork
sausage, drop by this designer
temple-deli where otherwise
beautifully behaved locals jostle
at the counter for the day's
home-made *botifarra*, plus
rigorously sourced hams,
cheese, pâtés and salamis. True
disciples can even buy the
T-shirt.

CASA GISPERT

BUBÓ

C/Caputxes 10 Ⓜ Jaume I Ⓦ www.bubo
.ws. Daily 10am–10pm (Fri & Sat until 1am).
MAP P.80, POCKET MAP E14

There are chocolates and then
there are Bubó chocolates –
jewel-like creations and playful
desserts by pastry maestro
Carles Mampel. This very classy
shop is complemented by their
minimalist new-wave tapas
place, *Bubóbar*, a couple of
doors down at no.6.

LA CAMPANA

C/Princesa 36 Ⓜ Jaume I. Daily 10am–9pm.
MAP P.80, POCKET MAP F13

This lovely old shop from 1890
presents handmade pralines
and truffles, but is best known
for its beautifully packaged
squares and slabs of *turrón*,
traditional Catalan nougat.

CASA GISPERT

C/Sombrerers 23 Ⓜ Jaume I Ⓦ www
.casagispert.com. Tues–Fri 9.30am–2pm &
4–7.30pm (also Mon in Oct, Nov & Dec), Sat
10am–2pm & 5–8pm. MAP P.80, POCKET MAP F13

Roasters of nuts, coffee and
spices for over 150 years. It's a
truly delectable store of
wooden boxes, baskets, stacked
shelves and tantalizing smells,
and there are organic nuts and
dried fruit, teas and gourmet
deli items available too.

CUSTO BARCELONA

Pl. de les Olles 7 Ⓜ Barceloneta Ⓦ www
.custo-barcelona.com. Mon–Sat 10am–9pm,
Sun noon–8pm. MAP P.80, POCKET MAP F14

Where the stars get their
T-shirts – hugely colourful
(highly priced) designer tops
and sweaters for men and
women. There are other
branches around town (at
Ramblas 109, c/de Ferran
36, and at L'Illa shopping),
while last season's gear gets
another whirl at Pl. del Pi in
the Barri Gòtic.

IRIARTE IRIARTE

C/Esquirol 1 ⓜ Jaume I ⓦ www
.iriarteiriarte.com. Tues–Fri 10am–2pm &
4–8.30pm, Sat noon–8.30pm.
MAP P.80, POCKET MAP E13

Atelier-showroom for
sumptuous handmade leather
bags and belts. The alley (off
c/Cotoners) has several other
interesting craft workshops and
galleries to browse.

OLD CURIOSITY SHOP

C/Volta dels Tamborets 4 ⓜ Barceloneta.
Mon–Fri 5–9pm, Sat 11.30am–3pm & 5–9pm.
MAP P.80, POCKE MAP F13

Through the arch and down the
alley from Passeig del Born,
this place is a suitably
mysterious location for a
collection of antique and repro
curios, from Russian porcelain
tea sets to chunky vintage
diaries and ledgers.

U-CASAS

C/Espaseria 4 ⓜ Jaume I ☎ 933 100 046,
ⓦ www.casasclub.com. Mon–Sat
10.30am–8.30pm (Fri & Sat until 9pm).
MAP P.80, POCKET MAP F14

Casas has four lines of shoe
stores across Spain, with the
U-Casas brand at the young
and funky end of the market.
Never mind the shoes, the
stores are pretty spectacular,
especially here in the Born
where an enormous
shoe-shaped bench-cum-sofa
takes centre-stage. Other
branches are at c/Tallers 2
(Raval), c/Portaferrissa 25
(Barri Gòtic) and L'Illa and
Maremàgnum shopping
centres.

VILA VINITECA

C/Agullers 7 & 9 ⓜ Jaume I ☎ 937 777 017,
ⓦ www.vilaviniteca.es. Mon–Sat
8.30am–8.30pm (closes Sat at 2.30pm in July
& Aug). MAP P.80, POCKET MAP E14

A very knowledgeable specialist
in Catalan and Spanish wines.

CUSTO BARCELONA

Pick your vintage and then nip
over the road for the gourmet
deli part of the operation.

Cafés

LA BASCULA

C/Flassaders 30 ⓜ Jaume I ☎ 933 199 866.
Wed–Sat 11.30am–11.30pm, Sun 1–7pm.
MAP P.80, POCKET MAP F13

A hippy-chic makeover for an
old backstreet chocolate
factory. It's a welcoming veggie
place, serving speciality pastas,
gourmet sandwiches, crepes,
dipping platters, salads and the
like, and there are dozens of
organic teas, coffees, wines,
juices and shakes.

CAFÉ DEL BORN

Pl. Comercial 10 ⓜ Barceloneta ☎ 932 683
272. Daily 9am–1am (Fri & Sat until 3am).
MAP P.80, POCKET MAP F13

No gimmicks, no fusion food,
and dodgy local art kept to a
bare minimum – the recipe
for success at this
ever-popular neighbourhood
café-bar. There's a simple
Mediterranean menu on
offer, while Sunday brunch is
the big weekend draw.

Restaurants and tapas bars

SENYOR PARELLADA

CAL PEP

Pl. de les Olles 8 ⓜ Barceloneta ☎ 933 107 961, ⓦ www.calpep.com. Mon 7.30–11.30pm, Tues–Fri 1–3.45pm & 7.30–11.30pm, Sat 1.15–3.45pm; closed Easter week & Aug. MAP P.80, POCKET MAP F14

There's no equal in town for off-the-boat and out-of-the-market tapas. You may have to queue, and prices are high for what's effectively a bar meal (up to €40), but it's definitely worth it for the likes of impeccably fried shrimp, grilled sea bass, Catalan sausage, or squid and chickpeas – all overseen by Pep himself, bustling up and down the counter.

CASA DELFIN

Pg. del Born 36 ⓜ Jaume I ☎ 933 195 088. Daily noon–1am. MAP P.80, POCKET MAP F13

A revamp for an old cheap-and-cheerful classic has resulted in a designer look and contemporary Catalan dishes, from crispy artichokes to roast mountain lamb. It's served tapas-style, so you can snack or dine, with dishes from €5 to €17. The *terrassa*, outside the old market, is the best in the neighbourhood.

EUSKAL ETXEA

Pl. de Montcada 1–3 ⓜ Jaume I ☎ 933 102 185. Mon 6.30pm–midnight, Tues–Sat noon–4pm & 6.30pm–midnight. MAP P.80, POCKET MAP F13

The bar at the front of the local Basque community centre is great for sampling *pintxos* – elaborately fashioned pint-sized tapas, held together by a stick. Just point to what you want (and keep the sticks so the bill can be tallied).

SALERO

C/Rec 60 ⓜ Barceloneta ☎ 933 198 022. Mon–Sat 1.30–4pm & 8.30pm–midnight, Sun 8.30pm–midnight; closed 2 weeks in Aug. MAP P.80, POCKET MAP F14

A crisp, modern space fashioned from a former salt-cod warehouse – if white is your colour, you'll enjoy the experience. The food's Mediterranean-Asian, presenting delights like vegetable tempura or a *mee goreng* (fried noodle) of the day (most dishes €10–18).

SENYOR PARELLADA

C/Argenteria 37 ⓜ Jaume I ☎ 933 105 094, ⓦ www.senyorparellada.com. Daily 1–3.45pm & 8.30–11.30pm. MAP P.80, POCKET MAP F13

A gorgeous renovation of an eighteenth-century building is the mellow background for genuine Catalan food – home-style cabbage rolls, duck with figs, a papillote of beans with herbs – served from a long menu that doesn't bother dividing starters from mains. You can eat well for around €30.

WUSHU

Av. del Marquès de l'Argentera 1
Ⓜ Barceloneta ☎ 933 107 313, Ⓦ www
.wushu-restaurant.com. Tues–Sat 1–5pm &
8–11.45pm, Sun 2–5pm & 7–11pm.
MAP P.80, POCKET MAP F14

Aussie-chef Brad Ainsworth's
cool Asian wok bar turns out
super-authentic *pad Thais*,
laksas, rice paper rolls, red and
green curries, Chinese noodles
and the like. Around €30.

EL XAMPANAYET

C/de Montcada 22 Ⓜ Jaume I ☎ 933 197
003. Tues–Sat noon–4pm & 6.30–11pm, Sun
noon–4pm; closed Aug. MAP P.80, POCKET MAP F13

Traditional blue-tiled bar doing
a roaring trade in sparkling
cava, cider and traditional
tapas (anchovies are the
speciality). The drinks are
cheap and the tapas turn out
to be rather pricey, but there's
usually a good buzz about
the place.

Bars

ESPAI BARROC

Palau Dalmases, c/de Montcada 20 Ⓜ Jaume
I ☎ 933 100 673. Tues–Sat 8pm–2am, Sun
6–10pm. MAP P.80, POCKET MAP F13

The handsome Baroque
mansion of Palau Dalmases is
open in the evenings for wine,
champagne or cognac in

DINERS AT LA FIANNA

refined surroundings or, once a
week, the billowing strains of
live opera (Thurs at 11pm; €20,
first drink included).

LA FIANNA

C/Banys Vells 19 Ⓜ Jaume I ☎ 933 151 810,
Ⓦ www.lafianna.com. Mon–Wed & Sun
6pm–1.30am, Thurs–Sat 6pm–2.30am.
MAP P.80, POCKET MAP F13

Flickering candelabras, rough
plaster walls and deep colours
set the Gothic mood in this
stylish lounge-bar. Relax on the
chill-out beds and velvet sofas,
or book ahead to eat – the
fusion-food restaurant is open
from 8.30pm.

MUDANZAS

C/Vidriería 15 Ⓜ Barceloneta ☎ 933 191 137.
Daily 10am–2.30am, Aug opens at 6pm.
MAP P.80, POCKET MAP F14

Locals like the relaxed
atmosphere, while those in the
know come for the wide
selection of rums, whiskies and
vodkas from around the world.

EL NUS

C/Mirallers 5 Ⓜ Jaume I ☎ 933 195 355.
Daily except Wed 7.30pm–2.30am.
MAP P.80, POCKET MAP F13

Still has the feel of the shop it
once was, down to the antique
cash register, though now it's a
kind of jazz-bar-cum-gallery –
a quiet, faintly old-fashioned,
late-night place.

LA VINYA DEL SENYOR

Pl. Santa Maria 5 Ⓜ Jaume I ☎ 933 103 379.
Tues–Thurs noon–1am, Fri & Sat noon–2am,
Sun noon–midnight.
MAP P.80, POCKET MAP F14

A great wine bar with
front-row seats onto the lovely
church of Santa María del Mar.
The wine list is really good –
with a score available by the
glass – and there are oysters,
smoked salmon and other
classy tapas available.

Parc de la Ciutadella

The city's favourite green space holds a full set of attractions – the Catalan parliament building (not open to the public), plant houses, museums and a zoo – though on lazy summer days there's little incentive to do any more than stroll the garden paths and pilot rowboats across the ornamental lake. The park itself (open daily 8am until dusk) was laid out in the nineteenth century and subsequently chosen as the site of the 1888 Universal Exhibition – from which period dates a series of vibrant monuments by the city's pioneering *modernista* architects. The park's main gates are on Passeig de Picasso, a short walk from La Ribera, and there's also an entrance on Passeig de Pujades (Metro Arc de Triomf); for direct access to the zoo, use Metro Ciutadella-Vila Olímpica.

ARC DE TRIOMF

Pg. Lluís Companys Ⓜ Arc de Triomf.
MAP P.87, POCKET MAP G11

A giant brick arch announces the architectural splendours to come in the park itself. Conceived as a bold statement of Catalan intent, it's studded with ceramic figures and motifs and topped by two pairs of bulbous domes. The reliefs on the main facade show the city of Barcelona welcoming visitors to the 1888 Universal Exhibition, held in the park to the south.

CASCADA

Parc de la Ciutadella Ⓜ Arc de Triomf.
MAP P.87, POCKET MAP K6

Ciutadella's monumental
fountain in the northeast
corner of the park displays a
Baroque extravagance in its
statuary (notably the dragons).
The young Antoni Gaudí had a
hand in its design, which is
certainly suggestive of the
flamboyant decoration that
became one of his trademarks.
For a few euros you can rent a
rowboat and paddle about on
the nearby lake.

MUSEU DE ZOOLOGIA

Pg. de Picasso Ⓜ Arc de Triomf ☎ 932 562
200, ⓦ www.museuciencies.bcn.cat. Tues–Fri
10am–6pm, Sat, Sun & hols 10am–8pm.
€5.30, Sun after 3pm & first Sun of the month
free. MAP P.87, POCKET MAP G12

The Natural Science Museum
divides its collections between

two buildings in Ciutadella
park, on either side of the
Hivernacle plant house. The
one housing the zoological
museum is an impressive
red-brick, castle-like structure,
originally a café and later a
centre for *modernista* arts and
crafts dubbed the "Castell dels
Tres Dragons". The building
itself has long knocked spots
off the rather dry collection of
stuffed Iberian birds, insects
and animals inside, though a
museum revamp during 2010
should inject a livelier tone,
while temporary popular
science exhibitions always
create much interest. You can
also liven up a visit for the
under-12s by asking for the free
educational activities kit. Note
that the ticket is also valid for
the nearby Geological Museum
and the Botanical Garden at
Montjuïc.

HIVERNACLE AND UMBRACLE

Pg. de Picasso Ⓜ Arc de Triomf. Both open daily 8am–dusk. Free. MAP P.87, POCKET MAP G13

The two unsung glories of Ciutadella are its plant houses, arranged either side of the Geological Museum. The larger Hivernacle (conservatory) features enclosed greenhouses separated by a soaring glass-roofed terrace. If anything, the Umbracle (palm-house) is even more imposing, with a vaulted wood-slat roof supported by cast-iron pillars, which allows shafts of light to play across the assembled palms and ferns. Traditionally, there's always been a café-bar in the Hivernacle, set among the plants and trees, though it was closed at the time of writing while restoration work continued on the building. There are also a couple of other kiosk-cafés in the park grounds for snacks and drinks.

MUSEU DE GEOLOGIA

Pg. de Picasso Ⓜ Arc de Triomf ☎ 932 562 222, Ⓦ www.museuciencies.bcn.cat. Tues–Fri 10am–6pm, Sat, Sun & hols 10am–8pm. €5.30, Sun after 3pm & first Sun of the month free. MAP P.87, POCKET MAP G13

The other building of the Natural Science Museum is the city's Geological Museum. It was the first public museum to be founded in Barcelona, opened in 1882. It's another period piece, also due a major reorganization, after which you can expect its rocks, minerals and fossils to be displayed within a more up-to-date context. There are certainly some fascinating artefacts, from fluorescent rocks to mammoth bones, many of them found in Catalunya.

MUSEU DE CARROSSES FÚNEBRES

C/Sancho de Ávila 2 Ⓜ Marina ☎ 934 841 700. Mon–Fri 10am–1pm & 4–6pm, Sat & Sun 10am–1pm. Free. MAP P.87, POCKET MAP L5

Go to the front desk of the Serveis Funeraris (funerary services) de Barcelona (by the Banc Sabadell sign) for one of the city's more esoteric attractions. You'll be escorted into the bowels of the building and the lights will be thrown on to reveal a staggering set of 22 funerary carriages, each parked on its own cobbled stage, complete with ghostly attendants, horses and riders suspended in frozen animation. Used for city funeral processions from the end of the nineteenth century onwards, most of the carriages and

hearses are black or white, and extravagantly decorated in gilt. Old photographs show some of them in use in the city's streets, while showcases highlight antique uniforms, mourning wear and formal riding gear.

PARC ZOOLÒGIC

C/de Wellington ⓂCiutadella-Vila Olímpica ☎ 932 256 780, ⓦ www.zoobarcelona.com. Daily: June–Sept 10am–7pm; March–May & Oct 10am–6pm; Nov–Feb 10am–5pm. €16. MAP P.87, POCKET MAP J7–K7

Ciutadella's most popular attraction by far is the city zoo, which takes up most of the southeastern part of the park (main entrance on c/Wellington, signposted from ⓂCiutadella-Vila Olímpica). It boasts 7500 animals from over 400 different species – which is simply too many for a zoo that is still essentially nineteenth century in character, confined to the formal grounds of a public park. Nonetheless it's hugely popular with families,

PARC ZOOLÒGIC

as there are mini-train and pony rides, a petting zoo and daily dolphin shows alongside the main animal attractions. There's a nod to conservation issues, while the many endangered species on show include the Iberian wolf, and big cats such as the Sri Lankan leopard, snow leopard and the Sumatran tiger.

Restaurants and tapas bars

IKIBANA

Pg. Picasso 32 ⓂBarceloneta ☎ 932 956 732, ⓦ www.ikibana.es. Mon–Sat 1.30–4pm & 8.30pm–midnight, Sun 8.30pm–midnight. MAP P.87, POCKET MAP G13

Barcelona's latest sensation – Japanese-Brazilian fusion in a glam lounge-bar setting – offers a great weekday lunch deal, just a step or two out of the park. A series of dainty little dishes presents a mix of zingy rice- and seaweed-roll combos and exotic tempuras, with the full menu also running to ceviches and Kobe beef burgers (dishes €6–13, tasting menu €33).

SANTA

Av. Meridiana 2 ⓂMarina ☎ 933 097 078, Daily 1–4pm, Mon & Thurs–Sun 8.30pm–midnight. MAP P.87, POCKET MAP K6

New-wave chef Paco Guzmán's restaurant on the north side of the park is definitely on the modern side of Catalan cooking (there's a good lunch deal, otherwise mains €10–15), and there's a similar slant on the tapas at his nearby bar, *Santa Maria* (c/Comerç 17, Mon–Sat 8pm–midnight), where a glass-fronted kitchen turns out taste sensations like octopus confit, yucca chips or quail with salsa. Signature dessert at restaurant or bar is the famous "Dracula" – a crackling shot glass of raspberries and vanilla cream.

Montjuïc

For art and gardens you need to head across the city to the verdant park area of Montjuïc, site of the 1992 Olympics. The hill is topped by a sturdy castle and anchored around the heavyweight art collections in the Museu Nacional d'Art de Catalunya (MNAC). Two other superb galleries also draw visitors, namely Caixa Forum and the celebrated Fundació Joan Miró, not to mention a whole host of family-oriented attractions, from the open-air Poble Espanyol (Spanish Village) to the cable-car ride to the castle. Meanwhile, the various gardens that spill down the hillsides culminate in Barcelona's excellent botanical gardens. For Caixa Forum, Poble Espanyol and MNAC use Metro Espanya; the Trasbordador Aeri (cable car from Barceloneta) and Funicular de Montjuïc (from Metro Paral.lel) drop you near the Fundació Joan Miró.

PLAÇA D'ESPANYA

Ⓜ Espanya. MAP P.92, POCKET MAP C4

Montjuïc's characteristic gardens, terraces, fountains and monumental buildings were established for the International Exhibition of 1929. Gateway to the Exhibition was the vast Plaça d'Espanya and its huge Neoclassical fountain, with striking twin towers, 47m high, standing at the foot of the imposing Avinguda de la Reina Maria Cristina. This avenue heads up towards Montjuïc, and is lined by exhibition halls used for trade fairs. At the end, monumental steps (and modern escalators) ascend the hill to the Palau Nacional (home of MNAC), past water cascades and under the flanking walls of two grand Viennese-style pavilions. The higher you climb, the better the views, while a few café-kiosks put out seats on the way up to MNAC.

BUS MONTJUÏC TURÍSTIC

☎ 934 414 982. Daily Easter week & last week June to first week Sept, otherwise weekends & hols only. Departures every 40min, 10am–9.20pm. €4.

Montjuïc's open-top bus service runs on two routes, one starting at Plaça d'Espanya (Ⓜ Espanya), the other at the foot of the Ramblas at Plaça Portal de la Pau (Ⓜ Drassanes). The service covers all

PLAÇA D'ESPANYA

Montjuïc's sights, including out-of-the-way attractions like the castle and botanic gardens. You can switch routes at connecting stops, and use the ticket all day. The city bus designated "PM" (city transport tickets and passes valid) covers much the same route, while the sightseeing Bus Turístic also stops at the main Montjuïc attractions. There are stops for all these services right outside the upper station of the Funicular de Montjuïc.

CAIXA FORUM

Av. del Marquès de Comillas 6–8. ⓜ Espanya. ☎ 934 768 600, ⓦ www.fundacio.lacaixa.es. Daily 10am–8pm (Sat until 10pm). Free. MAP P.92, POCKET MAP C4

The former Casamarona textile factory (1911) at the foot of Montjuïc conceals a terrific arts and cultural centre. The exhibition halls were fashioned from the former factory buildings, whose external structure was left untouched – girders, pillars, brickwork and crenellated walls appear at every turn. The undulating roof (signposted "terrats") offers unique views, while the high Casamarona tower, etched in blue and yellow tiling, is as readily recognizable as the huge Miró starfish logos emblazoned across the building. The contemporary art collection focuses on the period from the 1980s to the present, and works are shown in partial rotation alongside an excellent free programme of changing exhibitions across all aspects of the arts. There's also the Mediateca multimedia space, plus an arts bookshop, children's activities and a 400-seat auditorium for music, art and literary events. The café-restaurant occupies a converted space within the old factory walls, and serves breakfast and light meals.

FONT MÀGICA

Pl. de Carles Buïgas ⓜ Espanya. May–Sept Thurs–Sun 8–11.30pm, music starts 9.30pm; Oct–April Fri & Sat only at 7pm, 7.30pm, 8pm & 8.30pm. Free. MAP P.92, POCKET MAP C5

On selected evenings, the "Magic Fountain" at the foot of the Montjuïc steps becomes the centrepiece of an impressive, if slightly kitsch, sound-and-light show, as the sprays and sheets of brightly coloured water dance to the music.

PAVELLÓ MIES VAN DER ROHE

Av. del Marquès de Comillas Ⓜ Espanya
☎ 934 234 016, Ⓦ www.miesbcn
.com. Daily 10am–8pm; guided visits Wed &
Fri 5–7pm. €4.50. MAP P.92, POCKET MAP C5

The German contribution to the 1929 International Exhibition was a pavilion designed by Mies van der Rohe (and reconstructed in 1986 by Catalan architects). It's considered a major example of modern rationalist architecture – a startling conjunction of dark-green polished onyx, shining glass and watery surfaces. Unless there's an exhibition in place (a fairly regular occurrence) there is little to see inside, though you can buy postcards and books from the small shop and debate quite how much you want a Mies mousepad or a "Less is More" T-shirt.

POBLE ESPANYOL

Av. del Marquès de Comillas Ⓜ Espanya
☎ 935 086 330, Ⓦ www.poble-espanyol.com.
Mon 9am–8pm, Tues–Thurs 9am–2am, Fri
9am–4am, Sat 9am–5am, Sun 9am–midnight.
€8.50, family ticket €20, night ticket €5,
combined ticket with MNAC €12.
MAP P.92, POCKET MAP B5

"Get to know Spain in one hour" is what's promised at the Spanish Village – an open-air park of reconstructed Spanish buildings, such as the medieval walls of Ávila, through which you enter. The echoing main square is lined with cafés, while the surrounding streets and alleys contain around forty workshops, where you can witness engraving, weaving, pottery and other crafts. Inevitably, it's one huge shopping experience, and prices are inflated, but children will love it (they can run free as

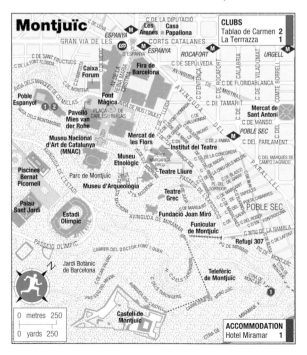

MUSEU NACIONAL D'ART DE CATALUNYA

there's no traffic) and there are plenty of family activities. Get to the village early to enjoy it in relatively crowd-free circumstances – once the tour groups arrive, it becomes a bit of a scrum. You could always come instead at the other end of the day, to venues like *Tablao de Carmen* or *La Terrrazza*, when the village transforms into a vibrant centre of Barcelona nightlife.

MUSEU NACIONAL D'ART DE CATALUNYA (MNAC)

Palau Nacional ⓂEspanya ☎936 220 376, ⓦwww.mnac.cat. Tues–Sat 10am–7pm, Sun & hols 10am–2.30pm. €8.50, ticket valid 48hr, first Sun of the month free; special exhibitions, varied charges apply. MAP P.92, POCKET MAP C5/6

Catalunya's national art gallery is one of Barcelona's essential visits, showcasing a thousand years of Catalan art in stupendous surroundings. For first-time visitors it can be difficult to know where to start, but if time is limited it's recommended you concentrate on the medieval collection. It's split into two main sections, one dedicated to Romanesque art and the other to Gothic

– periods in which Catalunya's artists were pre-eminent in Spain.

The collection of Romanesque frescoes in particular is the museum's pride and joy – removed from churches in the Catalan Pyrenees, and presented in a reconstruction of their original setting. MNAC also boasts an unsurpassed nineteenth- and twentieth-century Catalan art collection (until the 1940s – everything from the 1950s onwards is covered by MACBA in the Raval). It's particularly strong on *modernista* and *noucentista* painting and sculpture, the two dominant schools of the period, while there are some fascinating diversions into subjects like *modernista* interior design, avant-garde sculpture and historical photography.

Blockbuster exhibitions, and special shows based on the museum's archives, are popular (separate charges sometimes apply). There's also a café-bar, gift shop and art bookshop, and a museum restaurant called *Oleum* (Tues–Sun lunch only) with extraordinary city views.

MUSEU ETNOLÒGIC

Pg. Santa Madrona 16–22 ⓂEspanya ☎934
246 807, ⓦwww.museuetnologic.bcn.cat.
June–Sept Tues–Sat 10am–6pm, Sun & hols
11am–3pm; Oct–May Tues–Sun 10am–2pm
(Tues & Thurs until 7pm). €3.50.
MAP P.92, POCKET MAP C6

The Ethnological Museum
boasts extensive global cultural
collections and puts on
excellent exhibitions, which
usually last for a year or two
and focus on a particular
subject or geographical area.
Refreshingly, pieces close to
home aren't neglected, which
means that there's also often a
focus on local and national
themes, like rural life and work
or Spanish carnival
celebrations.

MUSEU D'ARQUEOLÒGIA

Pg. Santa Madrona 39–41 ⓂEspanya
☎934 232 129, ⓦwww.mac.cat. Tues–Sat
9.30am–7pm, Sun & hols 10am–2.30pm. €3,
free last Sun of month. MAP P.92, POCKET MAP C6

The city's main archeological
collection spans the centuries
from the Stone Age to the time
of the Visigoths, with the
Roman and Greek periods
particularly well represented.
Finds from Catalunya's
best-preserved archeological
site – the Greek remains at
Empúries on the Costa Brava –
are notable, while life in
Barcino (Roman Barcelona) is
interpreted through a vivid
array of tombstones, statues,
inscriptions and friezes.

LA CIUTAT DEL TEATRE

Mercat de les Flors ⓂPoble Sec ☎934 261
875, ⓦwww.mercatflors.org; Teatre Lliure
☎932 289 747, ⓦwww.teatrelliure.cat;
Institut del Teatre ☎932 273 900, ⓦwww
.institutdelteatre.org. MAP P.92, POCKET MAP C5–D6

At the foot of Montjuïc the
theatre area known as La Ciutat
del Teatre ("Theatre City")
occupies a corner of the old
working-class neighbourhood
of Poble Sec. Here, off c/de
Lleida, you'll find the **Mercat
de les Flors** – once a flower
market, now a centre for dance
and the "movement arts" – and
the progressive **Teatre Lliure**
("Free Theatre"), while the
sleek **Institut del Teatre** brings
together the city's major drama
and dance schools.

Teatre Grec and the Barcelona Festival

Centrepiece of Barcelona's annual summer cultural festival (ⓦwww
.barcelonafestival.com) is the **Teatre Grec** (Greek theatre), cut into a
former quarry on the Montjuïc hillside. Starting in late June (and
running throughout July and Aug), the festival incorporates drama, music
and dance, with some of the most atmospheric events staged in the Greek
theatre, from Shakespearean productions to shows by avant-garde
performance artists.

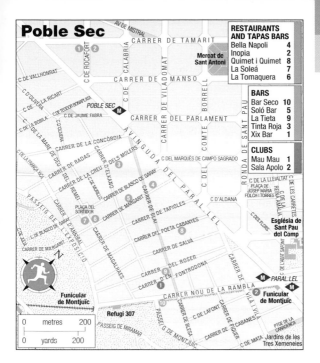

Poble Sec

RESTAURANTS AND TAPAS BARS	
Bella Napoli	4
Inopia	2
Quimet i Quimet	8
La Soleá	7
La Tomaquera	6

BARS	
Bar Seco	10
Soló Bar	5
La Tieta	9
Tinta Roja	3
Xix Bar	1

CLUBS	
Mau Mau	2
Sala Apolo	1

POBLE SEC

Ⓜ Poble Sec. MAP P.95, POCKET MAP D5–E6

The Poble Sec neighbourhood provides a complete contrast to the landscaped slopes of Montjuïc. The name ("Dry Village") is derived from the fact that this working-class neighbourhood originally had no water supply. Today, the hillside grid of streets is lined with down-to-earth grocery stores and good-value restaurants, while Poble Sec is also emerging as an "off-Raval" nightlife destination, with its fashionable bars and music clubs – pedestrianized Carrer de Blai is the epicentre of the scene. It has its own metro station, or it's an easy walk from El Raval, while the Montjuïc funicular has its lower station at nearby Ⓜ Paral.lel.

REFUGI 307

C/Nou de la Rambla 169 Ⓜ Paral.lel ☎ 932 562 100, Ⓦ www.museuhistoria.bcn .cat. Guided tours Sat & Sun at 11am, noon & 1pm. €3. MAP P.92, POCKET MAP D7/8

For a fascinating look at one of the city's hidden corners, visit Poble Sec's old Civil War air-raid shelter, dug into the hillside by local people in 1936. The tunnels could shelter up to 2000 people from Franco's bombs – you follow your guide into the labyrinth to the sound of screaming sirens, which at the time gave the locals just two minutes to get safely underground. Storyboards and photographs by the entrance explain the gripping history of the Civil War in Barcelona. Tours are in Spanish or Catalan, though someone usually speaks English, and you can just turn up on the day.

ESTADI OLÍMPIC

Museu Olímpic i de l'Esport, Av. de l'Estadi 21 🚇 Espanya ☎ 932 925 379, 🌐 www .museuolimpicbcn.com. Tues–Sat 10am–6pm (April–Sept until 8pm), Sun & hols 10am–2.30pm. €4. MAP P.92, POCKET MAP B6

The 65,000-seater Olympic Stadium was the ceremonial venue for the 1992 Barcelona Olympics. From the front, a vast *terrassa* provides one of the finest vantage points in the city, while the space-age curve of Santiago Calatrava's communications tower dominates the skyline.

Around the other side, across the road from the stadium, the history of the Games – and Barcelona's successful hosting – are covered in the Olympic and Sports Museum. It's a fully interactive experience, with lots of sports gear and memorabilia displayed, but even so it's probably one for hardcore Olympics fans only.

FUNDACIÓ JOAN MIRÓ

Parc de Montjuic 🚇 Espanya ☎ 934 439 470. 🌐 www.fundaciomiro-bcn.org. Tues–Sat 10am–7pm, July–Sept until 8pm, Thurs until 9.30pm, Sun & hols 10am–2.30pm. €8.50, exhibitions €4. MAP P.92, POCKET MAP C6

Barcelona's most adventurous art museum houses the life's work of the great Catalan artist Joan Miró (1893–1983). Inside the stark white building is a permanent collection of works largely donated by Miró himself and covering the period from 1914 to 1978. The paintings and drawings in particular are instantly recognizable, being among the chief links between Surrealism and abstract art, while there's also a selection of fascinating original sketches – Miró's enormous tapestries and outdoor sculptures, for example, often started life as a doodle on a scrap of notepaper.

The museum's Sala K provides a rapid appraisal of Miró's entire *oeuvre* in a representative selection of works. Elsewhere are pieces by other artists in homage to Miró, and exhibitions by young experimental artists in the Espai 13 gallery.

The museum sponsors temporary exhibitions, film shows, lectures and children's theatre. There's also a café-restaurant with outdoor tables on a sunny patio – and you don't need a museum ticket to go in.

FUNICULAR DE MONTJUÏC

Av. del Paral.lel 🚇 Paral.lel 🌐 www .tmb.cat. Every 10min, Mon–Fri 7.30am–8pm, Sat, Sun & hols 9am–8pm (April–Oct daily until 10pm). €1.40, transport tickets and passes valid. MAP P.92, POCKET MAP D6

The quickest way to reach the lower heights of Montjuïc is to take the funicular, from inside the station at 🚇 Paral.lel. At the upper station you can switch to the Montjuïc cable car, or you're only a few minutes' walk from the Fundació Joan Miró.

TELEFÈRIC DE MONTJUÏC

Av. de Miramar ⓜ Paral.lel, then Funicular
ⓦ www.tmb.cat. Daily, June–Sept 10am–9pm;
April, May & Oct 10am–7pm; Nov–March
10am–6pm. €6.30 one-way, €9 return.
MAP P.92, POCKET MAP D7

The cable car up to the castle
and back is an exciting ride,
and the views, of course, are
stupendous. There's an
intermediate station, called
Mirador, where you can get out
and enjoy more sweeping
vistas.

CASTELL DE MONTJUÏC

Carretera de Montjuïc ☎ 932 564 445,
ⓦ www.bcn.cat/castelldemontjuic. Grounds,
Tues–Sun 9am–7pm (April–Sept until 9pm).
Free. MAP P.92, POCKET MAP C7/8

Barcelona's fortress served as a
military base and prison for
decades, and was where the last
president of the prewar Catalan
government, Lluís Companys,
was executed on Franco's
orders on October 15, 1940.
However, in 2008 the castle was
symbolically handed over to
the city and restoration work is
transforming the site into a
combined peace museum,
memorial space and Montjuïc
interpretation centre.
Exhibitions may take place here
in the meantime, though the
cable-car ride and dramatic

location merit a visit in any
case. The rampart views are
magnificent, while below the
walls the panoramic **Camí del
Mar** pathway looks out over
port and ocean. It runs for 1km
to the Mirador del Migdia
viewpoint, where there's a great
open-air bar called *La Caseta*
(weekends from noon, plus
summer weekend DJ nights).

JARDÍ BOTÀNIC DE BARCELONA

C/Dr Font i Quer 2 ⓜ Espanya ☎ 934 245
053, ⓦ www.museuciencies.bcn.cat. Daily,
June–Aug 10am–8pm; April, May & Sept
10am–7pm; Feb, March & Oct 10am–6pm,
Nov–Jan 10am–5pm. €3.50, free Sun after
3pm & last Sun of month.
MAP P.92, POCKET MAP D7

Principal among Montjuïc's
many gardens is the city's
Botanical Garden, laid out on
terraced slopes offering fine
views of the city. The Montjuïc
buses run here directly, or it's a
five-minute walk around the
back of the Olympic Stadium.
The beautifully kept
contemporary garden has
landscaped zones representing
the flora of the Mediterranean,
Canary Islands, California,
Chile, South Africa and
Australia. Just don't come in
the full heat of the summer day,
as there's very little shade

Restaurants and tapas bars

TINTA ROJA

BELLA NAPOLI

C/Margarit 14 Ⓜ Poble Sec ☎ 934 425 056.
Tues 8.30pm–midnight, Wed–Sun
1.30–4.30pm & 8.30pm–midnight.
MAP P.95, POCKET MAP E6

Authentic Neapolitan pizzeria
serving the city's finest pizzas
straight from a beehive-shaped
oven. Or there's a huge range of
pastas, risottos and veal
scaloppine (most dishes
between €9 and €15).

INOPIA

C/Tamarit 104 Ⓜ Poble Sec ☎ 934 245 231.
Ⓦ www.barinopia.com. Tues–Fri 7–11pm, Sat
1.30–3.30pm & 7–11pm; closed Aug.
MAP P.95, POCKET MAP D5

The brainchild of Albert Adrià,
brother of Ferran Adrià (of
best-restaurant-in-the-world
fame, *El Bulli*, on the Costa
Brava) there are often queues
for its renowned "classic tapas".
Don't miss the signature dish
patatas bravas (spicy fried
potatoes), but everything's
good and you can eat for
around €25.

QUIMET I QUIMET

C/Poeta Cabanyes 25 Ⓜ Paral.lel ☎ 934 423
142. Tues–Sat noon–4pm & 7–11pm, Sun
noon–4pm; closed Aug. MAP P.95, POCKET MAP E6

Poble Sec's cosiest tapas bar is a
place of pilgrimage for classy
finger food – delicacies like
roast onions, marinaded
mushrooms, stuffed cherry
tomatoes or anchovy-wrapped
olives.

LA SOLEÁ

Pl. del Sortidor 14 Ⓜ Poble Sec ☎ 934 410
124. Tues–Sat noon–midnight, Sun noon–5pm.
MAP P.95, POCKET MAP D6

A sunny-day place, with a
terrassa in a down-to-earth

square. It's a bistro menu
(lunch from 1.30pm, dinner
from 8.30pm, dishes €5–10), so
expect salads and dips, proper
hamburgers, stir-fries and
pasta.

LA TOMAQUERA

C/Margarit 58 Ⓜ Poble Sec. Tues–Sat
1.30–3.45pm & 8.30–10.45pm; closed Aug.
MAP P.95, POCKET MAP D6

Sit down in this chatter-filled
tavern to a dish of olives and
two quail's eggs – and there any
delicacy ends, as the chefs set
to hacking steaks and chops
from great hunks of meat. It's
not for the faint-hearted, but
the grilled chicken is
sensational and the *entrecôtes*
enormous (most mains €8–15).

Bars

BAR SECO

Pg. Montjuïc 74 Ⓜ Paral.lel ☎ 933 296 374.
Mon 9am–8pm, Tues–Thurs 9am–1am (Nov–
April Tues & Wed closes at 8pm), Fri
9am–2am, Sat 10am–2am, Sun 10am–1am.
MAP P.95, POCKET MAP E6

The "Dry Bar" is a local hit,
with its mellow vibe, freshly
squeezed juices, Free Trade
drinks and artisan beers.
Stand-out dish from the
veggie-friendly menu is *patatas
salvajes* (wild potatoes) – fried
organic skin-on spuds with a
fiery *alioli*.

SOLÓ BAR

C/Margarit 18 Ⓜ Poble Sec ☎ 933 297 618.
Mon, Tues & Thurs–Sun 7.30pm–2.30am.
MAP P.95, POCKET MAP E6

Bare-bones boho music bar with free live gigs most nights around 9pm, from Latin American beats to alt-rock.

LA TIETA

C/de Blai 1 Ⓜ Paral.lel ☎ 646 077 936.
Tues–Sun 11am–11pm. MAP P.95, POCKET MAP E6

Small but perfectly formed, "The Aunt" is a cool drinks and tapas place with an open window onto the street and just enough room inside for a dozen or so good friends.

TINTA ROJA

C/Creu dels Molers 17 Ⓜ Poble Sec ☎ 934 433 243, Ⓦ www.tintaroja.net. Wed, Thurs & Sun 8pm–1.30am, Fri & Sat 8pm–3am; closed 2 weeks in Aug. MAP P.95, POCKET MAP D6

Theatrical tango bar with cabaret and live music (tango, rumba, Cuban, flamenco) a couple of nights a week (often free, special shows €10).

XIX BAR

C/Rocafort 19 Ⓜ Poble Sec ☎ 934 234 314,
Ⓦ www.xixbar.com. Daily 6.30pm–3am.
MAP P.95, POCKET MAP D5

An old *granja* (milk bar) turned candlelit cocktail bar. It's big on gin, and you can limber up for tapas at *Inopia*, just over the road.

LA TERRRAZZA

Clubs

MAU MAU

C/Fontrodona 33 Ⓜ Paral.lel ☎ 934 418 015,
Ⓦ www.maumaunderground.com. Thurs
11pm–2.30am, Fri & Sat 11pm–3am.
MAP P.95, POCKET MAP E6

Underground lounge-club, cultural centre and chill-out space, with nightly video projections, all sorts of exhibitions and guest DJs playing deep, soulful grooves.

SALA APOLO

C/Nou de la Rambla 113 Ⓜ Paral.lel
☎ 934 414 001, Ⓦ www.sala-apolo.com.
MAP P.95, POCKET MAP A13

Old-time ballroom turned hip concert venue with gigs on two stages (local acts to big names) and an eclectic series of club nights, from punk or Catalan rumba sounds to the weekend's long running *Nitsa Club* (Ⓦ www.nitsa.com). Admission €10–20.

TABLAO DE CARMEN

Poble Espanyol Ⓜ Espanya ☎ 933 256 895,
Ⓦ www.tablaodecarmen.com. Tues–Sun,
shows at 7.45pm & 10pm.
MAP P.92, POCKET MAP B5

Poble Espanyol's famous flamenco club is situated in a replica Andalucian street, and features a variety of shows from seasoned performers and new talent. From €35, rising to €70 for the show plus dinner. Reservations required.

LA TERRRAZZA

Poble Espanyol Ⓜ Espanya ☎ 932 724 980.
May–Oct Thurs–Sat midnight–6am.
MAP P.92, POCKET MAP B5

Open-air summer club for nonstop dance, house and techno. Don't get there until at least 3am and be prepared for the style police. Admission €15–20.

Port Olímpic and Poble Nou

The main waterfront legacy of the 1992 Olympics was the Port Olímpic, the marina development which lies fifteen minutes' walk along the promenade from Barceloneta. Locals make full use of the beach and boardwalks, descending in force at the weekends for a leisurely lunch or late drink in one of the scores of restaurants and bars. There are also spruced-up beaches further north near the old working-class neighbourhood of Poble Nou, whose pretty *rambla* makes for an offbeat diversion. Access is by metro to Ciutadella-Vila Olímpica or Poble Nou, or bus #59 runs from the Ramblas through Barceloneta and out to Port Olímpic.

PORT OLÍMPIC

Ⓜ Ciutadella-Vila Olímpica.
MAP P.101, POCKET MAP K8–M8

Approaching the Olympic port, the golden mirage above the promenade slowly reveals itself to be a huge **copper fish** (courtesy of Frank Gehry, architect of the Bilbao Guggenheim). It's the emblem of the seafront development constructed for the 1992 Olympics, incorporating the port itself – site of many of the Olympic watersports events – which is backed by the city's two tallest buildings, the **Torre Mapfre** and the steel-framed **Hotel Arts Barcelona**, both 154m tall. Two wharves contain the bulk of the action: the Moll de Mestral has a lower deck by the marina lined with bars, while the Moll de Gregal sports a double-decker tier of seafood restaurants. The beach, meanwhile, turns into a full-on summer resort, backed by class-conscious clubs along Passeig Marítim appealing to local rich kids and A-list celebs.

PORT OLÍMPIC

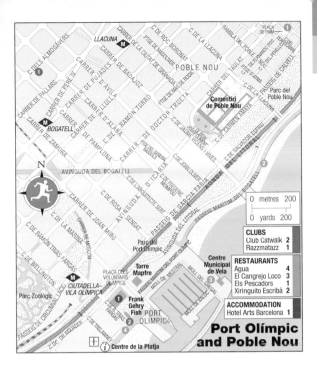

Port Olímpic and Poble Nou

CLUBS	
Club Catwalk	2
Razzmatazz	1

RESTAURANTS	
Agua	4
El Cangrejo Loco	3
Els Pescadors	1
Xiringuito Escribà	2

ACCOMMODATION	
Hotel Arts Barcelona	1

CITY BEACHES

Centre de la Platja, Pg. Marítim
Ⓜ Yellow line 4, between Barceloneta and Poble Nou ☎ 932 210 348.
Ⓦ www.bcn.cat/platges. June–Sept daily 10am–7pm, plus March May weekends only.
MAP P.101, POCKET MAP L8-M8

A series of sandy beaches stretches for 5km north of Port Olímpic, providing a sparkling waterfront that has been reclaimed from a former industrial zone. Split into different named sections (Nova Icària, Bogatell etc), which boast showers, playgrounds and open-air café-bars, it's a pretty extraordinary facility to find so close to a city centre. A sunny day, even in winter, brings the locals out in force, and the sands are regularly swept and replenished. The local water quality has improved massively over recent years, too, and most of the beaches have Blue Flag (ie, clean beach) status, though conditions can change from year to year.

CENTRE DE LA PLATJA

Pg. Marítim Ⓜ Ciutadella-Vila Olímpica
☎ 932 210 340, Ⓦ www.bcn.cat/platges.
June–Sept daily 10am–7pm, plus March May weekends only. MAP P.101, POCKET MAP K8

On the boardwalk arcade, in front of the Hospital del Mar, the city council has opened a beach visitor centre – a kind of one-stop shop for information and activities along the seafront. There's a full programme of walks, talks and sports, a small summer lending library for beach reading, as well as buckets and spades for kids and frisbees, volleyball and beach tennis gear available for pick-up games on the sands.

THE EDIFICI FÒRUM

RAMBLA DEL POBLE NOU

Ⓜ Poble Nou. MAP P.101

A twenty-minute walk up the beach promenade from Port Olímpic, the tree-lined Rambla de Poble Nou runs inland through the most attractive part of **Poble Nou** ("New Village"). The old industrial neighbourhood is at the heart of a huge city regeneration scheme, known as 22@ Barcelona, but the local avenue remains unchanged – a run of modest shops, cafés and restaurants, including the classic juice and milk bar of *El Tio Che* (Rambla de Poble Nou 44–46), which serves orange or lemon *granissat* (crushed ice) and their famous *orxata* (milky tiger-nut drink). Poble Nou metro (yellow line 4) will save you the walk back to the city centre.

CEMENTIRI DE POBLE NOU

Av. d'Icaria Ⓜ Bogatell. Daily 8am–6pm. MAP P.101. POCKET MAP M7

This vast nineteenth-century mausoleum has its tombs set in walls 7m high, tended by families who climb stepladders to reach the uppermost tiers. With birdsong accompanying a stroll around the flower-lined pavements, quiet courtyards and chapels, this village of the dead is a rare haven of peace in the city.

Diagonal Mar

The waterfront district north of Poble Nou was developed in the wake of the Universal Forum of Cultures Expo (held in 2004). It's promoted as **Diagonal Mar**, anchored by the Diagonal Mar shopping mall (Ⓜ El Maresme Fòrum or tram T4) and with several classy hotels, convention centres and exhibition halls grouped nearby. The dazzling **Edifici Fòrum** building is the work of Jacques Herzog (architect of London's Tate Modern), while the main open space is claimed to be the second-largest square in the world after Beijing's Tiananmen Square. This immense expanse spreads towards the sea, culminating in a giant solar-panelled canopy that overlooks the marina, beach and park areas. In summer, temporary bars, dancefloors and chill-out zones are established at the **Parc del Fòrum**, and the city authorities have shifted some of the bigger annual music festivals and events down here to inject a bit of life outside convention time. At other times it can be a bit soulless, but it's definitely worth the metro or tram ride if you're interested in heroic-scale public projects.

Restaurants

AGUA

Pg. Marítim 30 Ⓜ Ciutadella-Vila Olímpica
☎ 932 251 272, Ⓦ www.aguadeltragaluz.com.
Daily 1–3.45pm & 8–11.30pm (Fri & Sat until
4.30pm & 12.30am). MAP P.101, POCKET MAP K8

Nicest boardwalk restaurant on
the strip, with a contemporary
Mediterranean menu, from
salads to grills. Prices are
pretty fair (around €30), so it's
usually busy.

EL CANGREJO LOCO

Moll de Gregal 29–30 Ⓜ Ciutadella-Vila
Olímpica ☎ 932 211 748, Ⓦ www
.elcangrejoloco.com. Daily 1pm–1am.
MAP P.101, POCKET MAP L8

The terrace at the "Crazy Crab"
offers ocean views, and the
food is first rate. A mixed
fried-fish plate is a typically
Catalan starter, and the rice
dishes are thoroughly
recommended. From around
€40.

ELS PESCADORS

Pl. Prim 1 Ⓜ Poble Nou ☎ 932 252 018,
Ⓦ www.elspescadors.com. Daily 1–4pm &
8–11.30pm; closed Easter. MAP P.101

The best top-class fish
restaurant in Barcelona? It's a
tough call, but many would
choose this hideaway place in a
pretty Poble Nou square. The
menu offers daily fresh fish
dishes, and plenty more
involving rice, noodles or
salt-cod. Don't go mad and
you'll escape for €50–60.

XIRINGUITO ESCRIBÀ

Ronda del Litoral 42, Platja Bogatell
Ⓜ Ciutadella-Vila Olímpica ☎ 932 210 729,
Ⓦ www.escriba.es. Tues–Sat 11am–1am, Sun
11am–4pm; restricted hours in winter.
MAP P.101, POCKET MAP M8

Beachfront restaurant that's
enough off the beaten track (a
15min walk from Port Olímpic)
to mark you out as in the know.

High points are paellas and
daily fish specials (€18–20),
followed by sensational cakes
and pastries from the Escribà
family patisserie.

Clubs

CLUB CATWALK

C/Ramon Trias Fargas 2–4 Ⓜ Ciutadella-Vila
Olímpica ☎ 932 216 161, Ⓦ www.clubcatwalk
.net. Thurs–Sun midnight–5am.
MAP P.101, POCKET MAP K8

Portside club of choice playing
house, funk, soul and r'n'b for
well-heeled locals and visitors.
It's under the *Hotel Arts*;
admission €15–20.

RAZZMATAZZ

C/dels Almogavers 122 & c/Pamplona 88
Ⓜ Bogatell ☎ 933 208 200, Ⓦ www
.salarazzmatazz.com. Fri & Sat 1–6am.
MAP P.101, POCKET MAP L5

Razzmatazz hosts the biggest
in-town rock gigs, and at
weekends turns into "five clubs
in one", spinning mixed sounds
in variously named bars.
Admission €15.

CLUB CATWALK

Dreta de l'Eixample

The nineteenth-century street grid north of Plaça de Catalunya is the city's main shopping and business district. It was designed as part of a revolutionary urban plan – the Eixample in Catalan ("Extension" or "Widening") – that divided districts into regular blocks, whose characteristic wide streets and shaved corners survive today. Two parallel avenues, Passeig de Gràcia and Rambla de Catalunya, are the backbone of the Eixample, with everything to the east known as the Dreta de l'Eixample (the right-hand side). It's here that the bulk of the city's famous *modernista* (Catalan Art Nouveau) buildings are found, along with an array of classy galleries and some of the city's most stylish shops. Start your exploration from either Metro Passeig de Gràcia or Metro Diagonal.

PASSEIG DE GRÀCIA

Ⓜ Passeig de Gràcia. MAP P.105, POCKET MAP H1/4

The prominent avenue, which runs northwest from Plaça de Catalunya, was laid out in its present form in 1827. It later developed as a showcase for *modernista* architects, eagerly commissioned by status-conscious merchants and businessmen. Walk the length of Passeig de Gràcia from Plaça de Catalunya to Avinguda Diagonal (a 25min stroll) and you'll pass some of the city's most extraordinary architecture, notably the famous group of buildings (including casas Amatller and Batlló) known as the Mansana de la Discòrdia, or "Block of Discord", as they show off wildly varying manifestations of the *modernista* style and spirit. Further up is Antoni Gaudí's iconic apartment building La Pedrera, while, in between, wrought-iron Art Nouveau street lamps, fashion stores and designer hotels set the tone for this resolutely upscale avenue.

Dreta de l'Eixample

RESTAURANTS AND TAPAS BARS

La Bodegueta	3
Casa Calvet	11
Ciudad Condal	8
El Japonés	1
El Mussol	4, 10
TapaÇ24	7
Tragaluz	2

CAFÉS

Café del Centre	6
Forn de Sant Jaume	5
Laie Llibreria Café	9

SHOPS

Antonio Miró	8
Armand Basi	5
Casa del Llibre	4
Colmado Quilez	6
Cubiñá	2
Mango	3, 10
Muxart	1, 7
Purificacion Garcia	9

ACCOMMODATION

Centric Point Hostel	4
Hostal L'Antic Espai	5
Hostal Girona	8
Hostal Goya	7
Hostal D'Uxelles	6
Hotel Condes de Barcelona	2
Hotel Majestic	3
Hotel Omm	1
the5rooms	9

CASA AMATLLER

MUSEU DEL PERFUM

Pg. de Gràcia 39 ⓂPasseig de Gràcia
☏ 932 160 121, ⓦwww.museodelperfume
.com. Mon–Fri 10.30am–1.30pm & 4.30–8pm,
Sat 11am–2pm. €5. MAP P.105, POCKET MAP H3

At the back of the Regia
perfume store is a private
collection of over five thousand
perfume and essence bottles
from Egyptian times onwards.
There are some exquisite pieces,
including Turkish filigree-and-
crystal ware and bronze and
silver Indian elephant flasks,
while more modern times are
represented by scents made for
Brigitte Bardot, Grace Kelly
and Elizabeth Taylor.

CASA AMATLLER

Fundació Amatller, Pg. de Gràcia 41
ⓂPasseig de Gràcia ☏ 934 877 217, ⓦwww
.amatller.org. Tours, Mon–Fri mornings,
reservations required. €10. MAP P.105,
POCKET MAP G3

Josep Puig i Cadafalch's striking
Casa Amatller (1900) was
designed for Antoni Amatller, a
Catalan chocolate
manufacturer, art collector,
photographer and traveller. It's
awash with coloured ceramic
decoration, while inside the
hallway twisted stone columns
are interspersed by dragon
lamps. Guided tours of the
house include a visit to
Amatller's photographic studio
as well as chocolate-tasting in
the original kitchen. The house
also displays temporary
exhibitions under the auspices
of the Amatller Institute of
Hispanic Art.

CASA BATLLÒ

Pg. de Gràcia 43 ⓂPasseig de Gràcia
☏ 932 160 306, ⓦwww.casabatllo.es. Daily
9am–8pm, access occasionally restricted.
€18. Advance sales from TelEntrada on
☏ 902 101 212, ⓦwww.telentrada.com.
MAP P.105, POCKET MAP G3

The most extraordinary
creation on the "Block of

Modernisme

The Catalan offshoot of Art Nouveau, **modernisme**, was the expression
of a renewed upsurge in Catalan nationalism in the 1870s. Its most
famous exponent was **Antoni Gaudí i Cornet** (1852–1926), whose
buildings are apparently lunatic flights of fantasy, which at the same time
are perfectly functional. His architectural influences were Moorish and
Gothic, while he embellished his work with elements from the natural world.
The imaginative impetus he provided inspired others like **Lluís Domènech i
Montaner** (1850–1923) – perhaps the greatest *modernista* architect – and
Josep Puig i Cadafalch (1867–1957), both of whom also experimented
with the use of ceramic tiles, ironwork, stained glass and stone carving.
This combination of traditional methods with modern technology became
the hallmark of *modernisme* – producing some of the most exciting
architecture to be found anywhere in the world.

Discord" is the Casa Batlló, designed for the industrialist Josep Batlló and finished in 1907. Antoni Gaudí created an undulating facade that Salvador Dalí later compared to "the tranquil waters of a lake". The sinuous interior, meanwhile, resembles the inside of some great organism, complete with meandering, snakeskin-patterned walls. Self-guided audio tours show you the main floor, the patio and rear facade, the ribbed attic and celebrated mosaic roof-top chimneys. Advance tickets are recommended (by phone, in person or online); the scrum of visitors can be a frustrating business at peak times.

FUNDACIÓ ANTONI TÀPIES

C/Aragó 255 Ⓜ Passeig de Gràcia ☎ 934 870 315, Ⓦ www.fundaciotapies.org. Tues–Sun 10am–8pm. €7. MAP P.105, POCKET MAP G3

The definitive collection of the work of Catalan abstract artist Antoni Tàpies i Puig is housed in *modernista* architect Lluís Domènech i Montaner's first important building, the Casa Montaner i Simon (1880). You can't miss it – the foundation building is capped by Tàpies's own striking sculpture, *Núvol i Cadira* ("Cloud and Chair", 1990), a tangle of glass, wire and aluminium. The artist was born in Barcelona in 1923 and was a founding member (1948) of the influential avant-garde Dau al Set ("Die at Seven") artists' group. Tàpies's abstract style matured in the 1950s, with underlying messages and themes signalled by the inclusion of everyday objects and symbols on the canvas. Changing exhibitions focus on selections of Tàpies's work, while other shows highlight works by other contemporary artists.

MUSEU EGIPCI DE BARCELONA

C/de València 284 Ⓜ Passeig de Gràcia ☎ 934 880 188, Ⓦ www.museuegipci.com. Mon–Sat 10am–8pm, Sun 10am–2pm. €11 MAP P.105, POCKET MAP H3

Barcelona's Egyptian Museum is an exceptional private collection of over a thousand ancient artefacts, from amulets to sarcophagi – there's nothing else in Spain quite like it. Visitors are given a detailed English-language guidebook, but the real pleasure is a serendipitous wander, turning up items like cat mummies or the rare figurine of a spoonbill (ibis) representing an Egyptian god. There are temporary exhibitions, plus a good shop and terrace café, while the museum also hosts children's activities and themed events.

JARDINS DE LES TORRES DE LES AIGÜES

C/Roger de Llúria 56, between c/Consell de Cent and c/Diputació ⓜ Girona. Daily 10am-dusk. Free. MAP P.105, POCKET MAP H3

The original nineteenth-century Eixample plan – by utopian architect Ildefons Cerdà – was drawn up with local inhabitants very much in mind. Space, light and social community projects were part of the grand design, and something of the original spirit can be seen in this enclosed square centred on a Moorish-style water tower. It's been handsomely restored by the city council, which turns it into a backyard beach every summer, complete with sand and paddling pool.

MERCAT DE LA CONCEPCIÓ

Between c/de Valencia and c/d'Aragó ⓜ Girona ☎ 934 575 329, ⓦ www .laconcepcio.com. Mon–Sat 8am–3pm. MAP P.105, POCKET MAP J3

Flowers, shrubs and plants are a Concepció speciality (the florists on c/Valencia are open 24 hours a day), and there are some good snack bars inside the market and a few outdoor cafés to the side. The market takes its name from the nearby church of **La Concepció** (entrance on c/Roger de Llúria), whose quiet cloister is a surprising haven of slender columns and orange trees.

PALAU MONTANER

C/de Mallorca 278 ⓜ Passeig de Gràcia ☎ 933 177 652, ⓦ www.rutadelmodernisme .com. Guided visits: Sat at 10.30am in English, plus 11.30am & 12.30pm, and Sun at 10.30am, 11.30am & 12.30pm in Spanish/Catalan. €5. MAP P.105, POCKET MAP H3

The Palau Montaner (1896) has a curious history – after the original architect quit, Lluís Domènech i Montaner took over halfway through construction, and the top half of the facade is clearly more elaborate than the lower part. Meanwhile, the period's most celebrated craftsmen were set to work on the interior, which sports rich mosaic floors, painted glass, carved woodwork and a monumental staircase. The building is now the seat of the Madrid government's delegation to Catalunya, but there are tours at the weekend that show you the public rooms, grand dining room and courtyard.

FUNDACIÓ JOAN BROSSA

C/Provença 318 ⓜ Diagonal ☎ 934 676 952, ⓦ www.fundaciojoanbrossa.cat. Mon–Fri 10am–2pm & 3–7pm. Free. MAP P.105, POCKET MAP H2

Joan Brossa (1919–98) was a most unusual poet and playwright, seeing poetry not just on the page or stage but also in everyday items and deconstructed words, which

FLOWERS AT THE MERCAT DE LA CONCEPCIÓ

LA PEDRERA

he incorporated into objects, installations, sculptures and posters. The foundation's permanent exhibition explores these different genres, particularly his fascinating "object" and "visual" poems, while an English-language guidebook available from the foundation leads you around some of his more famous public works in Barcelona – like his "Homage to the Book" on Passeig de Gràcia (at Gran Via).

LA PEDRERA

Pg. de Gràcia 92, entrance on c/Provença ⓂDiagonal ☎902 400 973 Ⓦwww .lapedreraeducacio.org. March–Oct daily 9am–8pm; Nov–Feb daily 9am–6.30pm. €10. La Pedrera de Nit, late June & July only, Fri & Sat 9–11.30pm; €15, advance sales from TelEntrada ☎902 101 212, Ⓦwww .telentrada.com. MAP P.105, POCKET MAP H2

Antoni Gaudí's weird apartment building at the top of Passeig de Gràcia is simply not to be missed – though you can expect queues whenever you visit. Popularly known as La Pedrera, "the stone quarry", its rippled facade, curving around the street corner in one smooth sweep, is said to have

been inspired by the mountain of Montserrat, while the apartments themselves resemble eroded cave dwellings. Indeed, there's not a straight line to be seen – hence the contemporary joke that the new tenants would only be able to keep snakes as pets. The self-guided visit includes a trip up to the extraordinary terrace to see the enigmatic chimneys, as well as an excellent exhibition about Gaudí's life and work displayed under the brick arches of the attic. "El Pis" on the building's fourth floor recreates the design and style of a *modernista*-era bourgeois apartment. During the early summer's **La Pedrera de Nit** (advance booking essential) you can enjoy the amazing rooftop by night with a complimentary glass of *cava* and music, while other concerts are also held at La Pedrera at various times.

Through the grand main entrance of the building there's access to the Pedrera **exhibition hall** (daily 10am–8pm; free; guided visits Mon–Fri at 6pm), which hosts temporary art shows of works by major international artists.

VINÇON

Pg. de Gràcia 96 Ⓜ Diagonal ☎ 932 156 050,
ⓦ www.vincon.com. Mon–Sat 10am–8.30pm.
MAP P.105, POCKET MAP H2

The Vinçon store emerged in the 1960s as the country's pre-eminent purveyor of household furniture and design, pioneered by Fernando Amat, the "Spanish Terence Conran". There are various separate street entrances, including separate sections for bedroom (Tinç Con, c/Rosselló 246) and kitchen (Kitchen Con, c/Pau Claris 179) stuff, while the extraordinary furniture floor gives access to a terrace with views of La Pedrera. The *Sala Vinçon* gallery (same hours as shop; admission free) puts on shows of graphic and industrial design and contemporary furniture.

CASA ÀSIA

PALAU ROBERT

Pg. de Gràcia 107 Ⓜ Diagonal ☎ 932 388 091, ⓦ www.gencat.cat/palaurobert. Mon–Sat 10am–7pm, Sun 10am–2.30pm. Free.
MAP P.105, POCKET MAP H2

Visit the information centre for the Catalunya region for regularly changing exhibitions on all matters Catalan, from art to business. There are several exhibition spaces, both inside the main palace – built as a typical aristocratic residence in 1903 – and in the old coach house. The centre is also an important concert venue for recitals and orchestras, while the gardens around the back are a popular meeting point for local nannies and their charges.

CASA ÀSIA

Av. Diagonal 373 Ⓜ Diagonal ☎ 933 680 836, ⓦ www.casaasia.es. Tues–Sat 10am–8pm, Sun 10am–2pm. Free. Café open Mon–Fri 9am–9pm. MAP P.105, POCKET MAP H2

The beautifully detailed Palau Quadras (a Josep Puig i Cadafalch work of 1904) now serves as a cultural and arts centre for Asia and the Pacific Region. Current exhibitions (usually free) are always worth a look, and there's a good café on the ground floor, a multimedia library and, best of all, the Jardi d'Orient roof terrace – take the elevator up for views of the neighbouring Casa de les Punxes and the Sagrada Família towers rising behind.

CASA DE LES PUNXES

Av. Diagonal 416–420 Ⓜ Diagonal. No public access. MAP P.105, POCKET MAP H2

Architect Josep Puig i Cadafalch's largest work, the soaring Casa Terrades, is more usually known as the Casa de les Punxes ("House of Spikes") because of its red-tiled turrets and steep gables. Built in 1903 for three sisters, and converted from three separate houses spreading around an entire corner of a block, the crenellated structure is almost northern European in style, reminiscent of a Gothic castle.

Shops

ANTONIO MIRÓ

C/Consell de Cent 349 Ⓜ Passeig de Gràcia Ⓦ www.antoniomiro.es. Mon–Sat 10.30am–8.30pm. MAP P.105, POCKET MAP G3

The showcase for Barcelona's most innovative designer, now also branding accessories and household design items.

ARMAND BASI

Pg. de Gràcia 49, outlets also at L'Illa and El Corte Inglés Ⓜ Passeig de Gràcia Ⓦ www .armandbasi.com. Mon–Sat 10am–8.30pm. MAP P.105, POCKET MAP H3

Colourful men's and women's clothes from this hot designer, plus branded accessories, including must-have tables and kitchenware created with superchef Ferran Adrià.

CASA DEL LLIBRE

Pg. de Gràcia 62 Ⓜ Passeig de Gràcia Ⓦ www.casadellibro.com. Mon–Sat 9.30am–9.30pm. MAP P.105, POCKET MAP H3

Barcelona's biggest book emporium, with lots of English-language titles and Catalan literature in translation.

COLMADO QUILEZ

Rambla de Catalunya 63 Ⓜ Passeig de Gràcia Ⓦ www.lafuente.es. Mon–Fri 9.30am–2pm & 4.30–8.30pm, Sat 9.30am–2pm, plus Sat afternoon Sept–Dec. MAP P.105, POCKET MAP G3

Classic Catalan grocery piled high with tins, jars and packets, overseen by sober gents in collar and tie and blue smocks.

CUBIÑÀ

C/Mallorca 291 Ⓜ Verdaguer Ⓦ www .cubinya.es. Mon–Sat 10am–2pm & 4.30–8.30pm. MAP P.105, POCKET MAP H3

The building is stupendous – Domènech i Montaner's *modernista* Casa Thomas – while inside holds the very latest in household design.

MANGO

Pg. de Gràcia 8–10 and Pg. de Gràcia 65, plus others Ⓜ Passeig de Gràcia Ⓦ www .mango.com. Mon–Sat 10.15am–9.30pm. MAP P.105, POCKET MAP H3, H4

Barcelona is where high-street fashion chain Mango began. For last season's gear at unbeatable prices, head to Mango Outlet (c/Girona 37).

MUXART

C/Rosselló 230 and Rambla de Catalunya 47 Ⓜ Diagonal Ⓦ www.muxart.com. Mon–Sat 10am–8.30pm. MAP P.105, POCKET MAP G2, G3

A suave showroom for Barcelona's top-class shoe designer, selling gorgeous footwear and handbags for men and women.

PURIFICACION GARCIA

Pg. de Gràcia 21 Ⓜ Passeig de Gràcia Ⓦ www.purificaciongarcia.es. Mon–Sat 10am–8.30pm. MAP P.105, POCKET MAP G4

A hot designer with an eye for fabrics – Garcia's first job was in a textile factory. She's also designed clothes for film and theatre, and her costumes were seen at the opening ceremony of the Barcelona Olympics.

Cafés

CAFÉ DEL CENTRE

C/Girona 69 Ⓜ Girona ☎ 934 881 101.
Mon–Fri 8am–11pm; closed Aug.
MAP P.105, POCKET MAP J3

This quiet coffee stop is only four blocks from the main drag of Passeig de Gràcia. It's been here since 1873 (a plaque outside honours its service to the city) and, with its timeworn *modernista* decor, seems largely unchanged.

FORN DE SANT JAUME

Rambla de Catalunya 50 Ⓜ Passeig de Gràcia ☎ 932 160 229. Mon–Sat 9am–9pm.
MAP P.105 POCKET MAP G3

Uptown *pastisseria* whose glittering windows are piled high with croissants, cakes, pastries and sweets. The small adjacent café has *rambla* seats, or you can take away your goodies for later.

LAIE LLIBRERIA CAFÉ

C/Pau Claris 85 Ⓜ Passeig de Gràcia ☎ 933 027 310, Ⓦ www.laie.es. Mon–Fri 9am–9.30pm, Sat 10am–9.30pm.
MAP P.105, POCKET MAP H4

The city's first and best bookshop-café is known for its popular weekday buffet breakfast spread, as well as its set lunch deals and à la carte dining.

Restaurants and tapas bars

LA BODEGUETA

Rambla Catalunya 100 Ⓜ Diagonal ☎ 932 154 894. Daily 8am–2am; closed mornings in Aug. MAP P.105, POCKET MAP G2

Long-established *bodega* with *cava* and wine by the glass, as well as ham, cheese, anchovies and other tapas to soak it up.

CASA CALVET

C/de Casp 48 Ⓜ Catalunya ☎ 934 124 012, Ⓦ www.casacalvet.es. Mon–Sat 1–3.30pm & 8.30–11.30pm. MAP P.105, POCKET MAP F10

Antoni Gaudí's earliest commissioned townhouse is a marvel of interior decoration, making for a truly glam night out. It offers a seasonally changing, modern Catalan menu, with desserts that are artworks in themselves, though with mains around the €30 mark (or tasting menus from €40 to €75) expect it to be a wallet-emptying experience.

CIUDAD CONDAL

Rambla de Catalunya 18 Ⓜ Passeig de Gràcia ☎ 933 181 997. Daily 7.30am–1.30am.
MAP P.105, POCKET MAP G4

Breakfast sees the bar groan under the weight of a dozen types of crispy baguette sandwich, plus croissants and pastries, while the daily changing tapas selection ranges far and wide – *patatas bravas* to octopus. It can be standing room only at lunch (and not much of that either), so get there early. Dinner doesn't really have the same buzz, but it's a useful stop for a drink at any time.

CASA CALVET

EL JAPONÉS

Ptge. de la Concepció 2 ⓜ Diagonal
☎ 934 872 592, ⓦ www.eljaponesdeltragaluz
.com. Daily 1.30–4pm & 8.30pm–midnight
(Fri & Sat until 1am). MAP P.105, POCKET MAP G2

Designer style – gunmetal grey interior, black-clad staff, sharp service – at moderate prices gives this minimalist Japanese restaurant the edge over its more traditional rivals. Tick your choices from the long menu of sushi, sashimi, noodles and tempura and hand it to the waiter; average cost is €20–25 a head.

EL MUSSOL

C/Aragó 261 ⓜ Passeig de Gràcia ☎ 934 876
151; branch at c/de Casp 19 ☎ 933 017 610.
Daily 1pm–1am. MAP P.105, POCKET MAP G3, E10

Chain of big rustic diners, known for their meat and vegetables *a la brasa* (on the grill), most of which run between €6 and €12. They're good places to sample hearty Catalan country cooking, with snails and wild mushrooms on the menu all year round and *calçots* (big spring onions) a spring speciality.

TAPAÇ24

C/Diputació 269 ⓜ Passeig de Gràcia
☎ 934 880 977, ⓦ www.carlesabellan.com.
Daily 9am–midnight. MAP P.105, POCKET MAP H4

Carles Abellan, king of pared-down designer cuisine at his restaurant *Comerç 24*, offers a simpler tapas menu at this retro basement bar-diner. There's a reassuringly traditional feel that's echoed in the menu – *patatas bravas*, Andalucian-style fried fish, *bombas* (meatballs), chorizo sausage and fried eggs. But the kitchen updates the classics too, so there's also *calamares romana* (fried squid) dyed black with squid ink or a burger with *foie gras*. Most tapas dishes cost around €4 to

TAPAÇ24

€16. And there's always a rush and bustle at meal times, so be aware that you might well have to queue.

TRAGALUZ

Ptge. de la Concepció 5 ⓜ Diagonal
☎ 934 870 621, ⓦ www.grupotragaluz.com
/tragaluz. Daily 1.30–4pm & 8.30pm–midnight
(Thurs–Sat until 1am). MAP P.105, POCKET MAP G2

A stylish uptown standby that attracts beautiful people by the score, and the classy Mediterranean-with-knobs-on cooking, served under a glass roof (*tragaluz* means "skylight"), doesn't disappoint. Mains cost €16–30, though cheaper options are available in a separate dining room courtesy of the *Tragarapid* menu (daily 1–4.30pm, dishes €9–11), where things like gourmet burgers, salads, fajitas and stir-fries cater for those fresh off the *modernista* trail (La Pedrera is just across the way).

Sagrada Família and Glòries

If there's one building that is an essential stop on any visit to Barcelona it's Antoni Gaudí's great church of the Sagrada Família (Metro Sagrada Família). In many ways this has become a kind of symbol for the city, representing the glory of Catalan design and endeavour. Most visitors make a special journey out to see the church and then head back into the centre, but it's worth taking in the few blocks south of the area known as Glòries for a further set of attractions, including the city's main concert hall and music museum, and Catalunya's flagship national theatre building.

SAGRADA FAMÍLIA

C/Mallorca 401 ⓜ Sagrada Família ☎ 932 080 414, ⓦ www.sagradafamilia.org. Daily, April–Sept 9am–8pm; Oct–March 9am–6pm. €12 (under-10s free), or €16 including guided tour; combination ticket with Casa Museu Gaudí at Parc Güell €14. MAP P.116–117, POCKET MAP K2

The metro drops you right outside the overpowering church of the Sagrada Família ("Sacred Family"). Begun in 1882 on a modest scale, the project changed the minute that 31-year-old architect Antoni Gaudí took charge in 1884 – he saw in the Sagrada Família an opportunity to reflect his own deepening spiritual feelings. Gaudí spent the rest of his life working on the church and was adapting the plans right up to his untimely death. Run over by a tram on June 7, 1926, his death was treated as a Catalan national disaster, and all of Barcelona turned out for his funeral procession.

Although the building survived, Gaudí's plans were mostly destroyed during the Spanish Civil War. Work restarted in the 1950s amid great controversy, and has continued ever since – as have the arguments. Some maintained that the Sagrada Família should be left incomplete as a memorial to Gaudí, others that the architect intended it to be the work of

CASA MACAYA

several generations. Either way, based on reconstructed models and notes, the project is now drawing inexorably towards completion (within the next twenty years, it's said), and the building is beginning to take final shape.

The size alone is startling (Gaudí's original plan was to build a church to seat over 10,000 people), while the carved spires, monumental bronze doors and vibrant facades are an imaginative and symbolic *tour de force*. Gaudí made extensive use of human, plant and animal models to exactly produce the likenesses he sought – the spreading stone leaves of the roof in the church interior, for example, were inspired by the city's plane trees. An **elevator** (€2.50) up one of the towers provides an unforgettable close-up view of the work, while in the **crypt** (where Gaudí is buried) a fascinating museum traces the history and construction of the church – you'll also be able to view sculptors and model-makers at work. English-language **guided tours** run daily at 11am and 1pm (plus 3pm and 5pm between May and Oct).

HOSPITAL DE LA SANTA CREU I DE SANT PAU

C/de Sant Antoni Maria Claret 167
Ⓜ Hospital de Sant Pau ☎ 933 177 652.
Ⓦ www.rutadelmodernisme.com. Tours daily at 10.15am and 12.15pm in English, plus others in Spanish/Catalan. €6. MAP P.116–117. POCKET MAP M1

Lluís Domènech i Montaner's *modernista* public hospital is possibly the one building that can touch the Sagrada Família for size and invention, its whimsical pavilions, turrets and towers adorned with sculpture, mosaics, stained glass and ironwork. The old buildings have been superseded by the modern hospital behind, but there are interesting guided tours of the historical complex – and it's an easy stroll up here from the Sagrada Família.

CASA MACAYA

Pg. de Sant Joan 108 Ⓜ Verdaguer.
MAP P.116–117, POCKET MAP J2

Just four blocks from the Sagrada Família, Josep Puig i Cadafalch's Casa Macaya (1898–1900) is well known for its imaginative exterior carvings by craftsman Eusebi Arnau – look for the angel holding a camera or the sculptor himself on his way to work by bike.

ACCOMMODATION
Barcelona Urbany   1
Hotel Eurostars Gaudí   2

RESTAURANTS AND TAPAS BARS
Alkimia   1
Piazzena   2

CAFÉ
Bar Gaudí   3

SHOPS
Centre Comercial
Barcelona Glòries   1

Sagrada Família and Glòries

PLAÇA DE LES GLÒRIES CATALANES

Ⓜ Glòries. MAP P.116–117, POCKET MAP M4

Barcelona's major avenues all meet at Plaça de les Glòries Catalanes, dedicated to the Catalan "glories", from architecture to literature. Glòries is at the centre of the city's latest bout of regeneration, which will include a design centre for applied art collections (by 2012). Signature building is Jean Nouvel's cigar-shaped **Torre Agbar**, a remarkable aluminium-and-glass tower inspired by Montserrat. Nearby **Parc del Clot** shows what can be done in an urban setting within the remains of a razed factory site. Trams speed down Avinguda Diagonal to the Diagonal Mar district, passing the **Parc del Centre del Poble Nou** (10min walk, or tram stop Pere IV), another park on an old industrial site – a surviving brick chimney stands in the centre, surrounded by willow trees.

TEATRE NACIONAL DE CATALUNYA

Pl. de les Arts 1 Ⓜ Glòries ☎ 933 065 700. Ⓦ www.tnc.cat. MAP P.116–117, POCKET MAP L4/5

Catalunya's National Theatre features an enterprising programme of classics, original works and productions by guest companies. The building itself makes a dramatic

ANTIQUES STALL AT ELS ENCANTS VELLS

statement, presenting a soaring glass box encased within a Greek temple, and there are guided **tours** for anyone interested in learning more (currently Tues & Thurs; €5; reservations required).

L'AUDITORI

C/Lepant 150 Ⓜ Glòries ☎ 932 479 300. Ⓦ www.auditori.cat. Museu de la Música, c/Padilla 155 ☎ 932 563 650. Ⓦ www .museumusica.bcn.cat. Mon & Wed–Sat 10am–6pm, Sun 10am–8pm. €4, Sun after 3pm free. MAP P.116–117. POCKET MAP L5

The city's main contemporary concert hall is home to the Barcelona Symphony Orchestra (OBC), though the programme also includes chamber, choral, jazz and world concerts, and the annual Early Music and Contemporary Music festivals. There's more in the city's entertaining music museum, including a unique collection of historic instruments.

Els Encants Vells

At the city's traditional open-air flea market, **Els Encants Vells** (Mon, Wed, Fri & Sat 7am–3pm, plus Sun & hols Dec 1 to Jan 5, Ⓦ www.encantsbcn.com, Ⓜ Glòries), you name it, you can buy it: old sewing machines, photograph albums, lawnmowers, clothes, antiques, furniture and out-and-out junk. However, the market is due a new home with the completion of the Glòries renovations, so access, hours and location are subject to change over the next few years.

Shops

CENTRE COMERCIAL BARCELONA GLÒRIES

Av. Diagonal 208, at Pl. de les Glòries Catalanes ⓜ Glòries ⓦ www.lesglories .com. Mon–Sat 10am–10pm.
MAP P.116–117, POCKET MAP M4

Anchoring the neighbourhood is this huge 230-store mall with all the national high-street fashion names represented (H&M, Zara, Bershka, Mango) as well as a big Carrefour supermarket, children's wear, toy shops, play areas, ice-cream parlours, a dozen bars, cafés and restaurants, and a seven-screen cinema complex.

Cafés

BAR GAUDÍ

Mercat de la Sagrada Família, c/de Padilla 255 ⓜ Sagrada Família ☎ 934 363 452, ⓦ www.mercatsbcn.com. Tues–Thurs 7am–2pm & 5.30–8.30pm, Fri 7am–8.30pm, Sat 7am–3pm. MAP P.116–117, POCKET MAP L2

Only two blocks east of the Sagrada Família – and not a tourist in sight. Browse the stalls and pick up your picnic lunch, and make for the stand-up market bar, which has pastries, sandwiches and tapas at local prices, and an internal courtyard with a small children's playground.

Restaurants and tapas bars

ALKIMIA

C/Indústria 79 ⓜ Sagrada Família ☎ 932 076 115, ⓦ www.alkimia.cat. Mon–Fri 1.30–3.30pm & 8.30–11pm; closed Easter week and 3 weeks in Aug.
MAP P.116–117, POCKET MAP K2

Ask Barcelona foodies which is the best Catalan new-wave restaurant in town, and once they've all stopped bickering this is the one they'll probably plump for. "Alchemy" is what's promised by the name, and that's what chef Jordi Vilà delivers in bitingly minimalist style – think *pa amb tomàquet* (bread rubbed with tomato and olive oil), only liquidized and served in a shot glass. It's a Michelin-starred operation, so reservations are vital – expect a €100-a-head bill too (though the €35 lunch is a comparative bargain).

PIAZZENZA

Av. Gaudí 27–29 ⓜ Sagrada Família ☎ 934 363 817. Daily 1pm–1am; closed 2 weeks in Aug. MAP P.116–117, POCKET MAP L2

A reliable standby, five minutes' walk from the Sagrada Família. There's tapas, drinks and pizzas, and you can eat for around €20. It's a pretty buzzy place at night, just as popular with locals as tourists.

Esquerra de l'Eixample

The long streets west of Rambla de Catalunya as far as Barcelona Sants station are perhaps the least visited on any city sightseeing trip. With all the major architectural highlights found on the Eixample's eastern (or right-hand) side, the Esquerra de l'Eixample (left-hand side) was intended by its nineteenth-century planners for public buildings and institutions, many of which still stand. However, the Esquerra does have its moments of interest – not least an eye-catching public park or two – while it's here that some of the city's best bars and clubs are found, particularly in the gay-friendly streets of the so-called Gaixample district, near the university.

UNIVERSITAT DE BARCELONA

Gran Via de les Corts Catalanes 585, at Pl. de la Universitat. Ⓜ Universitat.
MAP P.122-123, POCKET MAP F4-G4

Built in the 1860s, the grand Neoclassical university building is now largely used for ceremonies and administration purposes, but you can visit the main hall or the fine arcaded courtyards and extensive gardens. The traditional student meeting point is the *Bar Estudiantil*, outside in Plaça Universitat, where you can usually grab a pavement table.

FUNDACIÓ FRANCISCO GODIA

C/Diputació 250 Ⓜ Passeig de Gràcia
☎ 932 723 180, Ⓦ www.fundacionfgodia.org.
Mon & Wed–Sun 10am–8pm. €6.
MAP P.122-123, POCKET MAP G4

The private art collection of aesthete and 1950s racing driver Francisco Godia springs a real surprise, concentrating on medieval art, ceramics and modern Catalan art. Not all of the collection can be shown at any one time, so pieces are rotated on occasion, while special exhibitions run in tandem, for which there's usually no extra charge.

UNIVERSITY COURTYARDS

MERCAT DEL NINOT

C/Mallorca 133 ⓜ Hospital Clinic ☎ 934 536
512, ⓦ www.mercatsbcn.com. Mon–Fri
8am–9pm, Sat 8am–3pm.
MAP P.122–123, POCKET MAP F2/3

One of the oldest markets in
the city is currently undergoing
a major refurbishment (until
2012), but there's a large
temporary market building on
c/Casanova, in front of the
hospital. You won't find many
tourists here and the shops
around the market are
refreshingly down-to-earth
places to buy clothes, jewellery,
accessories and homeware.

Around the back of the
hospital, it's also worth having
a look at the **Escola Industrial**,
formerly a textile mill, which
boasts a 1920s chapel by Joan
Rubió i Bellvér, who worked
with Antoni Gaudí. Students
usually fill the courtyards, and
you're free to take a stroll
through to view the highly
decorative buildings.

MUSEU I CENTRE D'ESTUDIS DE L'ESPORT

C/de Buenos Aires 56–58 ⓜ Hospital Clinic
☎ 934 192 232. June to mid-Sept Mon–Fri
8am–3pm, otherwise Mon–Fri 10am–2pm &
3–5pm. Free. MAP P.122–123, POCKET MAP F1

Built as a private house in 1911
by *modernista* architect Josep
Puig i Cadafalch, this little
municipal sports museum
contains probably the most
unassuming sporting "Hall of
Fame" found anywhere in the
world. In a couple of
wood-panelled rooms
photographs of 1920s Catalan
rally drivers and footballers are
displayed alongside a collection
of memorabilia, including a
signed water-polo ball used in
the 1992 Olympics, Everest
mountaineer Carles Vàlles's ice
pick, and all manner of
mementoes from Catalan
sporting triumphs.

MUSEU I CENTRE D'ESTUDIS DE L'ESPORT

FILMOTECA

Av. de Sarrià 33 ⓜ Hospital Clinic
☎ 934 107 590, ⓦ www.gencat.cat/cultura
/icic/filmoteca. MAP P.122–123, POCKET MAP E1

Run by the Catalan
government, the FilmoTeca has
an excellent art-house cinema
programme, showing three or
four different films (original
language, marked "V.O.") every
day. The programme changes
every couple of weeks and
themed seasons, classic films,
retrospectives and obscure
world cinema releases are
FilmoTeca's stock in trade. It
can be a bit too worthy at
times, though English-language
visitors will generally find
something worth seeing during
their stay, and there's also a
children's club (*sessió infantil*)
on Sunday, and a decent café.
Tickets are a bargain at €2.70,
or you can buy a discounted
ten-film pass for €18. A new
cinema building is being
constructed in the Raval, but
for the time being the
FilmoTeca will still be based at
Avinguda de Sarrià.

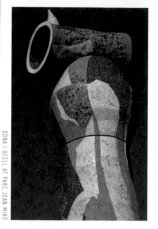

raised piazza whose only feature is Joan Miró's gigantic mosaic sculpture *Dona i Ocell* ("Woman and Bird"), towering above a shallow reflecting pool. The rear of the park is given over to games areas and landscaped sections of palms and firs, with a kiosk café and some outdoor tables found in among the trees. The children's playground here is one of the best in the city, with a climbing frame and aerial runway.

LES ARENES

Pl. d'Espanya ⓜ Espanya.
MAP P.122–123, POCKET MAP C4

The traditional bullring backing Parc Joan Miró is undergoing a massive Richard Rogers-inspired refit to convert it into a leisure and retail complex with enormous roof terrace, while retaining the circular Moorish facade of

PARC JOAN MIRÓ

C/de Tarragona ⓜ Tarragona. Daily 10am–dusk. MAP P.122–123, POCKET MAP C3/4–D3/4

Parc Joan Miró was laid out on the site of the nineteenth-century municipal slaughterhouse. It features a

Esquerra de l'Eixample

ACCOMMODATION	
Alternative Creative Youth Home	5
Expo Hotel Barcelona	2
Gran Hotel Torre Catalunya	1
Hotel Inglaterra	6
Residencia Australia	4
Somnio Barcelona	3

RESTAURANTS AND TAPAS BARS	
Cervesaria Catalana	6
Cinc Sentits	9
La Flauta	13
Gaig	10
Me	1
Out of China	7
Racó d'en Balta	4

BARS	
Aire	8
Belchica	14
Dietrich	12
Dry Martini	3
La Fira	5
Punto BCN	11
Quilombo	2

CLUBS	
Antilla BCN Latin Club	3
Arena Madre	4
Danzarama	5
Luz de Gas	1
Metro	6
Opium	2

SHOPS	
Altaïr	3
Jamonísimo	2
Jean-Pierre Bua	1

1900. Also spared the wrecker's ball is the six-storey *modernista* **Casa Papallona** (1912), on the eastern side of Les Arenes on c/de Llança. It's one of the city's favourite house facades, crowned by a huge ceramic butterfly.

PARC DE L'ESPANYA INDUSTRIAL

C/de Sant Antoni ⓂSants-Estació. Daily 10am -dusk. MAP P.122-123, POCKET MAP B2/3-C2/3

If you have time to kill at Barcelona Sants station, nip around the south side to Basque architect Luis Peña Ganchegui's urban park. Built on the site of an old textile factory, there's a line of concrete lighthouses contrasting with an incongruously classical Neptune, as well as boating lake, café kiosk, playground and sports facilities. It's a decent attempt at reconciling

On the Miró trail

When you've seen one Miró – well, you start to see them everywhere in Barcelona, starting with the large ceramic mural visible on the facade at the airport. The towering *Dona i Ocell* in the Parc Joan Miró is unmissable, but you should also look down at your feet on the Ramblas for the pavement mural at Plaça de la Boqueria. Miró also designed the *Caixa de Pensions* starfish logo splashed across the Caixa Forum arts centre. In many ways, it's a Miró city, whatever Picasso fans might think.

local interests with the otherwise mundane nature of the surroundings, typical of the city's approach to revitalizing unkempt urban corners.

Shops

ALTAÏR

Gran Via de les Corts Catalanes 616
Ⓜ Passeig de Gràcia Ⓦ www.altair.es. Mon-
Sat 10am–8.30pm. MAP P.122–123, POCKET MAP G4

Europe's biggest travel
superstore has a massive
selection of travel books,
guides, maps and world music,
plus a programme of
travel-related talks and
exhibitions.

JAMONÍSIMO

C/Provença 85 Ⓜ Hospital Clinic Ⓦ www
.jamonisimo.com. Mon-Fri 9.30am–2.30pm
& 5–9pm, Sat 9.30am–2.30pm.
MAP P.122–123, POCKET MAP E2

When Ferran Adrià, Heston
Blumenthal and other kitchen
maestros are in town, this is
where they come to taste and
buy the world's finest
artisan-made cured hams.

JEAN-PIERRE BUA

Av. Diagonal 469 Ⓜ Hospital Clinic Ⓦ www
.jeanpierrebua.com. Mon-Sat 10am–2pm &
4.30–8.30pm. MAP P.122–123, POCKET MAP F1

The city's high temple for
fashion victims: a postmodern
shrine for Yamamoto, Gaultier,
Miyake, Galliano, McQueen,
McCartney, Westwood and
other international stars.

JAMONÍSIMO

Restaurants and tapas bars

CERVESARIA CATALANA

C/Mallorca 236 Ⓜ Passeig de Gràcia
☎ 932 160 368. Daily 9am–1am.
MAP P.122–123, POCKET MAP G3

A place that is serious about its
tapas and beer – the counters
are piled high, supplemented by
a blackboard list of daily
specials, while the walls are
lined with bottled brews from
around the world. It gets busy
after work and at meal times,
and you might have to wait for
a table.

CINC SENTITS

C/Aribau 58 Ⓜ Universitat ☎ 933 239 490,
Ⓦ www.cincsentits.com. Tues-Sat
1.30–3.30pm & 8.30–11pm. MAP P.122–123,
POCKET MAP F3

Jordi Artal's "Five Senses" wows
diners with its contemporary
Catalan cuisine – and the
restaurant now has a Michelin
star to boot, so you'll need to
book. Six- and eight-course
"tasting menus" (€50 and €70,
matching wines available) use
rigorously sourced ingredients
(wild fish, mountain lamb,
seasonal vegetables, farmhouse
cheeses) in elegant, pared-down
dishes that are all about flavour.

LA FLAUTA

C/d'Aribau 23 Ⓜ Universitat ☎ 933 237 038.
Mon-Sat 8am–1am. MAP P.122–123, POCKET MAP F4

One of the city's best-value
lunch menus sees diners
queuing for tables early – get
there before 2pm to avoid the
rush. It's a handsome bar-
restaurant of dark wood and
deep colours, and, while the
name is a nod to the house
speciality gourmet sandwiches
(a *flauta* is a crispy baguette)
there are also tapas served
all day.

CINC SENTITS

GAIG

C/Aragó 214 ⓜ Universitat ☎ 934 291 017.
Mon 9–11pm, Tues–Sat 1–3.30pm & 9–11pm;
closed 3 weeks in Aug. MAP P.122–123,
POCKET MAP F3

The Gaig family restaurant was
first founded in 1869 out in the
Horta neighbourhood, but
under fourth-generation family
member, Carles Gaig, it has a
sleek downtown home at the
Hotel Cram. Its towering
reputation rests on innovative
reinterpretations of traditional
Catalan dishes, so a typical
arròs (rice) dish might combine
foie gras, endive and citrus. But
when starters can cost €35, and
the *menu degustació* is over
€100, you're talking about a
true special-occasion place –
though at the associated *Fonda
Gaig* (c/Corsega 200, ☎ 934 532
020, mains €15–22) you can
sample something of the style
at less stratospheric prices.

ME

C/Paris 162 ⓜ Provença ☎ 934 194 933.
ⓦ www.catarsiscuisine.com. Tues–Thurs
8.45–11.30pm, Fri & Sat 1.45–3.30pm &
8.45–11pm. MAP P.122–123, POCKET MAP F2

All the rage for its clever
fusion of cuisines from
Vietnam and New Orleans by
way of Barcelona – all places
dear to owner Javier's heart.
Expect gumbo and marinated
shrimp alongside papaya salad
or grilled Saigon rib-eye with
lemongrass, all in a stylish
neo-Colonial setting. Mains
are €15–23 though the
weekend lunch is a cheaper
affair.

OUT OF CHINA

C/Muntaner 100 ⓜ Provença ☎ 934 515 555.
Mon–Sat 1–4pm & 8pm–midnight, Sun
1–4pm. MAP P.122–123, POCKET MAP F3

Most Chinese restaurants in
Barcelona are pretty bland, but
not *Out of China*.
Black-and-red decor, lanterns
and jazz-lounge sounds set the
tone for a contemporary
Chinese menu that's
particularly hot on veggie
options, from fried aubergine
to tofu curry. Lunch is a good
deal but even at night prices
won't break the bank, with
most dishes around €8–10.

RACÓ D'EN BALTA

C/Aribau 125 ⓜ Provença ☎ 934 531 044.
Mon 1–3.45pm, Tues–Sat 1–3.45pm &
9–11pm (bar until 2am); closed 1 week in Jan,
Easter week & 3 weeks in Aug. MAP P.122–123,
POCKET MAP F2

This funky hangout serves a
popular weekday lunch, while
at night you can eat for around
€30 from a Mediterranean
market-led menu. Meanwhile,
it's drinks and tapas at the cool
Balta Bar next door, which has
been around for a century or so
but is lent a certain style by the
trendy local punters.

Bars

AIRE

C/de Valencia 236 Ⓜ Passeig de Gràcia
☎ 934 515 812, Ⓦ www.arenadisco.com.
Thurs–Sat 11pm–3am, July & Aug also Tues
& Wed. MAP P.122–123, POCKET MAP G3

The hottest, most stylish lesbian bar in town is a relaxed place for a drink and a dance to pop, house and retro sounds. Gay men are welcome too.

BELCHICA

C/Villaroel 60 Ⓜ Urgell ☎ 625 814 001.
Tues–Sat 6pm–3am, Sun & Mon 7pm–1am.
MAP P.122–123, POCKET MAP F4

Barcelona's first Belgian beer bar guarantees a range of decent brews (including Trappist beers) that you can't get anywhere else. It's a cosy haunt, playing electronica, new jazz, lounge, reggae and other left-field sounds, and there are music and poetry nights.

DIETRICH

C/Consell de Cent 255 Ⓜ Universitat
☎ 934 517 707. Daily 10pm–2.30am (Fri & Sat until 3am). MAP P.122–123, POCKET MAP F3

Cornerstone of the Gaixample scene is this well-known music bar and "teatro-café" – *tranquilo* during the week, but ever more hedonistic as the weekend wears on, with drag shows, acrobats and dancers punctuating the DJ sets.

DRY MARTINI

C/d'Aribau 166 Ⓜ Provença ☎ 932 175 072,
Ⓦ www.drymartinibcn.com. Mon–Fri 1pm–2.30am (opens 6.30pm in Aug), Sat & Sun 6.30pm–3am. MAP P.122–123, POCKET MAP F2

White-jacketed bartenders, dark wood and brass fittings, a self-satisfied air – it could only be Barcelona's legendary uptown cocktail bar. To be fair, though, no one in town mixes drinks better.

DRY MARTINI

LA FIRA

C/Provença 171 Ⓜ Provença
☎ 939 781 096. Wed–Sat 10pm–3am.
MAP P.122–123, POCKET MAP F2

One of the city's most bizarre drinking emporiums comes complete with old-fashioned fairground rides and circus paraphernalia – sit at the bar fashioned from a circus awning or cosy up in the dodgem cars.

PUNTO BCN

C/Muntaner 63–65 Ⓜ Universitat
☎ 934 536 123, Ⓦ www.arenadisco.com.
Daily 6pm–2.30am. MAP P.122–123, POCKET MAP F3

Gaixample classic that attracts a lively crowd for drinks, chat and music. Wednesday happy hour is a blast, while Friday night is party night.

QUILOMBO

C/d'Aribau 149 Ⓜ Provença ☎ 934 395 406.
Mon–Thurs & Sun 9pm–3am, Fri & Sat 7.30pm–3.30am. MAP P.122–123, POCKET MAP F2

Unpretentious music bar that's rolled with the years since 1971, featuring live guitarists, Latin American bands and a clientele that joins in enthusiastically, maracas in hand.

Clubs

ANTILLA BCN LATIN CLUB

C/Aragó 141–143 Ⓜ Urgell ☎ 934 514 564, Ⓦ www.antillasalsa.com. Daily 11pm–5am (Fri & Sat until 6am). MAP P.122–123, POCKET MAP E3

Latin and Caribbean tunes galore – rumba, son, salsa, merengue, mambo, you name it – for out-and-out good-time dancing. There are live bands, killer cocktails and dance classes most nights.

ARENA MADRE

C/Balmes 32 Ⓜ Passeig de Gràcia ☎ 934 070 342, Ⓦ www.arenadisco.com. MAP P.122–123, POCKET MAP G4

The "mother" club sits at the helm of *Arena*'s gay empire, all within a city block (pay for one, get in to all) – frenetic house at *Arena Madre* (daily 12.30–5.30am), high-disco antics at *Arena Classic* (c/de la Diputació 233; Fri & Sat 12.30–6am), more of the same plus dance, r'n'b, pop and rock at the more mixed *Arena VIP* (Gran Via de les Corts Catalanes 593; Fri & Sat 12.30–6am), and vintage chart hits at *Arena Dandy* (same address and hours).

DANZARAMA

Gran Vía de les Corts Catalanes 604 Ⓜ Universitat ☎ 933 425 070, Ⓦ www .danzarama.com. Daily 7am–2am (Fri & Sat until 3am). MAP P.122–123, POCKET MAP G4

One of the stalwarts of the uptown gastro-club scene, with a flashy fusion restaurant (open day and night), summer *terrassa* and cool bar and lounge, great for starting the night before some serious dancing elsewhere.

LUZ DE GAS

C/Muntaner 246 Ⓜ Provença ☎ 932 097 711, Ⓦ www.luzdegas.com. Daily 11.30pm–5am, occasional gigs from 9.30pm. MAP P.122–123, POCKET MAP F1

Smart venue popular with a slightly older crowd, with live bands (rock, blues, soul, jazz and covers) every night around midnight. Foreign acts appear regularly too, mainly jazz-blues types but also old soul acts and up-and-coming rockers. Admission up to €20.

METRO

C/Sepúlveda 158 Ⓜ Universitat ☎ 933 235 227, Ⓦ www.metrodiscobcn.com. Daily midnight–5am. MAP P.122–123, POCKET MAP A10

A gay institution in Barcelona, with cabaret nights and other events midweek, and extremely crowded club nights at weekends in its two rooms playing either current dance and techno or retro disco.

OPIUM

C/de Paris 193–197 Ⓜ Provença ☎ 934 146 362, Ⓦ www.opiumcinema.com. Tues–Sat 9pm–3am. MAP P.122–123, POCKET MAP F1

A once-decayed cinema, now restyled as a very handsome galleried restaurant, lounge-bar and club. You don't have to pay to get in, and the restaurant runs from 9pm until midnight, after which you're looking at jazz, funk and chill-out sounds

ARENA MADRE

Gràcia and Parc Güell

Gràcia was a village for much of its early existence, before being annexed as a suburb in the late nineteenth century. It still feels set apart from the city in many ways, and though actual sights are few and far between it's well known for its cinemas, bars and restaurants. The one unmissable attraction, meanwhile, is just on the neighbourhood fringe, nearby Parc Güell, an extraordinary flight of fancy by architectural genius Antoni Gaudí. To get to Gràcia take the FGC train from Plaça de Catalunya to Gràcia station, or the metro to either Diagonal (south) or Fontana (north). From any of the stations, it's around a 500m walk to Gràcia's main square, Plaça del Sol, hub of the neighbourhood's renowned nightlife.

MERCAT DE LA LLIBERTAT

Pl. Llibertat 27 Ⓜ Fontana ☎ 932 170 995,
Ⓦ www.mercatsbcn.com. Mon–Fri
8am–8.30pm, Sat 8am–3pm. MAP P.129
You may as well start where the locals start, first thing in the morning, shopping for bread and provisions in the neighbourhood market. The red-brick and iron structure has been beautifully restored and at *El Tast de Joan Noi* (next to the Joan Noi fish counter) you can sample the breakfast of champions – oysters, grilled razor clams and a glass of *cava*.

CASA VICENS

C/de les Carolines 24 Ⓜ Fontana. No public access. MAP P.129
Antoni Gaudí's first major private commission (1883–85) took its inspiration from the Moorish style, covering the

facade of the house in green and white tiles with a flower motif. The decorative iron railings are a reminder of Gaudí's early training as a metalsmith (and he also designed much of the mansion's original furniture).

PLAÇA DE LA VIRREINA

Ⓜ Fontana. MAP P.129

This pretty square, backed by the parish church of Sant Joan, is one of Gràcia's favourites, with a couple of bars providing a place to rest and admire the handsome houses, most notably the Casa Rubinat (1909). Nearby streets, particularly **Carrer Verdi**, contain many of the neighbourhood's most fashionable boutiques, galleries and cafés.

VERDI AND VERDI PARK

C/Verdi 32 and c/Torrijos 49 Ⓜ Fontana
☎ 932 387 990. ⓦ www.cines-verdi.com.
MAP P.129

Barcelona's favourite art-house cinemas have sister locations in adjacent streets, with nine screens showing original-language movies from around the world. Tickets are €7.50, or €5 for the first screening on weekdays and all day Monday.

PLAÇA DE RIUS I TAULET

Ⓜ Diagonal. MAP P.129, POCKET MAP H1

The 30m-high clock tower in the heart of Gràcia was a rallying point for nineteenth-century radicals – whose twenty-first-century counterparts prefer to meet for brunch at the square's popular café *terrassas*.

PILLARED WALKWAY IN PARC GÜELL

PARC GÜELL

C/d'Olot Ⓜ Vallcarca/Lesseps. Daily, March &
Oct 10am–7pm; April & Sept 10am–8pm;
May–Aug 10am–9pm; Nov–Feb 10am–6pm.
Free. MAP P.130

Gaudí's Parc Güell (1900–14)
was his most ambitious project
after the Sagrada Família,
conceived as a "garden city" of
the type popular at the time in
England, but opened as a
public park instead in 1922.
Laid out on a hill, which
provides fabulous views back
across the city, the park is an
almost hallucinatory
expression of the imagination.
Pavilions of contorted stone,
giant decorative lizards,
meandering rustic viaducts, a
vast Hall of Columns, carved
stone trees – all combine in
one manic swirl of ideas and
excesses, like the famous
meandering ceramic bench
that snakes along the edge of

the terrace above the columned hall. The displays at the **Centre d'Interpretació** (daily 11am–3pm; free), at the main park entrance, provide useful background information on the whole project.

The most direct route to Parc Güell is on bus #24 from Plaça de Catalunya, Passeig de Gràcia or c/Gran de Gràcia, which drops you at the eastern side gate. From Ⓜ Vallcarca, walk a few hundred metres down Avinguda de l'Hospital Militar until you see the mechanical escalators on your left, ascending Baixada de la Glòria – follow these to the western side park entrance (15min in total). From Ⓜ Lesseps, turn right along Travessera de Dalt and then left up steep c/Larrard, which leads (10min) straight to the main entrance on c/Olot.

CASA-MUSEU GAUDÍ

Parc Güell Ⓜ Vallcarca/Lesseps ☎ 932 193 811, ⓦ www.casamuseugaudi.org. Daily: April–Sept 10am–8pm; Oct–March 10am–6pm. €5.50, combination ticket with Sagrada Família €14. MAP P.130

One of Gaudí's collaborators, Francesc Berenguer, designed and built a turreted house within Parc Güell for the architect (though he only lived in it intermittently). This contains a diverting collection of some of the furniture Gaudí designed for other projects – a typical mixture of wild originality and brilliant engineering – as well as plans and objects related to the park and to Gaudí's life. His study and bedroom have been preserved and there's an inkling of his personality, too, in the displayed religious texts and pictures, along with a silver coffee cup and his death mask, made at the Santa Pau hospital where he died.

PARC DE LA CREUETA DEL COLL

Pg. de la Mare de Deu del Coll 89 Ⓜ Vallcarca. Daily 10am–dusk. Free. MAP P.130

For a different kind of experience altogether, combine a trip to Gaudí's extravagant park with this contemporary urban space laid out on the site of an old quarry, whose sheer walls were retained in the landscaping. You're greeted at the top of the park steps by an Ellsworth Kelly metal spike, while suspended by steel cables over water is a massive concrete claw by the Basque artist Eduardo Chillida. There are also palms, promenades and a kiosk-café.

Bus #28 from Plaça de Catalunya, up Passeig de Gràcia, stops 100m from the park, or you can walk from Ⓜ Vallcarca in about twenty minutes (there's a neighbourhood map at the metro station). It's worth knowing that if you visit Creueta del Coll first and then walk down the main Passeig de la Mare de Deu del Coll, there are signposts leading you into Parc Güell the back way.

GAUDÍ'S DESK IN THE CASA-MUSEU GAUDÍ

HIBERNIAN BOOKS

of Carrer Verdi – they make Portuguese specialities daily (including the famous *pasteis de Belém*, little custard tarts), and have a full programme of wine tastings, food festivals and other events.

LA NENA

C/Ramon i Cajal 36 Ⓜ Joanic ☎ 932 851 476. Daily 9am–2pm & 4–10pm.
MAP P.129, POCKET MAP J1

Great for home-made cakes, waffles, quiches, organic ice cream, squeezed juices and the like. But parents also like the "little girl" as it's very child-friendly, from the changing mats in the loos to the little seats, games and puzzles.

Restaurants and tapas bars

BO

Pl. Rius i Taulet 11 Ⓜ Diagonal ☎ 933 683 529. Daily 10am–1am (Fri & Sat until 2am).
MAP P.129, POCKET MAP H1

Gràcia's nicest square also has its best selection of café-bars, including this contemporary *tasca* that serves tapas and sandwiches all day and night. You can easily rustle up a decent meal here, from mussels to Caesar salad (most dishes €5–7), and it's an honourable alternative if you can't get a *terrassa* table (or it's Tuesday) at the almost adjacent Nou Candanchu.

FLASH, FLASH

C/de la Granada del Penedès 25 Ⓜ Diagonal ☎ 932 370 990, Ⓦ www .grup7portes.com. Daily 1pm–1.30am (bar open 11am–2am). MAP P.129, POCKET MAP G1

A classic 1970s survivor with a keen sense of style, *Flash, Flash* does tortillas (€6–9) served any time you like, any way you like,

Shop

HIBERNIAN BOOKS

C/Montseny 17 Ⓜ Fontana Ⓦ www .hibernian-books.com. Mon 4.30–8.30pm, Tues–Sat 10.30am–8.30pm.
MAP P.129

Barcelona's only secondhand English bookstore has around 40,000 titles in stock – you can part-exchange, and there are always plenty of giveaway bargains available.

Cafés

A CASA PORTUGUESA

C/Verdi 58 Ⓜ Fontana ☎ 933 683 528, Ⓦ www.acasaportuguesa.com. Tues–Fri 5–11pm, Sat & Sun 11am–3pm & 5–11pm.
MAP P.129

A sleek café and deli on Gràcia's buzziest street that's a showcase for the food, wine and culture of Portugal. Call in for a break while trawling the designer and streetwear stores from plain and simple to elaborately stuffed, with sweet ones for dessert. If that doesn't grab you, try the reasonably priced menu of salads, steaks, burgers and fish. Either way, you'll love the original white leatherette booths and monotone photo-model cutouts – very Austin Powers.

NOU CANDANCHU

Pl. Rius i Taulet 9 Ⓜ Diagonal ☎ 932 377 362. Mon, Wed, Thurs & Sun 7am–1am, Fri & Sat 7am–3am. MAP P.129, POCKET MAP H1

Good for lunch on a sunny day or a leisurely night out on a budget, when you can sit beneath the clock tower and soak up the atmosphere in the ever-entertaining local square. There's a wide menu – tapas and hot sandwiches, but also steak and eggs, steamed clams and mussels, or cod and hake cooked plenty of different ways. It's managed by an affable bunch of young guys, and there's lots of choice for €8–12.

FLASH, FLASH

LA SINGULAR

C/Francesc Giner 50 Ⓜ Diagonal ☎ 932 375 098. Mon–Fri 1.30–4pm & 9pm–midnight (Fri until 1am), Sat 9pm–1am. MAP P.129, POCKET MAP H1

The tiny kitchen turns out refined Mediterranean food at moderate prices (most dishes €9–15) – think aubergine and smoked fish salad or chicken stuffed with dates and ham. There's always something appealing on the menu for veggies, too. It's a cornerstone of the neighbourhood, with a friendly atmosphere, but there are only nine tables, so go early or reserve.

SURENY

Pl. de la Revolució 17 Ⓜ Fontana ☎ 932 137 556. Tues–Sat 8.30pm–midnight, Sun 1–3.30pm & 8.30pm–midnight. MAP P.129, POCKET MAP H1

Although, strictly speaking, a tapas place, this is more of a gourmet choice as you're served at restaurant tables with inventive little dishes from a seasonally changing menu. For around €7 or €8 a time sample clever concoctions like venison tartare with pineapple preserve, a scallop on artichoke cream or monkfish with baby asparagus. Alternatively, a €35 tasting menu gets you seven of the best plus dessert.

TAVERNA EL GLOP

C/Sant Lluís 24 Ⓜ Joanic ☎ 932 137 058, Ⓦ www.tavernaelglop.com. Daily 1–4pm & 8pm–1am. MAP P.129

The rusticity (stone-flagged floors, baskets of garlic) stops just the right side of parody and the lunch *menú del dia* is one of the city's best deals; otherwise expect to spend around €20–25 a head for grills and other tavern specials prepared in front of you on the open kitchen ranges.

Bars

LA BAIGNOIRE

C/Verdi 6 ⓂFontana. Mon–Sat 7.30pm–1am
(Fri & Sat until 2am), Sun 4pm–1am.
MAP P.129, POCKET MAP H1

Cosy little wine bar offering a
small corner of sophistication –
Ella Fitzgerald on CD, a dozen
good wines by the glass and
cheesy nibbles.

CAFÉ SALAMBO

C/Torrijos 51 ⓂFontana ☎ 932 186 966,
ⓌWwww.cafesalambo.com. Tues–Sat 4pm–1am
(Fri & Sat until 3am), Sun noon–11pm.
MAP P.129

Where the pre- and post-
cinema crowd meets (both
Verdi cinemas are on the
doorstep). It's a long-standing
neighbourhood hangout, with
something of a colonial feel,
and there are lots of wines and
cava by the glass, and good
food too.

CAFÉ DEL SOL

Pl. del Sol 16 ⓂFontana ☎ 934 155 663.
Daily 1pm–2.30am. MAP P.129, POCKET MAP H1

The grandaddy of the Plaça del
Sol scene sees action day and
night. On summer evenings,
when the square is packed with
revellers, there's not an outdoor
table to be had, but even in
winter this is a popular
drinking den with a cosy
pub-like interior.

CANIGÓ

Pl. de la Revolució 10 ⓂFontana. Tues–Sun
11am–midnight. MAP P.129, POCKET MAP H1

Family-run neighbourhood bar
now entering its third
generation. It's not much to
look at, but the drinks are
cheap and it's a Gràcia
institution with a loyal
following, packed out at
weekends especially with a
young, largely local crowd.

ELÈCTRIC BAR

Trav. de Gràcia 233 ⓂJoanic Ⓦwww
.myspace.com/electricbarcelona. Daily
7pm–2am (Fri & Sat until 3am).
MAP P.129, POCKET MAP J1

The bar of choice for a boho,
counterculture crowd who
come for the wildly varied
live programming, with
something on every night,
from poetry slams to
electro-folk gigs. It's free in
if you just fancy a drink at
the bar – performances in the
space out back start at 10pm
(weekends at 11pm) with
admission usually €3–5.

HELIOGABAL

C/Ramon i Cajal 80 ⓂJoanic Ⓦwww
.heliogabal.com. Daily 9pm–2am (Fri & Sat
until 3am). MAP P.129, POCKET MAP J1

Not much more than a boiler
room given a lick of paint, but
filled with a cool, twenty-
something crowd, here for the
live poetry and music – expect
something different every night
(Catalan versifying, jazz jam
sessions and earnest singer-
songwriters), starting at 10pm.
Admission is usually €3–10,
depending on the act, and
drinks aren't expensive.

TERRACE AT CAFÉ DEL SOL

SAMSARA

C/Terol 6 ⓜ Fontana ☎ 932 853 688.
Mon–Wed 8.30pm–1am, Thurs 8.30pm–2am,
Fri & Sat 8.30pm–3am, Sun 7.30pm–1am.
MAP P.129, POCKET MAP H1

It's totally Gràcia – low tables, low lighting and painted concrete walls, plus a chillout soundtrack and a projection screen above the bar. There's also contemporary tapas and "platillos" (little plates) but it's a bar first and foremost, with DJs cracking out house and techno sets at the weekend.

VINILO

C/Matilde 2 ⓜ Diagonal ☎ 626 464 759.
Daily 7pm–2am (Fri & Sat until 3am).
MAP P.129, POCKET MAP H1

Wear a beret, smoke like crazy, favour Bladerunner, Jeff Buckley and Band of Horses? This bar's for you – a dive bar with the lighting set at perpetual dusk, where time slips easily away.

VIRREINA

Pl. de la Virreina 1 ⓜ Fontana ☎ 932 379 880. Daily 10am–1am (Fri & Sat until 2am).
MAP P.129

Another real Gràcia favourite, on one of the neighbourhood's prettiest squares, with a very popular summer *terrassa*. Cold beer and sandwiches are served to a laidback crowd – it's one of those places where you drop by for a quick drink and find yourself staying for hours.

Clubs

CENTRE ARTESÀ TRADICIONÀRIUS

Trav. de Sant Antoni 6–8 ⓜ Fontana ☎ 932 184 485, ⓦ www.tradicionarius.cat. MAP P.129

The best place in town for folk, traditional and world music by Catalan, Spanish and visiting performers,

OTTO ZUTZ

including some occasional big names. Admission is usually €5–15, and you can expect anything from Basque bagpipes to Brazilian singers. There are also music and instrument workshops, while CAT sponsors all sorts of outreach concerts and festivals, including an annual international folk and traditional dance festival between January and April.

OTTO ZUTZ

C/de Lincoln 15 ⓜ Fontana ☎ 932 300 722, ⓦ www.grupo-ottozutz.com. Tues–Sat midnight–6am. MAP P.129

It first opened in 1985, and has lost some of its erstwhile glam cachet, but this three-storey former textile factory still has a shedload of pretensions. The sounds are basically hip-hop, r'n'b and house, and with the right clothes and face you're in (you may or may not have to pay, depending on how impressive you are, the day of the week, the mood of the door staff, etc).

Camp Nou, Pedralbes and Sarrià-Sant Gervasi

On the northwestern edge of the centre, the city's famous football stadium, Camp Nou, draws locals and visitors alike, both to the big game and to the FC Barcelona museum. Nearby, across Avinguda Diagonal, a former royal palace contains the city's applied art collections (of clothes and textiles, decorative art and ceramics), while a half-day's excursion can be made by walking from the palace, past the Gaudí dragon gate at Pavellons Güell, to the calm cloister at the Gothic monastery of Pedralbes. You can complete the day by returning via Sarrià, to the east, more like a small town than a suburb, with a pretty main street and market to explore. At night, the focus shifts to the bars and restaurants of neighbouring Sant Gervasi in the streets north of Plaça de Francesc Macià.

AVINGUDA DIAGONAL

Ⓜ Maria Cristina. MAP P.138–139

The uptown section of Avinguda Diagonal runs through the heart of Barcelona's flashiest business and shopping district. The giant **L'Illa** shopping centre flanks the avenue – the stepped design is a prone echo of New York's Rockefeller Center. Designer fashion stores are ubiquitous, particularly around **Plaça de Francesc Macià** and Avinguda Pau Casals – at the end of the latter, **Turó Parc** (daily 10am–dusk) is a good place to rest weary feet, with a small children's playground and a café-kiosk. Meanwhile, behind

CAMP NOU STADIUM

L'Illa, it's worth seeking out **Plaça de la Concordia**, a surprising survivor from the past amid the uptown tower blocks – the pretty little square is dominated by its church belltower and ringed by local businesses (florist, pharmacy, hairdresser), with an outdoor café or two for a quiet drink.

CAMP NOU AND FC BARCELONA

Av. Arístides Maillol Ⓜ Collblanc/Maria Cristina ☎ 902 189 900 or ☎ 934 963 600 from outside Spain, Ⓦ www.fcbarcelona.com. Match tickets (€40–100) also from ServiCaixa ☎ 902 332 211, Ⓦ www.servicaixa.com. MAP P.138-139

In Barcelona, football is a genuine obsession, with support for the local giants FC (Futbol Club) Barcelona raised to an art form. "More than just a club" is the proud boast, and during the dictatorship years the club stood as a Catalan symbol around which people could rally. Arch rivals, Real Madrid, on the other hand, were always seen as Franco's club. The swashbuckling team – past European champions and darling of football neutrals everywhere – plays at the magnificent Camp Nou football stadium, built in 1957, and enlarged for the 1982 World Cup semi-final to accommodate 98,000 spectators. A new remodelling (by architect Norman Foster) plans to update the stadium over the next few years, but even today Camp Nou provides one of the world's best football-watching experiences.

The **football season** runs from August until May, with league games usually played on Sundays. Tickets are relatively easy to come by, except for the biggest games, and go on general sale up to a month before each match – buy them

online, at the ticket office, or by calling ServiCaixa.

The stadium complex hosts basketball, handball and hockey games with FC Barcelona's other professional teams, and there's also a public ice rink, souvenir shop and café.

MUSEU DEL FUTBOL AND STADIUM TOUR

Camp Nou, Av. Arístides Maillol, enter through Gates 7 & 9 Ⓜ Collblanc/Maria Cristina ☎ 902 189 900 or ☎ 934 963 600. Ⓦ www.fcbarcelona.com. Mon–Sat 10am–6.30pm (April–Sept until 8pm), Sun 10am–2.30pm; tours until 1hr before closing. €17, children 6–13 years €14. MAP P.138-139

No soccer fan should miss the Camp Nou stadium tour and football museum. The self-guided tour winds through the changing rooms, onto the pitch and up to the press gallery and directors' box for stunning views. The museum, meanwhile, is jammed full of silverware and memorabilia, while displays and archive footage trace the history of the club back to 1901. Finally, you're directed into the massive **FC Botiga**, where you can buy anything from a replica shirt to a branded bottle of wine.

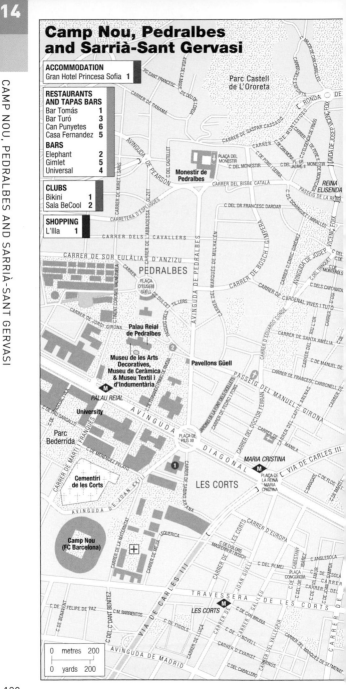

Camp Nou, Pedralbes and Sarrià-Sant Gervasi

ACCOMMODATION	
Gran Hotel Princesa Sofia	1

RESTAURANTS AND TAPAS BARS	
Bar Tomás	1
Bar Turó	3
Can Punyetes	6
Casa Fernandez	5
BARS	
Elephant	2
Gimlet	5
Universal	4

CLUBS	
Bikini	1
Sala BeCool	2

SHOPPING	
L'Illa	1

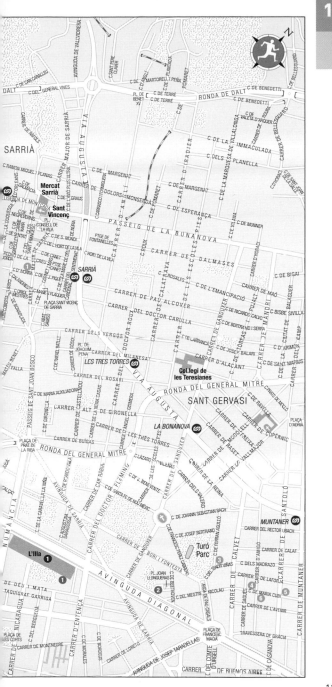

THE PALAU REIAL DE PEDRALBES GARDENS

PALAU REIAL DE PEDRALBES

Av. Diagonal 686 Ⓜ Palau Reial. Gardens daily 10am–dusk. Free. MAP P.138–139

Opposite the university on Avinguda Diagonal stands a small palace, originally built for the royal family on their visits to Barcelona, but since 1990 used by the city to show off its applied art collections. Until the Design Centre at Glòries is completed, palace rooms contain separate museums of ceramics, decorative arts, and textiles and clothing, which can be visited on the same ticket (note that all are closed on Mon). The gardens, meanwhile, are a calm oasis, where the "Hercules fountain", an early work by Antoni Gaudí, sits hidden in a bamboo thicket.

MUSEU DE CERÀMICA

Av. Diagonal 686 Ⓜ Palau Reial ☎ 932 563 465, Ⓦ www.museuceramica.bcn.cat. Tues–Sat 10am–6pm, Sun & hols 10am–3pm. €5, first Sun of the month free. MAP P.138–139

Spain's most significant collection of historic ceramics includes typical Moorish-influenced work as well as unusual decorated terracotta panels displaying demons and erotic scenes. Barcelona also has its own ceramics tradition, the most vivid example being the large *azulejo* (tile) panel of 1710 depicting a party centred on the craze of the period – drinking hot chocolate.

MUSEU DE LES ARTS DECORATIVES

Av. Diagonal 686 Ⓜ Palau Reial ☎ 932 563 465, Ⓦ www.dhub-bcn.cat. Tues–Sat 10am–6pm, Sun & hols 10am–3pm. €5, first Sun of the month free. MAP P.138–139

Arranged around the upper gallery of the Palau Reial's former throne room, the Decorative Arts Museum provides a fair old romp from Romanesque art through to contemporary Catalan design. Side rooms showcase the various periods, with displays of highly polished Baroque cabinets, Art Deco glassware and *modernista* furniture. The second half of the gallery traces the development of industrial design from the 1930s to the present day, which is actually an excuse to showcase an extraordinary range of Catalan *disseny* (design), from chairs to espresso machines, lighting to sink taps.

MUSEU TEXTIL I D'INDUMENTÀRIA

Av. Diagonal 686 Ⓜ Palau Reial ☎ 932 563 465, Ⓦ www.dhub-bcn.cat. Tues–Sat 10am–6pm, Sun & hols 10am–3pm. €5, first Sun of the month free. MAP P.138–139

In "Dressing the body", the city's extensive textile and clothing collections are put to work to explain how clothes have modified body image through the ages. It's basically a history of fashion and design from the sixteenth century onwards, from court gowns to Parisian silk stockings by way of 1930s cocktail dresses and contemporary haute couture.

PAVELLONS GÜELL

Av. de Pedralbes 7 Ⓜ Palau Reial ☏ 933 177 652, Ⓦ www.rutadelmodernisme.com. Tours Mon, Fri, Sat & Sun at 10.15am & 12.15pm in English, plus 11.15am & 1.15pm in Spanish/Catalan. €6. MAP P.138-139

As an early test of his capabilities, Antoni Gaudí was asked by his patron, Eusebi Güell, to rework the entrance, gatehouse and stables of the Güell summer residence. The resultant brick and tile buildings are frothy, whimsical affairs, though it's the gateway that's the most famous element. An extraordinary winged dragon of twisted iron snarls at the passers-by, its razor-toothed jaws spread wide in a fearsome roar. During the week you can't go any further than the gate, but guided visits show you the grounds and Gaudí's innovative stables, now used as a library by the university's historical architecture department.

SARRIÀ

FGC Sarrià, or bus #64 from Pl. Universitat or Pedralbes. MAP P.138-139

The Sarrià district was once an independent small town and still looks the part, with a narrow, traffic-free main street – c/Major de Sarrià – a handful of pretty Old Town squares and restored churches, and a handsome market, housed in a *modernista* red-brick building of 1911.

MONESTIR DE PEDRALBES

Biaxada del Monestir Ⓜ Palau Reial and 20min walk, or FGC Reina Elisenda and 10min walk, or bus #64 from Pl. Universitat ☏ 932 563 434, Ⓦ www.museuhistoria.bcn .cat. Tues-Sat 10am-2pm (April-Sept until 5pm), Sun 10am-8pm, hols 10am-3pm. €7. MAP P.138-139

Founded in 1326 for the nuns of the Order of St Clare, this is in effect an entire monastic village set within medieval walls on the outskirts of the city. The cloisters in particular are the finest in Barcelona, built on three levels and adorned by the slenderest of columns. Side rooms and chambers give a clear impression of medieval convent life, and also display a selection of the monastery's treasures, while the adjacent church contains the carved marble tomb of the convent's founder, Elisenda de Montcada, wife of King Jaume II.

MONESTIR DE PEDRALBES

Shopping

L'ILLA

Av. Diagonal 555–559 Ⓜ Maria Cristina
Ⓦ www.lilla.com. Mon–Sat 10am–9.30pm.
MAP P.138–139

The landmark uptown
shopping mall is stuffed full of
designer fashion, plus Camper
(shoes), FNAC (music, film and
books), Sfera (cosmetics),
Decathlon (sports), El Corte
Inglés (department store),
Caprabo (supermarket), food
hall and much more.

You can get here by metro
(Maria Cristina) or tram (from
Pl. de Francesc Macià), or on
the **Tomb Bus shopping line
service**, which visits other
uptown stores as well on a
circular route from Plaça de
Catalunya (departures every
6–8min; tickets available on
board).

Restaurants and tapas bars

BAR TOMÁS

C/Major de Sarrià 49, FGC Sarrià ☎ 932 031
077. Mon, Tues & Thurs–Sun 8am–10pm;
closed Aug. MAP P.138–139

The best *patatas bravas* in
Barcelona? Everyone will
point you here, to this
utterly unassuming, white-
Formica-table bar in
the suburbs (which is a 12min
train ride from Plaça de
Catalunya FGC station) for a
taste of their unrivalled spicy
fried potatoes with garlic mayo
and salsa picante. It's not all
they serve, but it might as
well be.

They fry noon to 3pm and
6pm to closing, so if it's *patatas
bravas* you want, be sure to
take a note of the hours.

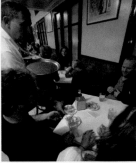

BAR TOMÁS

BAR TURÓ

C/del Tenor Viñas 1, FGC Muntaner
☎ 932 006 953. Mon–Sat 9am–midnight, Sun
9am–4.30pm. MAP P.138–139

A reliable place for tapas, fresh
pasta and home-made pizzas
(€9–10), right by Turó Parc. It's
a modern bar with big
windows that overlook a
year-round street *terrassa*, and
the food is pretty good value
for uptown.

CAN PUNYETES

C/Marià Cubí 189, FGC Muntaner ☎ 932 009
159, Ⓦ www.canpunyetes.com. Daily 1–4pm &
8pm–midnight. MAP P.138–139

Traditional grillhouse-tavern –
well, since 1981, anyway – that
offers diners a taste of older
times. Simple salads and tapas,
open grills turning out *botifarra*
(sausage), lamb chops, chicken
and pork – accompanied by
grilled country bread, white
beans and char-grilled potato
halves. It's cheap (almost
everything under €10) and
locals love it.

CASA FERNANDEZ

C/Santaló 46, FGC Muntaner ☎ 932 019 308,
Ⓦ www.casafernandez.com. Daily
1pm–12.30am. MAP P.138–139

The long kitchen hours are a
boon for the bar-crawlers in
this neck of the woods. It's a
contemporary place featuring

market cuisine, though they are specialists in – of all things – fried eggs, either served straight with chips or with Catalan sausage, garlic prawns or other variations. Most dishes are in the range of €6 to €15.

Bars

ELEPHANT

Pg. dels Til.lers ⓜ Palau Reial ☎ 933 340 258, ⓦ www.elephantbcn.com. Thurs–Sat 11pm–4am. MAP P.138–139

A gorgeous designer bar for gorgeous designer people. There's dancing, but mostly there's preening, in a series of fabulously appointed interior spaces and ornamental, Oriental-style gardens.

GIMLET

C/Santaló 46, FGC Muntaner ☎ 932 015 306. Daily 7pm–3am. MAP P.138–139

This favoured cocktail joint is especially popular in summertime, when the streetside tables offer a great vantage point for watching the party unfold. There are also two or three other late-opening bars on the same stretch.

UNIVERSAL

C/Marià Cubí 182, FGC Muntaner ☎ 932 013 596, ⓦ www.universalbcn.com. Mon–Sat 11pm–3.30am (Fri & Sat until 4.30am). MAP P.138–139

A classic designer music bar that's been part of the Barcelona style scene since 1985. Sounds range from house to back-to-the-80s, but be warned: drinks are fairly pricey and they operate a strict door policy, so if your face doesn't fit you might not get in.

Clubs

BIKINI

C/Deu i Mata 105 ⓜ Les Corts ☎ 933 220 800, ⓦ www.bikinibcn.com. Wed–Sun midnight–5am; closed Aug. MAP P.138–139

This traditional landmark of Barcelona nightlife (behind the L'Illa shopping centre) offers a regular diet of great indie, rock, roots and world gigs followed by club sounds, from house to Brazilian, according to the night. Admission usually €15–25, though some big-name gigs up to €40.

SALA BECOOL

Pl. Joan Llongueras 5 ⓜ Hospital Clinic ☎ 933 620 413, ⓦ www.salabecool.com. MAP P.138–139

Thumping uptown club venue for local and national rock, indie and electro/techno bands and DJs. Gigs usually Thursday to Saturday nights at around 10pm, followed by DJ sessions from midnight or 1am, with admission for either running from €10 to €20, depending on who's appearing. They also sponsor Friday-night acoustic nights at the next-door Irish bar *Dublin* (music Fri at 11pm, free admission, bar open daily until 3am).

Tibidabo and Parc de Collserola

The views from the heights of Tibidabo (550m), the peak that signals the northwestern boundary of the city, are legendary. On a clear day you can see across to the Pyrenees and out to sea even as far as Mallorca. However, while many make the tram and funicular ride up to Tibidabo's amusement park, few realize that beyond stretches the Parc de Collserola, an area of peaks, wooded river valleys and hiking paths – one of Barcelona's best-kept secrets. You can walk into the park from Tibidabo, but it's actually better to start from the park's information centre, across to the east above Vallvidrera, where hiking-trail leaflets are available. Meanwhile, families won't want to miss CosmoCaixa, the city's excellent science museum, which can easily be seen on the way to or from Tibidabo.

PARC D'ATRACCIONS

Pl. del Tibidabo ☎ 932 117 942, Ⓦ www
.tibidabo.es. Days and hours vary, but basically
June–Sept Wed–Sun, rest of the year Sat, Sun
& hols only, closed Jan & Feb. Park open from
noon until 7–11pm depending on season.
Skywalk ticket €11, full admission €25, plus
family/discount tickets. MAP P.145

Barcelona's self-styled "magic mountain" amusement park takes full advantage of its hillside location to offer jaw-dropping perspectives over the city. Some of the most famous rides (like the aeroplane – spinning since 1928 – and the carousel) are grouped under the discounted "Skywalk" ticket. Summer weekends finish with parades, concerts and a noisy *correfoc*, a theatrical fireworks display.

VIEW OVER THE PARC D'ATRACCIONS

Tibidabo and Parc de Collserola

ACCOMMODATION	
Gran Hotel La Florida	1

BAR	
Mirablau	1

SAGRAT COR

Elevator operates daily 10am–2pm
& 3–7pm. €1.50. MAP P.145

Next to Tibidabo's amusement park climb the shining steps of the Templo Expiatorio de España – otherwise known as the Sagrat Cor (Sacred Heart). This is topped by a huge statue of Christ, and inside the church an elevator climbs to a viewing platform from where the city, surrounding hills and shimmering sea glisten in the distance.

Getting to Tibidabo

Reaching the heights of Tibidabo takes up to an hour, all told, from the city centre. First, take the FGC train (line 7) from Plaça de Catalunya station to **Avinguda Tibidabo** (the last stop), where you cross the road to the tram/bus shelter (the Bus Turístic stops here too). The **Tramvia Blau**, an antique tram service (mid-June to mid-Sept daily 10am–8pm; rest of year weekends & hols, plus Christmas and Easter weeks 10am–6pm; departures every 15–30min; €4.50 return) then runs you up the hill to Plaça Doctor Andreu; out of season there's a bus service instead during the week. Here, you change to the **Funicular del Tibidabo**, with connections every 15min to Tibidabo at the top (operates when the Parc d'Atraccions is open; €4 return, fare reimbursed with park admission). Alternatively, the **Tibibus** runs direct to Tibidabo from Plaça de Catalunya, outside El Corte Inglés (from 10.30am every day that the park is open; €2.60, reimbursed with park admission).

TORRE DE COLLSEROLA

Carretera de Vallvidrera al Tibidabo
☎ 932 117 942, ⓦ www.torredecollserola.com.
June–Sept Wed–Sun 11am–2.30pm &
3.30–8pm, rest of the year weekends & hols
only 11am–2.30pm & 3.30–7pm, closed Jan &
Feb. €5. MAP P.145

Follow the road from the
Tibidabo car park and it's
only a few minutes' walk
to Norman Foster's soaring
communications tower, built
for the 1992 Olympics. This
features a glass elevator that
whisks you up ten floors
(115m) for extensive views –
70km, they claim, on a good
day. Note that there's a combo
ticket for the tower available at
the Tibidabo amusement park.

PARC DE COLLSEROLA

Centre d'Informació, FGC Baixada de
Vallvidrera (on the Sabadell or Terrassa line
from Pl. de Catalunya; 15min) ☎ 932 803
552, ⓦ www.parccollserola.net.
Daily 10am–3pm. MAP P.145

Given a half-decent day, local
bikers, hikers and outdoor
enthusiasts all make a beeline
for the city's ring of wooded

TORRE DE COLLSEROLA

hills beyond Tibidabo. The
park information centre lies in
oak and pinewoods, an easy
ten-minute walk up through
the trees from the FGC
Baixada de Vallvidrera train
station. There's a bar-restaurant
here with an outdoor terrace,
plus an exhibition on the
park's history, flora and fauna,
while the staff hand out
English-language leaflets
detailing the various
park walks. Some of the
well-marked paths – like the
oak-forest walk – soon gain
height for marvellous views
over the tree canopy, while
others descend through the
valley bottoms to springs and
shaded picnic areas. Perhaps
the nicest short walk from
the information centre is to
the **Font de la Budellera** (1hr
15min return), a landscaped
spring deep in the woods. If
you follow the signs instead
from the *font* to the Torre de
Collserola (another 20min),
you can return to Barcelona on
the funicular from the nearby
suburban village of **Vallvidrera**
(daily 6am–midnight; every
6–10min), which connects
to Peu del Funicular, an FGC
train station on the line from
Plaça de Catalunya.

MUSEU-CASA VERDAGUER

Villa Joana, Carretera de l'Església 4 ☎ 932
047 805, ⓦ www.museuhistoria.bcn.cat.
Sat, Sun & hols 10am–2pm. Free. MAP P.145

If you're up at the park at the
weekend, it's worth having a
quick look inside the country
house that sits just below the
Collserola information centre.
Jacint Verdaguer (1845–1902),
the Catalan Renaissance poet,
lived here briefly before his
death, and the house has been
preserved as an example of
well-to-do nineteenth-century
Catalan life.

COSMOCAIXA

C/Teodor Roviralta 47–51 ☎ 932 126 050,
ⓦ www.cosmocaixa.com. Tues–Sun
10am–8pm. €3, under-7s and first Sun of
the month free, children's activities €2,
planetarium €2. MAP P.145

A dramatic refurbishment in
2005 turned the city's science
museum into a must-see
attraction, certainly if you've got
children in tow – it's an easy
place to spend a couple of hours
and can break the journey on
your way to or from Tibidabo.
Partly housed in a converted
modernista hospice, the
museum retains the original
building but has added a
light-filled public concourse and
a huge underground extension
with four subterranean levels,
where hands-on experiments
and displays investigate life, the
universe and everything, "from
bacteria to Shakespeare". The
two big draws are the hundred
tonnes of "sliced rock" in the
Geological Wall and, best of all,
the Bosc Inundat – nothing less
than a thousand square metres
of real Amazonian rainforest,
complete with croc-filled
mangroves, anacondas and
giant catfish. Other levels of
the museum are devoted to

children's and family activities,
which tend to be held at
weekends and during school
holidays – pick up a schedule
when you arrive. There are
also daily shows in the
planetarium (in Spanish and
Catalan only), a great gift
shop and a café-restaurant
with outdoor seating.

The easiest way to reach
CosmoCaixa is by FGC train
from Plaça de Catalunya to
Avinguda del Tibidabo station,
and then walk up the avenue,
turning left just before the ring
road (10min) – or the Tramvia
Blau or Bus Turístic can drop
you close by.

Bar

MIRABLAU

Pl. del Dr. Andreu, Av. Tibidabo ☎ 934
185 879. Daily 11am–5am. MAP P.145
Unbelievable city views
from a chic bar near the
Tibidabo funicular that fills
to bursting at times. By day,
a great place for coffee and
views, by night a rich-kid
disco-tunes stomping
ground.

Montserrat

The mountain of Montserrat, with its rock crags, vast monastery and hermitage caves, stands just 40km northwest of Barcelona. It's the most popular day-trip from the city, reached in around ninety minutes by train and then cable car or rack railway for a thrilling ride up to the monastery. Once there, you can visit the basilica and monastery buildings and complete your day with a walk around the woods and crags, using the two funicular railways that depart from the complex. There are cafés and restaurants at the monastery, but they are relatively pricey and none too inspiring – you may wish to take a picnic instead.

AERI DE MONTSERRAT

Montserrat Aeri ☎ 938 350 005, ⓦ www .aeridemontserrat.com. Departures every 15min, daily 9.30am–2pm & 2.30–7pm.
MAP P.150

For the cable-car service, get off the train from Barcelona at Montserrat Aeri station (52min). You may have to wait in line fifteen minutes or so, but then it's only a five-minute swoop up the sheer mountainside to a terrace just below the monastery – probably the most exhilarating ride in Catalunya. Returning to Barcelona, the line R5 trains depart hourly from Montserrat Aeri (from 9.37am).

CREMALLERA DE MONTSERRAT

Monistrol de Montserrat ☎ 902 312 020, ⓦ www.cremalleirademontserrat.com. Departures every hour, daily 8.48am–5.38/7.38pm (later services at weekends April–Oct, plus daily July–Sept).
MAP P.150

The alternative approach to the monastery is by the Montserrat rack railway, which departs from Monistrol de Montserrat station (the next stop after Montserrat Aeri, another 4min), and takes twenty minutes to complete the climb. The original rack railway on Montserrat ran between 1892 and 1957, and this modern replacement recreates the

Getting to Montserrat

To reach the Montserrat cable-car/rack-railway stations, take the **FGC train** (line R5, direction Manresa), which leaves daily from **Plaça d'Espanya** (Ⓜ Espanya) at hourly intervals from 8.36am. All fare options are detailed at **Plaça d'Espanya**, including return through-tickets from Barcelona (around €20) either for the train/cable car or train/rack railway. There are also two combination tickets available: the **Trans Montserrat** (€25), which includes all transport services, including unlimited use of the mountain funiculars, and the audiovisual show; and the **Tot Montserrat** (€40), which includes the same, plus monastery museum and a cafeteria lunch. Both tickets are also available at the Plaça de Catalunya tourist office.

majestic engineering that allows the train to climb 550m in 4km. Returning to Barcelona, the line R5 trains depart hourly from Monistrol de Montserrat (from 9.33am).

MONESTIR DE MONTSERRAT

Visitor centre ☎ 938 777 701, Ⓦ www .montserratvisita.com. Daily 9am–5.45pm (Sat, Sun & July–Sept until 6.45pm). Walking maps and accommodation advice available. MAP P.158

Legends hang easily upon the monastery of Montserrat. Fifty years after the birth of Christ, St Peter is said to have deposited an image of the Virgin (known as La Moreneta), carved by St Luke, in one of the mountain caves. The icon was lost in the early eighth century after being hidden during the Moorish invasion, but reappeared in 880, accompanied by the customary visions and celestial music. A chapel was built to house it, and in 976 this was superseded by a Benedictine monastery, set at an altitude of nearly 1000m. Miracles abounded and the Virgin of Montserrat soon became the chief cult image of Catalunya and a pilgrimage centre second in Spain only to Santiago de Compostela – the main pilgrimages to

Montserrat take place on April 27 and September 8.

The monastery's various outbuildings – including hotel, post office, souvenir shop and bar – fan out around an open square, and there are extraordinary mountain views from the terrace. The best restaurant is inside the *Hotel Abat Cisneros* (meals around €40), though the finest views are from the cliff-edge *Restaurant de Montserrat* (around €25) – the self-service cafeteria, one floor up, is where you eat with the all-inclusive *Tot Montserrat* ticket.

MONASTERY BUILDING AT MONTSERRAT

ARTWORK IN THE BASÍLICA

BASÍLICA

Basílica daily 7.30am–8pm. Access to La Moreneta 8–10.30am & noon–6.30pm. Free. MAP P.150

Of the religious buildings, only the Renaissance basilica, dating largely from 1560 to 1592, is open to the public. **La Moreneta** stands above the high altar – reached from behind, by way of an entrance to the right of the basilica's main entrance. The approach to this beautiful icon reveals the enormous wealth of the monastery, as you queue along a corridor leading through the back of the basilica's rich side chapels. Signs at head height command "SILENCE" in various languages, but nothing quietens the line which waits to kiss the image's hands and feet.

The best time to be here is when Montserrat's world-famous **boys' choir** sings (Mon–Fri at 1pm & 6.45pm, Sun at noon & 6.45pm; not Sat and not during school holidays at Christmas/New Year and from late June to mid-Aug). The boys belong to the Escolania, a choral school established in the thirteenth century and unchanged in musical style since its foundation.

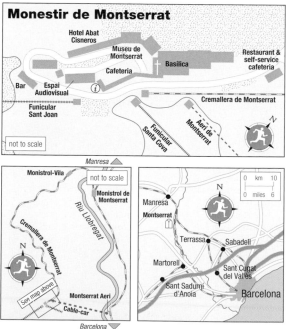

Monestir de Montserrat

Hotel Abat Cisneros
Museu de Montserrat
Cafeteria
Basílica
Restaurant & self-service cafeteria
Bar
Espai Audiovisual
Funicular Sant Joan
Cremallera de Montserrat
Aeri de Montserrat
Funicular Santa Cova
not to scale
N

Manresa

Monistrol-Vila
not to scale
Monistrol de Montserrat
Riu Llobregat
Cremallera de Montserrat
See map above
Montserrat Aeri
Cable-car
N

Barcelona

km 10
miles 6
N
Manresa
Montserrat
Terrassa
Sabadell
Martorell
Sant Cugat del Vallès
Sant Sadurní d'Anoia
Barcelona

THE HERMITAGE OF SANT JOAN

MUSEU DE MONTSERRAT

Daily 10am–5.30pm. €6.50. MAP P.150

The monastery museum presents a few archeological finds brought back by travelling monks, together with valuable painting and sculpture dating from the thirteenth century onwards, including works by Old Masters, French Impressionists and Catalan *modernistas*. There's also a collection of Byzantine icons, though other religious items are in surprisingly short supply, as most of the monastery's valuables were carried off by Napoleon's troops who sacked the complex in 1811. For more on the history, and to learn something of the life of a Benedictine community, visit the **Espai Audiovisual** (Mon–Fri 9am–6pm, Sat & Sun 9am–6.45pm; €2), near the information office.

MOUNTAIN WALKS

Funicular departures every 20min, daily 10am–6pm, weekends only Oct–March. Santa Cova €3 return, Sant Joan €7.50 return, combination ticket €8.50.

Following the mountain tracks to the caves and hermitages, you can contemplate Goethe's observation of 1816: "Nowhere but in his own Montserrat will a man find happiness and peace." The going is pretty good on all the tracks and the signposting is clear, but you do need to remember that you are on a mountain. Take water if you're hiking far and keep away from the edges.

Two separate funiculars run from points close to the cable-car station. One drops to the path for **Santa Cova**, a seventeenth-century chapel built where the Moreneta icon is said to have been found. It's an easy walk of less than an hour there and back. The other funicular rises steeply to the hermitage of **Sant Joan**, from where it's a tougher 45 minutes' walk to the **Sant Jeroni** hermitage, and another 15 minutes to the Sant Jeroni summit at 1236m. Several other walks are also possible from the Sant Joan funicular, perhaps the nicest being the 45-minute circuit around the ridge that leads all the way back down to the monastery.

Sitges

The seaside town of Sitges, 36km south of Barcelona, is definitely the highlight of the local coast – a great weekend escape for young Barcelonans, who have created a resort very much in their own image. It's also a noted gay holiday destination, with an outrageous annual carnival (February/March) and a summertime nightlife to match. During the heat of the day, though, the tempo drops as everyone hits the beach. Out of season Sitges is delightful: far less crowded, and with a temperate climate that encourages promenade strolls and Old Town exploration.

THE BEACHES

MAP P.153

There are clean sands on either side of the Old Town, though they become extremely crowded in high season. For more space keep walking west from Passeig de la Ribera along Passeig Marítim promenade, past eight interlinked beaches that run a couple of kilometres down the coast as far as the *Hotel Terramar*. Many of the handsome, nineteenth-century seafront mansions were built by successful local merchants (known as "Americanos") who had returned from Cuba and Puerto Rico.

THE OLD TOWN

MAP P.153

The knoll overlooking the town beaches is topped by the landmark Baroque parish church dedicated to Sant Bartolomeu, whose festival is celebrated in the last week of August. The views from the terrace sweep along the coast, while behind in the narrow streets of the Old Town you'll find whitewashed mansions, as well as the town hall and the **Mercat Vell** (Old Market), the latter now an exhibition hall. The pedestrianized shopping street, **Carrer Major**, is the best place for browsing boutiques.

OLD TOWN MANSION

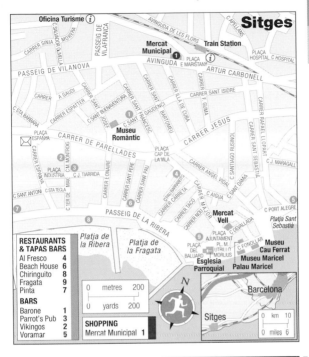

Oficina Turisme (i) Sitges

AVINGUDA DE LES FLORS

CARRER SINIA MORERA CARRER DE SALVADOR OLMELLA

PASSEIG DE VILAFRANCA

Mercat Municipal ❶ Train Station

PLAÇA HOSPITAL C HOSPITAL

PLAÇA E MARISTANY (i)

AVINGUDA ARTUR CARBONELL

PASSEIG DE VILANOVA

CARRER A. GAUDI

C.STA.BARBARA

C.STA BARBARA

CARRER SANT ISIDRE

CARRER SANT GAUDENCI BARTOMEU

CARRER SANT FRANCESC

CARRER ILLA DE CUBA

CARRER F. GUMA

CARRER ESPALTER CARRER SANT JOSEP CARRER SANT BENAVENTURA CARRER SANT

CARRER SANT GUMA

CARRER JESUS CARRER RAFAEL LLOPART

CARRER SANT SEBASTIA

CARRER SANTIAGO RUSINOL

CARRER SANT DAMIA

C.J. MARAGALL

Museu Romàntic ❶

CARRER DE PARELLADES PLAÇA CAP DE LA VILA

CARRER ANGEL. VIDAL

PLAÇA ESPANYA ✉

C SANT BENET

CARRER ESPANYA PLAÇA INDUSTRIA ❷ C.M. MONTROIG C.J. TIARRIDA

CARRER SANT PERE CARRER SANT PAU C/EN BARRANQUET CARRER CARRETA

CARRER AIGUA CARRER TACO C PORT ALEGRE ❺

C 1ER DE MAIG C STA TECLA

CARRER E ONAIRE

CARRER NOU Mercat Vell Platja Sant Sebastia

C SANT ANTONI

PASSEIG DE LA RIBERA CARRER MAJOR ❻ C.D'AVALLADA ❾

❼

❽

PLAÇA AJUNTAMENT

PLAÇA DEL BALUARD PL. M. I MORLIUS LITRILIO C FONOLLAR Museu Cau Ferrat

RESTAURANTS & TAPAS BARS	
Al Fresco	4
Beach House	6
Chiringuito	8
Fragata	9
Pinta	7
BARS	
Barone	1
Parrot's Pub	3
Vikingos	2
Voramar	5

Platja de la Ribera Platja de la Fragata

Esglesia Parroquial Museu Maricel Palau Maricel

0 metres 200
0 yards 200

N

SHOPPING
Mercat Municipal 1

Barcelona

Sitges

0 km 10
0 miles 6

CAU FERRAT, MARICEL AND ROMÀNTIC MUSEUMS

Tues-Sat 9.30am–2pm & 3.30–6.30pm (July–Sept afternoons 4–7pm), Sun 10am–3pm. €3.50 each, or €6.50 combined ticket. MAP P.153

Three museums showcase the town's artistic heritage, not least **Museu Cau Ferrat** (c/Fonollar), the former house of *modernista* artist Santiago Rusiñol (1861–1931). Next door, the **Museu Maricel** contains minor art works, ceramics and sculpture, while in July and August (usually two evenings a week) the main part of the mansion itself is open for guided tours and concerts. Meanwhile, occupying a stately bourgeois house of 1793, the **Museu Romàntic** (c/Sant Gaudenci 1) shows the lifestyle of a rich Sitges family in the nineteenth century (guided tours every hour).

Shopping

MERCAT MUNICIPAL

Av. Artur Carbonell ☎ 938 940 466.
Mon–Thurs 8am–2pm, Fri & Sat 8am–2pm &
5.30–8.30pm. MAP P.153

The town market is a great
place to put together a picnic of
cured meats, olives, cheese,
fresh bread and fruit.

Restaurants and tapas bars

AL FRESCO

Café, c/Major 33 ☎ 938 113 307, daily
10am–11pm. Restaurant, c/Pau Barrabeitg 4
☎ 938 940 600, ⓦ alfrescorestaurante.es.
Tues–Sat 8.30pm–1am. MAP P.153

The café is open for breakfast
and light meals, while an
associated restaurant (around
the corner and down the steps)
serves fancier Catalan cuisine
(monkfish on white beans,
gnocchi with wild mushrooms),
with meals for €25–35.

BEACH HOUSE

C/Sant Pau 34 ☎ 938 949 029, ⓦ www
.beachhousesitges.com. Easter–Oct, daily
4pm–2am. MAP P.153

Aussie owners have created a
highly relaxed restaurant,
offering a changing *table d'hôte*

BEACH PROMENADE

dinner menu (€25) of the best
Asian-Med fusion food, from
Thai fishcakes to barbecued
tuna. It's a cocktail joint, too
(with "happy hour" from
4–8pm), while the open-air
terrace adds a touch of
seaside romance.

CHIRINGUITO

Pg. de la Ribera ☎ 938 947 596. Daily
10am–10pm, reduced hours in winter. MAP P.153

With a prime position on the
prom, this claims to be Spain's
oldest beach bar, serving grilled
sardines, fried baby squid and
calamari, sandwiches and tapas
at reasonable prices (€5–15).

Sitges information

Trains to Sitges leave Passeig de Gràcia or Barcelona Sants stations
every twenty minutes, more frequently at peak times (destination
Vilanova/St Vicenç), and it's a thirty- to forty-minute ride depending on
the service. The main Oficina Turisme (c/Sínia Morera 1, behind Oasis
shopping centre ☎ 938 109 340, ⓦ www.sitgestour.cat; mid-June to
mid-Sept daily 9am–8pm; mid-Sept to mid-June Mon–Fri 9am–2pm &
4–6.30pm) is five minutes' walk from the train station. Note that Monday
isn't the best day to come, as the museums and many restaurants are
closed. As well as Carnival, Sitges is known for its celebrated annual sci-fi,
horror and fantasy fest, the Festival Internacional de Cinema (ⓦ www
.sitgesfilmfestival.com) every October.

The gay scene and Carnival

The Sitges gay scene is frenetic and ever-changing, but the bulk of the nightlife is centred on Plaça de l'Industria. Summer, of course, sees one long nonstop party, but Carnival time (Feb/March) is also notoriously riotous, with a full programme of parades, masked balls, concerts and beach parties. Highlights are Sunday night's Debauchery Parade and Tuesday's Extermination Parade, in which exquisitely dressed drag queens twirl lacy parasols, while bar doors stand wide open and the celebrations go on till dawn. The other big bash is Gay Pride Sitges (ⓦwww .gaypridesitges.com), a weekend of events plus street parade every July.

FRAGATA

Pg. de la Ribera 1 ☎ 938 941 086, ⓦwww .restaurantefragata.com. Daily 1–4pm & 8–11pm. MAP P.153

Typical of the new wave of classy seafood places in town, where catch-of-the-day choices like grilled scallops or wild sea bass cost €17 to €28.

PINTA

Pg. de la Ribera 58–59 ☎ 938 947 871. Daily 1–4pm & 8pm–midnight. MAP P.153

Every restaurant along the front does a paella with a promenade view, but this is better than most, with an enormous fish and seafood menu and a shady terrace. The lunchtime *menú del dia* (not available weekends) is a bargain, or eat *à la carte* for around €35.

Bars

BARONE

C/Sant Gaudenci 17 ☎ 938 942 279. Daily 9pm–2am. MAP P.153

Definitely not a style bar, but an old tavern that's a real slice of Sitges nonetheless. It's nowhere near the sea, so there's more of a down-to-earth local crowd.

PARROT'S PUB

Pl. de l'Industria ☎ 938 947 881. Daily 9pm–2am. MAP P.153

The stalwart of the gay bar scene in Sitges, with front-row seats on all the action.

VIKINGOS

C/Marqués de Montroig 7–9 ☎ 938 949 687, ⓦ www.lsvikingos.com. Daily 11am–1am (Fri & Sat until 2am). MAP P.153

Long-standing party-zone bar with an enormous air-conditioned interior and streetside terrace. This and the similar *Montroig* next door serve drinks, snacks and meals from morning until night to a really mixed crowd.

VORAMAR

C/Port Alegre 55 ☎ 938 944 404. Daily 6pm–2am. MAP P.153

Charismatic seafront bar, away from the main crowds, just right for an ice-cold beer or sundowner cocktail.

PARROT'S PUB

Accommodation

Finding a hotel vacancy in Barcelona at any time of year can be very difficult, so it's best to book in advance. The absolute cheapest rooms in a simple family-run *hostal* or *pension*, sharing a bathroom, cost around €50 (singles from €30), though if you want private facilities €70–80 a night is more realistic. Otherwise, there's a fair amount of choice around the €100 mark, while up to €200 gets you the run of decent hotels in most city areas. For Barcelona's most fashionable hotels count on €250–400 a night, while dorm beds in youth hotels go for €20 to €30 depending on the season. There is also a seven-percent tax (IVA) added to all accommodation bills (though it's sometimes included in the quoted price).

Breakfast isn't usually included, unless specifically stated in the reviews. Credit cards are accepted almost everywhere (though American Express isn't always). There's a lot of street noise in Barcelona, so bring earplugs if you're at all concerned.

You can reserve accommodation online with the city tourist board (ⓦwww.hotelsbcn.com) or make same-day bookings in person only at their tourist offices (ⓦwww.barcelonaturisme .com) at Plaça de Catalunya, the airport and elsewhere. For reliable apartment rental with a UK-based agency there's Barcelona Apartment Rentals (ⓦwww.barcelonaapartment rentals.co.uk), while My Favourite Things (ⓦwww.myft.net) has an eye for offbeat rooms and apartments in private houses.

Along the Ramblas

HOSTAL BENIDORM > Ramblas 37 ⓜ Drassanes ☏ 933 022 054, ⓦ www .hostalbenidorm.com. MAP P.35, POCKET MAP C13. Refurbished *pension* that offers real value for money, hence the tribes of young tourists. Rooms available for one to five people, and a balcony with a Ramblas view if you're lucky (and prepared to pay a bit more). From €75

HOTEL 1898 > Ramblas 109 ⓜ Catalunya ☏ 935 529 552, ⓦ www .hotel1898.com. MAP P.35, POCKET MAP C11. The former HQ of the Philippines Tobacco Company got an eye-popping boutique refit, adding four grades of rooms (the standard is "Classic") in deep red, green or black, plus sumptuous suites and dramatic public areas, including neocolonial lobby-lounge bar, heated rooftop pool and glam spa facilities. **Special rates from €160, otherwise from €250**

HOTEL EUROSTARS RAMBLAS BOQUERIA > Ramblas 91–93 ⓜ Liceu ☏ 933 435 461, ⓦ www .eurostarshotels.com. MAP P.35, POCKET MAP C12. Snappy little boutique rooms in a small three-star hotel right outside the Boqueria market. There's not much space, but all you need is on the doorstep, and the soundproofing is good so you get a street view without the racket. **From €85, weekends from €105**

HOTEL ORIENTE > Ramblas 45 ⓜ Liceu ☎ 933 022 558, ⓦ www.husa .es. MAP P.35, POCKET MAP C13. For somewhere on the Ramblas that's traditional but not too pricey, this historic three-star is your best bet – nineteenth-century style in the grand public rooms and tastefully updated bedrooms, some with Ramblas views (though the quieter ones face inwards). **From €85**

HOTEL RIVOLI RAMBLAS > Ramblas 128 ⓜ Catalunya ☎ 934 817 676, ⓦ www.hotelriviliramblas .com. MAP P.35, POCKET MAP D11. The elegant rooms in this four-star hotel are imaginatively furnished (Art Deco to contemporary), and all come with spacious bathrooms, while the front ones have floor-to-ceiling windows and classic Ramblas views. There's a lovely rooftop terrace and bar. **Special rates from €99, otherwise from €150**

Barri Gòtic

HOTEL EL JARDÍ > Pl. Sant Josep Oriol 1 ⓜ Liceu ☎ 933 015 900, ⓦ www.hoteljardi-barcelona.com. MAP P.44–45, POCKET MAP D12. Location is all – overlooking the charming Plaça del Pi – and though rooms can seem a bit bare and plain, some look directly onto the square. You can have breakfast at the hotel, though the *Bar del Pi* below is nicer. **From €85, terrace or balcony from €95**

HOTEL RACÓ DEL PI > c/del Pi 7 ⓜ Liceu ☎ 933 426 190, ⓦ www .h10hotels.com. MAP P.44–45, POCKET MAP D12. A stylish three-star hotel in a great location. Rooms – some with balconies over the street – have wood floors and granite-and-mosaic bathrooms. There's a glass of *cava* on check-in and free coffee and pastries during the day in the bar. **Special rates from €80, otherwise from €125**

ITACA HOSTEL > c/Ripoll 21 ⓜ Jaume I ☎ 933 019 751, ⓦ www.itacahostel .com. MAP P.44–45, POCKET MAP E12. Bright and breezy hostel close to the cathedral offering spacious rooms with balconies. Dorms are mixed, though you can also reserve a private room or apartment (sleeps up to six), and with a capacity of only 30 it feels more house party than hostel. **Dorm beds €15–25, rooms €55–65, apartments €100–150**

NERI HOTEL > c/de Sant Sever 5 ⓜ Liceu/Jaume I ☎ 933 040 655, ⓦ www.hotelneri.com. MAP P.44–45, POCKET MAP D12. A delightful eighteenth-century palace close to the cathedral houses this stunning boutique hotel of just 22 rooms and suites, featuring swags of flowing material, rescued timber and granite-toned bathrooms. Catalan designers have created eye-catching effects, like a tapestry that falls four floors through the central atrium, while a beamed library and stylish roof terrace provides a tranquil escape. Breakfast is served bento-box style, either out in the courtyard in summer or in chef Jordi Ruiz's fine contemporary Mediterranean restaurant. **From €285**

PENSIÓ ALAMAR > c/Comtessa de Sobradiel 1 ⓜ Liceu/Jaume I ☎ 933 025 012, ⓦ www.pensioalamar .com. MAP P.44–45, POCKET MAP D13. If you don't mind sharing a bathroom, this simply furnished *pension* makes a convenient base. There are twelve rooms (including five singles), most with little balconies, and there's a friendly welcome, laundry service and use of a kitchen. No credit cards. **€45**

PENSIÓN MARI-LUZ > c/de la Palau 4, 2° ⓜ Liceu/Jaume I ☎ 933 173 463, ⓦ www.pensionmariluz.com. MAP P.44–45, POCKET MAP D13. This old mansion, on a quiet Barri Gòtic street, offers inexpensive rooms and small dorms, plus a more personal touch than many other places of its kind. It can be a tight squeeze when full, but a dozen slick apartments (ⓦ www.apartmentsunio.com) a few minutes' walk away in the Raval offer more space. **Dorm beds €15–24, rooms €40–60, apartments €75–125**

What's the neighbourhood like?

If you hanker after a **Ramblas** view, you'll pay for the privilege – generally speaking, there are better deals to be had either side of the famous boulevard, often just a minute's walk away. Alongside some classy boutique choices, most of Barcelona's cheapest accommodation is found in the Old Town, principally the **Barri Gòtic** and **El Raval** neighbourhoods, which both still have their rough edges – be careful (without being paranoid) when coming and going after dark. North of Plaça de Catalunya, the **Eixample** – split into Right (**Dreta**) and Left (**Esquerra**) – has some of the city's most fashionable hotels. Those near **Sants** station are convenient for Montjuïc and the metro system, and those further north in **Les Corts** for the Avinguda Diagonal shopping district. For waterfront views look at **Port Vell** at the end of the Ramblas, and at the **Port Olímpic** southeast of the Old Town – while new four- and five-star hotels abound further out on the metro at the **Diagonal Mar** conference and events site. If you prefer neighbourhood living then **Gràcia** is the best base, as you're only ever a short walk away from its excellent bars, restaurants and clubs.

Port Vell and Barceloneta

BONIC BARCELONA > c/Josep
Anselm Clavé 9 Ⓜ Drassanes ☎ 626 053 434, Ⓦ www.bonic-barcelona .com. MAP P.58–59, POCKET MAP C14. This chic and charming "urban guesthouse" is located just a few steps from port and Ramblas, and features Gothic-Moorish decor and gorgeous tiled floors. The rooms are simple, and the three bathrooms are shared, but a maximum of six guests at any one time ensures peace and privacy. Advance reservations essential. €90

HOTEL DUQUESA DE
CARDONA > Pg. de Colom 12 Ⓜ Drassanes/Barceloneta ☎ 932 689 090, Ⓦ www.hduquesadecardona .com. MAP P.58–59, POCKET MAP D14. Step off the busy harbourfront highway into this soothing four-star haven, set in a remodelled sixteenth-century mansion. The rooms are calm and quiet, decorated in earth tones and immaculately appointed. Although not all of the rooms have harbour views, all guests have access to the stylish roof-deck overlooking the harbour. It's great for sundowner drinks, and boasts (if that's the word) probably the city's smallest outdoor pool. Special rates from €80, otherwise from €160

MARINA VIEW B&B > Pg. de Colom
Ⓜ Drassanes ☎ 609 206 493, Ⓦ www .marinaviewbcn.com. MAP P.58–59, POCKET MAP C14. Six classy rooms featuring bold colours, excellent bathrooms and nice touches, from minibars with normal drinks prices to hospitality trays. Breakfast included (served in the room), and advance reservations essential. From €120, harbour views €135

SEA POINT HOSTEL > Pl. del Mar
1–4 Ⓜ Barceloneta ☎ 932 312 045, Ⓦ www.seapointhostel.com. MAP P.58–59, POCKET MAP H8. The budget beachside choice is this neat little hostel with modern en-suite rooms sleeping six or seven people. The attached café looks right out onto the boardwalk. Dorm beds €18–25, includes breakfast

W BARCELONA > Pl. de la Rosa dels
Vents Ⓜ Barceloneta ☎ 932 952 800, Ⓦ www.starwoodhotels.com. MAP P.58–59, POCKET MAP G9. Signature building on the Barceloneta seafront is the stupendously cool, wave-shaped *W Barcelona*. The open-plan designer rooms offer fantastic views through floor-to-ceiling windows, while facilities are first rate, from ipod docks to an infinity pool. There's a hip, resort feel, with direct beach access, a chill-out lobby bar and rooftop lounge, while dining in *Bravo24* is courtesy of hot chef Carles Abellán. Special rates from €235, otherwise from €295

El Raval

BARCELÓ RAVAL > Rambla de Raval 17–21 ⓜ Liceu/Sant Antoni ☎ 933 201 490, ⓦ www.barceloraval .com. MAP P.64–65, POCKET MAP B12. Neighbourhood landmark is this glow-in-the-dark tower whose USP is the 360-degree top-floor terrace with plunge pool and city views. Sophisticated, open-plan rooms have a crisp, space-station-style sheen, plus ipod docks, coffee-makers and other cool comforts, while the slinky lobby "B-lounge" is the place for everything from breakfast to cocktails. From €100

HOSTAL CÈNTRIC > c/Casanova 13 ⓜ Universitat ☎ 934 267 573, ⓦ www .hostalcentric.com. MAP P.64–65, POCKET MAP B10. A good upper-budget choice a couple of minutes' walk from the Raval proper. Most rooms feature wood panelling and plenty of light; cheaper ones on the upper floors (no lift) share bathrooms, while some of the more expensive en-suite ones also have a/c. €65, en suite from €90

HOSTAL GAT RAVAL > c/Joaquín Costa 44, 2° ⓜ Universitat ☎ 934 816 670, ⓦ www.gatrooms.es. MAP P.64–65, POCKET MAP B10. Boutique style on a budget, with each lime-green room broken down to fundamentals – folding chair, wall-mounted TV, and signature back-lit street photograph/ artwork that doubles as a reading light. Only six of the 24 rooms are en suite, but communal facilities are good, and staff are on duty 24/7. €70, en suite €75

HOSTAL GAT XINO > c/Hospital 149–155 ⓜ Sant Antoni ☎ 933 248 833, ⓦ www.gatrooms.es. MAP P.64–65, POCKET MAP A11. Sister hotel to *Gat Raval* – the same style applies but all the rooms are en suite and breakfast is included. Four suites have more space, bigger bathrooms and less street noise (and one has a terrace). €90, suites €110, terrace suite €130

HOSTERIA GRAU > c/Ramelleres 27 ⓜ Catalunya ☎ 933 018 135, ⓦ www .hostalgrau.com. MAP P.64–65, POCKET MAP C10. A really friendly *pension* with attractive, colour-coordinated rooms – superior rooms also have balconies and a touch of modern Catalan style. Six small private apartments in the same building (sleeping two to five, available by the night) offer a bit more independence. From €70, en suites from €90, apartments from €95

HOTEL PENINSULAR > c/de Sant Pau 34 ⓜ Liceu ☎ 933 023 138, ⓦ www .hotelpeninsular.net. MAP P.64–65, POCKET MAP C13. The interesting old building originally belonged to a priestly order, which explains the slightly cell-like rooms. However, there's nothing spartan about the galleried courtyard (around which the rooms are ranged), hung with tumbling houseplants, while breakfast (included) is served in the arcaded dining room. €80

HOTEL SANT AGUSTÍ > Pl. Sant Agustí 3 ⓜ Liceu ☎ 933 181 658, ⓦ www.hotelsa.com. MAP P.64–65, POCKET MAP C12. Barcelona's oldest hotel occupies a former convent, with front balconies overlooking a restored square and church. It's of three-star standard, with the best rooms located in the attic, from where there are rooftop views. Special rates from €90, otherwise from €130

MARKET HOTEL > c/Comte Borrell 68, at Ptge. Sant Antoni Abad ⓜ Sant Antoni ☎ 933 251 205, ⓦ www .markethotel.com.es. MAP P.64–65, POCKET MAP E5. The designer-budget *Market* makes a splash with its part Japanese, part neocolonial look – think jet-black rooms with hardwood floors and boxy wardrobes topped with travel trunks. From €100

MESÓN CASTILLA > C/Valldonzella 5 ⓜ Universitat ☎ 933 182 182, ⓦ www .mesoncastilla.com. MAP P.64–65, POCKET MAP C10. A throwback to 1950s rural Spain, with every inch carved, painted and stencilled, from the grandfather clock in reception to the wardrobes. Large rooms with a/c (some with terraces) feature country-style furniture, and there's a vast rustic dining room (buffet breakfast included) and a lovely tiled rear patio on which to read in the sun. Parking available. €140, terrace room €155

Sant Pere

PENSIÓ 2000 > c/Sant Pere Més Alt
6, 1° Ⓜ Urquinaona ☎ 933 107 466,
Ⓦ www.pensio2000.com.
MAP P.75, POCKET MAP E11. As close
to a traditional family-style B&B as
Barcelona gets – seven rooms in a
welcoming mansion apartment strewn
with books, plants and pictures. A third
person could easily share most rooms
(€20 extra). **€55, en suites €70**

La Ribera

CHIC & BASIC > c/de la Princesa 50
Ⓜ Jaume I ☎ 932 954 652, Ⓦ www
.chicandbasic.com. MAP P.80, POCKET
MAP G13. From the babbling blurb
("it's fresh, it's cool, it's fusion") to the
all-in-white rooms with adjustable mood
lighting, everything is punchily boutique
and in-your-face. Chic, certainly – basic,
not at all, though the concept eschews
room service, mini-bars and tons of staff
at your beck and call. Meals are courtesy
of the attached – also effortlessly cool
– *thewhitebar* restaurant. There's a more
budget *Chic & Basic* on c/Tallers (near
Pl. Universitat, El Raval) and Barri Gòtic
apartments too (details on the website).
From €110, larger rooms from €135

GOTHIC POINT HOSTEL > c/Vigatans
5 Ⓜ Jaume I ☎ 932 312 045, Ⓦ www
.gothicpoint.com. MAP P.80, POCKET
MAP E13. Backpacker heaven, not far
from the Picasso museum. There's a
great roof terrace, and all sorts of tours
available, while each bunk bed gets its
own cabinet and reading light. **Dorm beds
€18–25, includes breakfast**

HOSTAL NUEVO COLÓN > Av.
Marquès de l'Argentera 19, 1°
Ⓜ Barceloneta ☎ 933 195 077,
Ⓦ www.hostalnuevocolon.com.
MAP P.80, POCKET MAP G14. Run by a
friendly family, featuring 32 spacious
rooms painted yellow and kitted out with
directors' chairs and double glazing.
Sunny front rooms all have side views to
Ciutadella park, while França station (for
trains from the airport) is right opposite.
€50, en suites €70

HOTEL BANYS ORIENTALS
> c/de l'Argenteria 37 Ⓜ Jaume I
☎ 932 688 460, Ⓦ www
.hotelbanysorientals.com. MAP P.80,
POCKET MAP E13. Funky boutique hotel
with 43 minimalist rooms, plus some
duplex suites in a nearby building.
Hardwood floors, sharp marble bathrooms
and urban-chic decor – not to mention
bargain prices for this sort of style –
make it a hugely popular choice. The
attached restaurant, *Senyor Parellada*, is
a great find too. **€100, suites €130**

Port Olímpic

HOTEL ARTS BARCELONA >
c/Marina 19–21 Ⓜ Ciutadella-Vila
Olímpica ☎ 932 211 000, Ⓦ www
.ritzcarlton.com/hotels/barcelona.
MAP P.101, POCKET MAP K8. Still the city
benchmark for five-star designer luxury,
service and standards. Effortlessly classy
rooms feature floor-to-ceiling windows
with fabulous views. Stunning duplex
apartments have their own perks (24hr
butler service, personal Mini Cooper),
and dining options range from the terrace
restaurant to Michelin-starred chef
Sergi Arola's contemporary tapas place,
Arola. Seafront gardens encompass an
open-air pool and hot tub, while the
jaw-dropping Six Senses spa occupies the
two top floors. **Special rates from €220,
otherwise from €400**

Dreta de l'Eixample

CENTRIC POINT HOSTEL > Pg. de
Gràcia 33 Ⓜ Passeig de Gràcia ☎ 932
312 045, Ⓦ www.centricpointhostel
.com. MAP P.105, POCKET MAP G3.
The biggest hostel in the city occupies
a refurbished *modernista* building in a
swish midtown location. Private twins,
doubles, triples and quads available, all
with shower room, balcony and views,
while dorms (all en suite) sleep up to
twelve. Excellent facilities (bar, laundry,
free wifi, common room with TV, music
and Wii) include a spectacular roof terrace
with views of the famous boulevard and
its buildings. **Dorm beds €18–25, rooms
€90–120, breakfast included**

HOSTAL L'ANTIC ESPAI > Gran Via de les Corts Catalanes 660 Ⓜ Passeig de Gràcia ☎ 933 041 945, Ⓦ www .lanticespai.com. MAP P.105, POCKET MAP H4. Camp and cosy, this beautifully ornate period piece springs a surprise in every room, from mosaic tile floors to antique pendants, with candles and flowers at every turn. Room 102 has an original glassed-in balcony, and 107 opens onto an internal terrace with a candelabra-topped table. Modern bathrooms and DVD players keep comforts up to date. From €100

HOSTAL GIRONA > c/Girona 24, 1° Ⓜ Urquinaona ☎ 932 650 259, Ⓦ www .hostalgirona.com. MAP P.105, POCKET MAP G10. Delightful family-run *pension* with a wide range of cosy, traditional rooms (some sharing a bathroom, others with a shower or full bath) – the best and biggest have balconies, though you can expect some noise. From €50, full en suites €75

HOSTAL GOYA > c/de Pau Claris 74, 1° Ⓜ Urquinaona ☎ 933 022 565, Ⓦ www.hostalgoya.com. MAP P.105, POCKET MAP E10. Boutique-style *pension* that offers stylishly decorated rooms on two floors of a mansion building. There's a fair range of options (not all are en suite), with the best rooms opening onto a balcony or terrace. Comfortable sitting areas, and free tea and coffee, are available on both floors. **€80, en suites €90, balcony/terrace €105**

HOSTAL D'UXELLES > Gran Via de les Corts Catalanes 688 Ⓜ Girona/Tetuan ☎ 932 652 560, Ⓦ www.hotelduxelles .com. MAP P.105, POCKET MAP J4. Elegant nineteenth-century townhouse rooms feature wrought-iron bedsteads, antique mirrors, typical tiled floors and country-decor bathrooms; some also have balconies and little private patios (it's quietest at the back). Extra beds can be placed in many rooms, while a few rooms are available in another building nearby. €105

HOTEL CONDES DE BARCELONA > Pg. de Gràcia 73–75 Ⓜ Passeig de Gràcia ☎ 934 450 000, Ⓦ www .condesdebarcelona.com. MAP P.105,

POCKET MAP H3. Straddling two sides of c/Mallorca, the *Condes* is fashioned from two former palaces, its rooms all turned out in contemporary style, some with jacuzzi, balcony or private terrace, some with views of Gaudí's La Pedrera. Meanwhile, Michelin-starred Basque chef Martín Berasategui offers fine dining in the hotel's acclaimed *Lasarte* restaurant and a more informal bistro menu in *Loidi*. Special rates from €120, otherwise from €200

HOTEL MAJESTIC > Pg. de Gràcia 68 Ⓜ Passeig de Gràcia ☎ 934 881 717, Ⓦ www.hotelmajestic.es. MAP P.105, POCKET MAP H3. Traditional grande-dame hotel, first opened in 1918, though refitted in contemporary style and muted colours to provide a tranquil city-centre base. The absolute clincher is the rooftop pool and deck, with amazing views over to the Sagrada Família, while the excellent *Drolma* restaurant is a boon. From €200

HOTEL OMM > c/Rosselló 265 Ⓜ Diagonal ☎ 934 454 000, Ⓦ www .hotelomm.es. MAP P.105, POCKET MAP H2. The glam designer experience that is *Omm* means minimalist, open-plan rooms, a studiously chic bar, the Michelin-starred *Moo* restaurant, terrace, pool and Spaciomm "relaxation centre", not to mention fearsomely handsome staff. It's not to everyone's taste – it's probably fair to say that the less annoyed you are by the endless Omm/Moo tagging of services and facilities, the more you'll like the hotel. From €200

THE5ROOMS > c/Pau Claris 72, 1° Ⓜ Urquinaona ☎ 933 427 880, Ⓦ www .thefiverooms.com. MAP P.105, POCKET MAP E10. The owner's impeccable taste and fashion background is evident in gorgeous contemporary-styled B&B rooms that are spacious and light-filled, with original artwork above each bed, exposed brick walls and terrific bathrooms. Breakfast is served whenever you like, drinks are always available, and Jessica is happy to sit down and talk you through her favourite bars, restaurants and galleries. Suites and apartments are also available. €135–165, apartments from €175 for 2 people

Sagrada Família and Glòries

BARCELONA URBANY > Av. Meridiana 97 Ⓜ Clot ☎ 932 458 414, Ⓦ www.barcelonaurbany.com. MAP P.116–117, POCKET MAP M3. Bumper steel-and-glass 400-bed hostel that's a bit off the beaten track, but on handy metro and airport train routes and with amazing views of Torre Agbar. The rooms are like space-shuttle pods – boxy en suites with pull-down beds (sleeping two to eight) – that are just as viable for couples on a budget as backpackers. There's a bar and terrace, plus free gym, jacuzzi and pool entry in the same building. **Dorm beds €12–28, private rooms €50–80, breakfast included**

HOTEL EUROSTARS GAUDÍ > c/Consell de Cent 498–500 Ⓜ Monumental ☎ 932 320 288, Ⓦ www.eurostarshotels.com. MAP P.116–117, POCKET MAP K3. An excellent-value four-star choice within walking distance of the Sagrada Família. The hotel doesn't overdo the Gaudí theme, staff are really helpful and the top-floor suites boast terrace views of the Gaudí church. **Special rates from €70, otherwise from €100, suites from €130**

Esquerra de l'Eixample

ALTERNATIVE CREATIVE YOUTH HOME > Ronda Universitat 17 Ⓜ Universitat/Catalunya ☎ 635 669 021, Ⓦ www.alternative-barcelona.com. MAP P.122–123, POCKET MAP G4. The hostel hangout for an art crowd who love the laid-back vibe, projection lounge, cool music and city-savvy staff. The regular hostel stuff is well designed too, with a walk-in kitchen and a maximum of 24 people spread across three small dorms. **Dorm beds €20–33**

EXPO HOTEL BARCELONA > c/Mallorca 1–23 Ⓜ Sants-Estació ☎ 936 003 020, Ⓦ www.expohotelbarcelona.com. MAP P.122–123, POCKET MAP C3. Bright, spacious rooms at a good-value four-star hotel. Each has a sliding window onto a capacious terrace and the best have views across to Montjuic. **From €80**

GRAN HOTEL TORRE CATALUNYA > Av. Roma 2–4 Ⓜ Sants-Estació ☎ 936 006 999, Ⓦ www.torrecatalunya.com. MAP P.122–123, POCKET MAP C2. The landmark four-star-deluxe hotel outside Sants station features sweeping views from all sides. Breakfast on the 23rd floor is a buzz; there's also a spa with indoor pool, and guests can use the nearby sister *Expo* hotel's outdoor pool. **Special rates from €80, otherwise from €125, superior from €150**

HOTEL INGLATERRA > c/Pelai 14 Ⓜ Universitat ☎ 935 051 100, Ⓦ www.hotel-inglaterra.com. MAP P.122–123, POCKET MAP C10. The boutique little three-star sister to the Dreta's *Hotel Majestic* has harmoniously toned rooms and snazzy bathrooms. Space is at a premium, but some rooms have cute private terraces, others street-side balconies, while best of all is the romantic roof terrace. Guests can also use the *Majestic*'s pool. **From €139**

RESIDENCIA AUSTRALIA > Ronda Universitat 11, 4° Ⓜ Universitat ☎ 933 174 177, Ⓦ www.residenciaustralia.com. MAP P.122–123, POCKET MAP G4. A very welcoming budget *pension*, overseen by Thomas, fount of city knowledge, musician and cheery host. Three of the four rooms have basins and balconies, and share two nice bathrooms; the other is a suite with private bathroom, while just down the street in another building are some more tidy suites with kitchen facilities. **€59, suites €85**

SOMNIO BARCELONA > c/Diputació 251 Ⓜ Passeig de Gràcia ☎ 932 725 308, Ⓦ www.somniohostels.com. MAP P.122–123, POCKET MAP G4. Sisters Lauren and Lee from Chicago bring their passion for Barcelona right into their upscale *pension*, dropping "tips for the day" into your room each morning. Simple but smart rooms with wood-block floors cater for singles, couples and friends (it's especially welcoming for women visitors), and there are two six-bed, single-sex dorms. **Dorm beds €25, singles €43, doubles €77, en suites €86**

Gràcia

HOSTAL HMB > c/Bonavista 21
Ⓜ Diagonal ☎ 933 682 013, Ⓦ www
.hostalhmb.com. MAP P.129, POCKET
MAP H2. Chic little budget *pension* with
a range of rooms, including some family
and friends "suites" sleeping four – a
safe, well-run, value-for-money choice if
you prefer to stay uptown near the Gràcia
nightlife. **From €60, weekends €70,
suites from €85, weekends €110**

HOTEL CASA FUSTER > Pg. de
Gràcia 132 Ⓜ Diagonal ☎ 932 553
000, Ⓦ www.hotelcasafuster.com.
MAP P.129, POCKET MAP H1. *Modernista*
architect Lluís Domènech i Montaner's
magnificent Casa Fuster (1908) is the
backdrop for five-star-deluxe luxury with
service to match. Rooms are in earth
tones, with huge beds, smart bathrooms,
and remote-controlled light and heat,
while public areas make full use of
the architectural heritage – from the
magnificent pillared lobby bar, the *Café
Vienés*, to the panoramic roof terrace
and pool. There's also a contemporary
restaurant, *Galaxó*, plus fitness centre,
sauna and 24hr room service. **From €200**

Les Corts

GRAN HOTEL PRINCESA SOFIA >
Pl. Pius XII 4 Ⓜ Maria Cristina ☎ 935
081 000, Ⓦ www.princesasofia.com.
MAP P.130, 132. A classic – one of the
first five-star hotels in town thirty years
ago – and well placed for shoppers, with
wide-ranging city views from the upper
floors. It still exudes old-school charm
(the concierges know everything) though
the warm-toned rooms, massages and
treatments in the Aqua Diagonal Wellness
Centre, pool (with retractable roof) and
superior club rooms and lounges offer
a more contemporary experience – the
Barcelona football team stays and
eats here before every home match. An
immense buffet breakfast is served in
the *Contraste* restaurant – which also
features an attractive patio for dining in
the summer. **From €140, club rooms
from €210**

Montjuïc

HOTEL MIRAMAR > Pl. Carlos
Ibañez 3 Ⓜ Paral.lel and Funicular de
Montjuïc ☎ 932 811 600, Ⓦ www
.hotelmiramarbarcelona.com. MAP P.92,
POCKET MAP E7. The remodelled *Miramar*
has 75 stylish rooms with sweeping views
over the city. From the architecture books
in the lounge to the terrace jacuzzis,
you're in designer heaven, augmented
by a stunning pool and tranquil gardens.
**Online advance bookings from €135,
otherwise from €250**

Tibidabo

GRAN HOTEL LA FLORIDA > Ctra.
Vallvidrera a Tibidabo 83–93, 7km from
the centre ☎ 932 593 000 Ⓦ www
.hotellaflorida.com. MAP P.145. This
five-star place on Tibidabo mountain
recreates the glory days of the 1950s,
when *La Florida* was at the centre of
Barcelona high society. Its terraces and
pools have amazing views, while some of
the seventy rooms and suites have private
gardens or terraces and jacuzzis. There's
also a spa, restaurant, poolside bar and
shuttle-bus service to town. **Online
advance bookings from €150, otherwise
from €300**

Horta

**ALBERG MARE DE DÉU DE
MONTSERRAT** > Pg. de la Mare
de Déu del Coll 41–51 Ⓜ Vallcarca
☎ 932 105 151, reservations on
☎ 934 838 363, Ⓦ www.xanascat.cat.
MAP P.130. This popular hostel is set
in a converted mansion with gardens,
terrace and great city views, with dorms
sleeping six, eight or twelve. It's a long
way from the centre (though it's close
to Parc Güell) – from the metro, follow
Av. República d'Argentina, c/Viaducte
de Vallcarca and then the signs, while
buses (#28 from Pl. de Catalunya, plus
night buses) stop just across the street.
Reception open 8am–3pm & 4.30–11pm;
main door closes at midnight, but opens
every 30min thereafter. **Dorms €18–26,
includes breakfast**

ESSENTIALS

Arrival

In most cases, you can be off the plane, train or bus and in your central Barcelona hotel room within the hour. Note that Ryanair flights (and some others) to Barcelona are actually to Girona (90km north) or Reus (110km south), and though there are reliable connecting bus and train services this means up to a 90-minute journey from either airport to Barcelona city centre.

By air

Barcelona's airport (☎ 902 404 704, Ⓦ www.aena.es) is 18km southwest of the city. A **taxi** to the centre costs up to €25, including the airport surcharge (plus other surcharges for travel after 9pm, at weekends or for luggage in the boot). Far cheaper is the **airport train** (6.08am–11.38pm; journey time 19min; €3; info on ☎ 902 240 202), which runs every thirty minutes to Barcelona Sants station (see "By train") and then continues on to Passeig de Gràcia (best stop for Eixample, Plaça de Catalunya and the Ramblas) and Estació de França (for La Ribera). It departs from Terminal T2, and there's a free shuttle bus to the station from T1 which takes around ten minutes. City travel passes and the Barcelona Card (available at the airport) are valid on the airport train.

Alternatively, the **Aerobús** service (Mon–Sat 6.05am–1.05am; €5, €9 return, departures every 5–10min; Ⓦ www.aerobusbcn.es) from T1 and T2 stops in the city at Plaça d'Espanya, Plaça Universitat, Plaça de Catalunya, Passeig de Gràcia and Barcelona Sants (travel time approx. 30min). Aerobus departures back to the airport leave from in front of El Corte Inglés in Plaça de Catalunya.

By train

The national rail service is operated by RENFE (☎ 902 240 202, Ⓦ www.renfe.es). The city's main station is **Barcelona Sants**, 3km west of the centre, with a metro station (Ⓜ Sants Estació) that links directly to the Ramblas (Ⓜ Liceu), Plaça de Catalunya and Passeig de Gràcia. The high-speed AVE line between Barcelona and Madrid has cut the fastest journey between the cities to under three hours. These services also arrive at and depart from Barcelona Sants, though a second high-speed station for the city is planned (probably not until 2013).

Some Spanish intercity services and international trains also stop at **Estació de França**, 1km east of the Ramblas and close to Ⓜ Barceloneta.

Regional and local commuter train services are operated by Ferrocarrils de la Generalitat de Catalunya, or **FGC** (☎ 932 051 515, Ⓦ www.fgc.es), with stations at **Plaça de Catalunya**, at the top of the Ramblas (for trains from coastal towns north of the city); **Plaça d'Espanya** (for Montserrat); and **Passeig de Gràcia** (Catalunya provincial destinations).

By bus

The main bus terminal is the **Estació del Nord** (☎ 902 260 606, Ⓦ www.barcelonanord.com; Ⓜ Arc de Triomf) on c/Ali-Bei, three blocks north of Parc de la Ciutadella. Various companies operate services across Catalunya, Spain and Europe from here – it's a good idea to reserve a ticket in advance on long-distance routes (a day before at the station is usually fine, or buy online). Some intercity and international services also make a stop at the bus terminal behind Barcelona Sants station. Either way, you're only a short metro ride from the city centre.

Getting around

Barcelona has an excellent integrated transport system which comprises the metro, buses, trams and local trains, plus a network of funiculars and cable cars. The local transport authority has a useful website (ⓦ www.tmb.net, English-language version available) with full timetable and ticket information, while a city transport map and information is posted at major bus stops and all metro and tram stations.

Tickets and travel passes

On all the city's public transport (including night buses and funiculars), you can buy a **single ticket** every time you ride (€1.40), but it's much cheaper to buy a **targeta** – a discount ticket card. They are available at metro, train and tram stations, but not on the buses.

Best general ticket deal is the T-10 ("tay day-oo" in Catalan) *targeta* (€7.95), valid for ten separate journeys, with changes between methods of transport allowed within 75 minutes. This card (also available at newsagents' kiosks) can be used by more than one person at a time – simply validate it the same number of times as there are people travelling.

Other useful (single-person) *targetes* include the T-Dia (1 day's unlimited travel; €6), and there are also multi-day combos up to the 5-Dies (5 days; €24.10). Prices given are for passes valid as far as the Zone 1 city limits, which in practice is everywhere you're likely to want to go except Montserrat and Sitges. For trips to these and other out-of-town destinations, buy a specific ticket.

The metro

The quickest way of getting around Barcelona is by **metro**, which currently runs on six main lines. A few stations on a new line, L9, are also now open – on its completion, by 2014, this will be the longest underground line in Europe (almost 50km) and will run between the airport, city centre and high-speed Sagrera train station.

There's a limited network of stations in the Old Town, but you can take the metro directly to the Ramblas (Catalunya, Liceu or Drassanes), and to the edge of the Barri Gòtic, El Raval and La Ribera.

Metro entrances are marked with a red diamond sign with an "M". Its **hours of operation** are Monday to Thursday, plus Sunday and public holidays 5am to midnight; Friday 5am to 2am; Saturday and the day before a public holiday, 24hr service. The system is safe, but many of the train carriages are heavily graffitied, and buskers and beggars are common.

Trams

The **tram** system (ⓦ www.trambcn .com) runs on six lines, with departures every eight to twenty minutes throughout the day from 5am to midnight. Lines **T1, T2 and T3** depart from Plaça Francesc Macià and run along the uptown part of Avinguda Diagonal to suburban destinations in the northwest – useful tourist stops are at L'Illa shopping and the Maria Cristina and Palau Reial metro stations. **Line T4** operates from Ciutadella-Vila Olímpica (where there's also a metro station) and runs up past the zoo and TNC (the National Theatre) to Glòries, before running down the lower part of Avinguda Diagonal to Diagonal Mar and the Fòrum site. You're unlikely to use the more suburban lines T5 and T6.

Buses

Most **buses** operate daily, roughly from 4am or 5am until 10.30pm, though some lines stop earlier and some run on until after midnight. Night bus services fill in the gaps on all the main routes, with services every twenty to sixty minutes from around 10pm to 4am. Many bus routes (including all night buses) stop in or near Plaça de Catalunya, but the full route is marked at each bus stop, along with a timetable.

Trains

The FGC **commuter train line** has its main stations at Plaça de Catalunya and Plaça d'Espanya, used when going to Sarrià, Vallvidrera, Tibidabo and Montserrat. The national rail service, RENFE, runs all the other services out of Barcelona, with local lines designated as **Rodiales/ Cercanías**. The hub is Barcelona Sants station, with services also passing through Plaça de Catalunya (heading north) and Passeig de Gràcia (south). Arrive in plenty of time to buy a ticket, as queues are often horrendous, though for most regional destinations you can use the automatic vending machines instead.

Funiculars and cable cars

As well as the regular city options, Barcelona also has some fun transport trips and historic survivors. A few **funicular railways** are still widely used, particularly up to Montjuïc and Tibidabo, while summer and year-round weekend visits to Tibidabo also combine a funicular trip with a ride on the clanking antique tram, the **Tramvia Blau**. Best of all, though, are the two **cable car** (telefèric) rides: from Barceloneta across the harbour to Montjuïc, and then from the top station of the Montjuïc funicular right the way up to the castle.

Taxis

There are taxi ranks outside major train and metro stations, in main squares, near large hotels and at places along the main avenues. To call a taxi in advance (few of the operators speak English, and you'll be charged an extra €3 or €4), try: Barna Taxis ☎ 933 577 755; Radio Taxi ☎ 933 033 033; Servi-Taxi ☎ 933 300 300; or Taxi Amic ☎ 934 208 088.

A fun way to get around the Old Town, port area and beaches is by **Trixi** (ⓦ www.trixi.com), a kind of love-bug-style bicycle-rickshaw. They tout for business between 11am and 8pm near the Columbus statue at the bottom of the Ramblas, and outside La Seu cathedral in the Barri Gòtic, though you can also flag them down if one cruises by. Fares are fixed (from €6 for 15min, tours also available) and the trixistas are an amiable, multilingual bunch for the most part.

Cycling and bike rental

The city council is investing heavily in cycle lanes and bike schemes, notably the **Bicing** pick-up and drop-off scheme (ⓦ www.bicing.cat), which is touted as Barcelona's new public transport system. You'll see the red bikes and bike stations all over the city, but Bicing is not aimed at tourists, rather at locals who are encouraged to use the bikes for short trips (users can register online or at the **Oficina de la Bicicleta**, Pl. Carles Pi i Sunyer 8–10, Barri Gòtic, between c/Canuda and c/Duran i Bas).

There are plenty of **bike rental** outfits more geared to tourist requirements. Rental costs around €20 a day with companies all over town, including Un Coxte Menys (ⓦ www.bicicletabarcelona.com) and Biciclot (ⓦ www.bikinginbarcelona.net).

Currently there are around 200km of **cycle paths** throughout the city, with plans to double the network in the future. Not all locals have yet to embrace the bike, and some cycle paths are still ignored by cars or clogged with pedestrians, indignantly reluctant to give way to two-wheelers. But, on the whole, cycling around Barcelona is not the completely hairy experience it was just a few years ago, while you can always get **off-road** in the Parc de Collserola, where there are waymarked trails through the woods and hills.

City tours

The number of available tours is bewildering, and you can see the sights on anything from a Segway to a hot-air balloon. A good place to start is the official Barcelona Turisme website (ⓦwww.barcelonaturisme .com), which has a dedicated tours section offering online sales and discounts.

Highest profile are the two tour-bus operators with daily board-at-will, open-top services (1 day €22, 2 days €29), which drop you outside every attraction in the city. The choice is between **Barcelona City Tour** (ⓦwww.barcelonatours.es) or the **Bus Turístic** (ⓦwww.barcelona turisme.com), with frequent departures from Plaça de Catalunya and many other stops – tickets are available on board.

Advance booking is advised (at Pl. de Catalunya tourist office) for **Barcelona Walking Tours** two-hour historical Barri Gòtic tour (daily all year, in English at 10am; €12.50). There are also "Picasso", "Modernisme"

and "Gourmet" walking tours on selected days.

The guides at **My Favourite Things** (ⓦwww.myft.net) reveal Barcelona in a new light, particularly on the signature tour "My Favourite Fusion", which gives an insider's view of the city. Tours (in English, flexible departures) cost from €26 per person and last around four hours, and there's always time for diversions, workshop visits and café stops. Altogether more idiosyncratic is **Follow the Baldie** (contact through website, ⓦwww.followthebaldie.com), with whom you can variously tour anarchist Barcelona, track tarantulas near Sitges or stagger from bar to tavern in rural Catalunya.

Bike tours now infest the city, with follow the leader cycle packs careering through the Old Town alleys. There are flyers and bike outfits everywhere and you'll pay around €25 for a guided 3hr tour.

At any time of year, the sparkling harbour waters invite a cruise and **Las Golondrinas** (ⓘ934 423 106, ⓦwww.lasgolondrinas.com) daily sightseeing boats depart (at least hourly June–Sept, less frequently Oct–May) from the quayside opposite the Columbus statue, at the bottom of the Ramblas (ⓜDrassanes). Two separate services visit either the port (35min; €6.50), or port and local coast (1hr 30min; €13.50).

There are also afternoon catamaran trips around the port with **Catamaran Orsom** (ⓦwww.barcelona-orsom.com; Easter week & June–Sept daily, May & Oct daily except Tues & Thurs; €12.50) plus summer evening jazz cruises (daily June–Aug; €15).

Emergency numbers

Call ⓘ112 for emergency ambulance, police and fire services; for the national police service call ⓘ091.

Directory A–Z

Addresses

The main address abbreviations are Av. (for Avinguda, avenue), c/ (Carrer, street), Pg. (Passeig, boulevard/ street), Bxda. (Baixada, alley), Ptge. (Passatge, passage) and Pl. (Plaça, square). The address "c/Picasso 2, 4°" means: Picasso street, number two, fourth floor.

Crime

Take all the usual precautions and be on guard when on public transport or on the crowded Ramblas and the medieval streets to either side. Easiest place to report a crime is the Gùardia Urbana (municipal police) station at Ramblas 43, opposite Pl. Reial (Ⓜ Liceu; ☎ 932 562 430, Ⓦ www.bcn.cat/guardiaurbana; 24hr, English spoken). For a police report for your insurance go to c/Nou de la Rambla 80, El Raval (Ⓜ Paral.lel ☎ 933 062 300).

Electricity

The electricity supply is 220v and plugs come with two round pins – bring an adapter (and transformer) to use UK and US cell phone chargers etc.

Embassies and consulates

Australia, Pl. Gala Placidia 1–3, Gràcia, Ⓜ Diagonal/FGC Gràcia ☎ 934 909 013, Ⓦ www.emb australia.es; Britain, Av. Diagonal 477, Eixample, Ⓜ Hospital Clinic ☎ 933 666 200, Ⓦ www.ukinspain .com; Canada, Pl. de Catalunya 9, Eixample, Ⓜ Catalunya ☎ 934 127 236, Ⓦ www.canadainternational .gc.ca; Republic of Ireland, Gran Via Carles III 94, Les Corts, Ⓜ Maria Cristina/Les Corts ☎ 934 915 021; New Zealand, Trav. de Gràcia 64, Gràcia, FGC Gràcia, ☎ 932 090 399, Ⓦ www.nzembassy.com; USA, Pg. de la Reina Elisenda 23, Sarrià, FGC Reina Elisenda, ☎ 932 802 227, Ⓦ www.embusa.es.

Gay and lesbian travellers

Epicentre of the gay scene is the so-called Gaixample, an area of a few blocks near the university in the Esquerra de l'Eixample. The annual pride march is on the nearest Saturday to June 28. General listings magazine *Guia del Ocio* can put you on the right track for bars and clubs, though there's also a good free magazine and blog called *Nois* (Ⓦ www.revistanois.com). For other information, contact the lesbian and gay city telephone hotline on ☎ 900 601 601 (daily 6–10pm only).

Health

The following central hospitals have 24hr accident and emergency services: Centre Perecamps, Av. Drassanes 13–15, El Raval, Ⓜ Drassanes ☎ 934 410 600; Hospital Clinic i Provincial, c/Villaroel 170, Eixample, Ⓜ Hospital Clinic ☎ 932 275 400; Hospital del Mar, Pg. Marítim 25–29, Vila Olímpica, Ⓜ Ciutadella-Vila Olímpica ☎ 932 483 000.

Usual pharmacy hours are 9am to 1pm and 4 to 8pm. At least one in each neighbourhood is open 24hr (and marked as such).

Lost property

Anything recovered by police, or left on public transport, is sent to the Oficina de Troballes (municipal lost property office) at Pl. Carles Pi Sunyer 8–10, Barri Gòtic Ⓜ Jaume I/Catalunya (Mon–Fri 9am–2pm; ☎ 010). You could also try the transport office at Ⓜ Universitat.

Money

Spain's currency is the euro (€), with notes issued in denominations of 5, 10, 20, 50, 100, 200 and 500 euros, and coins in denominations of 1, 2, 5, 10, 20 and 50 cents, and 1 and 2 euros. Normal banking hours are Monday to Friday from 8.30am to 2pm, and there are out-of-hours exchange offices down the Ramblas, as well as at the airport, Barcelona Sants station and the Pl. de Catalunya tourist office. ATMs are available all over the city, and you can usually withdraw up to €200 a day.

Museums and passes

Many museums and galleries offer free admission on the first or last Sunday of the month, and most museums are free on the saints' days of February 12, April 23 and September 24, plus May 18 (international museum day). The useful Barcelona Card (2 days €27, 3 days €33, 4 days €37.50 or 5 days €44; ⓦwww .barcelonaturisme.com) offers free public transport, plus museum and attraction discounts. The Articket (€22; valid six months; ⓦwww .articketbcn.org) covers free admission into seven major art galleries, while the *Ruta del Modernisme* (€12; valid one year; ⓦwww.rutadel modernisme.com) is an excellent English-language guidebook and discount-voucher package that covers 115 *modernista* buildings, plus other benefits.

Opening hours

Basic working hours are Monday to Saturday 9.30 or 10am to 1.30pm and 4.30 to 8 or 9pm, though many offices and shops don't open on Saturday afternoons. Local cafés, bars and markets open from around 7am, while shopping centres, major stores and large supermarkets tend to open all day from 10am to 9pm, with some even open on Sunday. Museums and galleries often have restricted Sunday and public holiday hours, while on Mondays most are closed all day.

Phones

Public telephones accept coins, credit cards and phone cards (the latter available in various denominations in tobacconists, newsagents and post offices). The cheapest way to make an international call is to go to a *locutorio* (phone centre); these are scattered throughout the old city, particularly in the Raval and Ribera. You'll be assigned a cabin to make your calls, and afterwards you pay in cash.

Post

The main post office (Correus) is on Pl. d'Antoni López, at the eastern end of Pg. de Colom, in the Barri Gòtic (Mon–Fri 8.30am–9.30pm, Sat 0.30am–2pm, ⓜBarceloneta/Jaume I). For stamps it's easier to visit a tobacconist (look for the brown-and-yellow *tabac* sign), found on virtually every street.

Public holidays

Official holidays are: Jan 1 (Cap d'Any, New Year's Day); Jan 6 (Epifanía, Epiphany); Good Friday & Easter Monday; May 1 (Dia del Treball, May Day/Labour Day); June 24 (Dia de Sant Joan, St John's Day); Aug 15 (L'Assumpció, Assumption of the Virgin); Sept 11 (Diada Nacional, Catalan National Day); Sept 24 (Festa de la Mercè, Our Lady of Mercy, Barcelona's patron saint); Oct 12 (Día de la Hispanidad, Spanish National Day); Nov 1 (Tots Sants, All Saints' Day); Dec 6 (Dia de la Constitució, Constitution Day); Dec 8 (La Imaculada, Immaculate Conception); Dec 25 (Nadal, Christmas Day); Dec 26 (Sant Esteve, St Stephen's Day).

Tickets

You can buy concert, sporting and exhibition tickets with a credit card using the ServiCaixa (ⓦwww.servicaixa.com) automatic dispensing machines in branches of La Caixa savings bank. You can also order tickets online through ServiCaixa or TelEntrada (ⓦwww.telentrada.com). For advance tickets for all city council (Ajuntament) sponsored concerts visit the Palau de la Virreina, Ramblas 99.

Time

Barcelona is one hour ahead of the UK, six hours ahead of New York and Toronto, nine hours ahead of Los Angeles, nine hours behind Sydney and eleven hours behind Auckland. This applies except for brief periods during the changeovers to and from daylight saving (in Spain the clocks go forward in the last week in March, back again in the last week of Oct).

Tipping

Locals leave only a few cents or round up the change for a coffee or drink, and a euro or two for most meals, though fancier restaurants will expect ten to fifteen percent. Taxi drivers normally get around five percent.

Tourist information

The city's tourist board, Turisme de Barcelona (ⓣ807 117 222 from within Spain, ⓣ932 853 834 from abroad, ⓦwww.barcelonaturisme.com), has its main office in Plaça de Catalunya (daily 9am–9pm; ⓜCatalunya), down the steps in the southeast corner of the square, where there's a tours service and accommodation desk. There's also an office in the Barri Gòtic at Plaça de Sant Jaume, entrance at c/Ciutat 2 (Mon–Fri 9am–8pm, Sat 10am–8pm, Sun & hols 10am–2pm;

ⓜJaume I), and staffed information booths dotted across the city. The city's ⓣ010 telephone enquiries service (Mon–Sat 8am–10pm; some English-speaking staff available) can help with questions about transport, public services and other matters. The city hall (Ajuntament; ⓦwww.bcn.cat) and regional government (Generalitat; ⓦwww.gencat.cat) websites are also mines of information about every aspect of cultural, social and working life in Barcelona. Concerts, exhibitions and festivals are covered in full at the walk-in office of the Institut de Cultura at the Palau de la Virreina, Ramblas 99, ⓜLiceu (ⓣ933 161 000, ⓦwww.bcn.cat/cultura; Mon–Sat 10am–8pm, Sun 11am–3pm). The most useful listings magazine is the Spanish-language *Guia del Ocio* (out every Thursday; ⓦwww.guiadelociobcn.es), available at any newspaper kiosk.

Travellers with disabilities

Barcelona's airport and Aerobús are fully accessible to travellers in wheelchairs. On the metro only lines 1, 2 and 11 are fully accessible, with elevators at major stations (including Pl. de Catalunya, Universitat, Pg. de Gràcia and Sagrada Família) from the street to the platforms. However, all city buses have been adapted for wheelchair use, while the city information line – ⓣ010 – has accessibility information for museums, galleries, hotels, restaurants, museums, bars and stores. Many Old Town attractions have steps, cobbles or other impediments to access.

Water

Water from the tap is safe to drink, but generally doesn't taste very nice. You'll be given bottled mineral water in a bar or restaurant.

Festivals and events

Almost any month you visit Barcelona you'll coincide with a festival, event or holiday. The best are picked out below, but for a full list check out the Ajuntament (city hall) website Ⓦ www.bcn.cat/cultura.

FESTES DE SANTA EULÀLIA

Mid-February Ⓦ www.bcn.cat/santaeulalia
Winter festival around February 12 in honour of the young Barcelona girl who suffered a beastly martyrdom at the hands of the Romans. There are parades, concerts, fireworks and *sardana* dancing.

CARNAVAL/CARNESTOLTES

Week before Lent (Feb or March)
Costumed parades and other carnival events across every city neighbourhood. Sitges, down the coast, has the most outrageous celebrations.

DIA DE SANT JORDI

April 23
St George's Day celebrates Catalunya's patron saint, with hundreds of book and flower stalls down the Ramblas and elsewhere.

PRIMAVERA SOUND

Usually late May
Ⓦ www.primaverasound.com
The city's hottest music festival attracts top names in the rock, indie and electronica world.

SÓNAR

June Ⓦ www.sonar.es
Europe's biggest, most cutting-edge electronic music, multimedia and urban art festival presents three days of brilliant noise and spectacle.

VERBENA/DIA DE SANT JOAN

June 23/24
The "eve" and "day" of St John herald a "night of fire", involving bonfires and fireworks (particularly on Montjuïc) and watching the sun come up on the beach.

FESTIVAL DE BARCELONA GREC

From end June to August
Ⓦ www.barcelonafestival.com
This is the city's main performing arts festival, with many events staged at Montjuïc's Teatre Grec.

FESTES DE LA MERCÈ

End September Ⓦ www.bcn.cat/bam
The city's main festival is celebrated for a week around September 24, with costumed giants, firework displays and human tower competitions.

FESTIVAL INTERNACIONAL DE JAZZ

October/November Ⓦ www.theproject.es
The annual jazz festival attracts big-name solo artists and bands to the clubs, as well as smaller-scale street concerts.

Celebrating Catalan-style

Central to any traditional Barcelona festival is the parade of *gegants*, five-metre-high giants with papier-mâché or fibreglass heads. Also typically Catalan is the *correfoc* ("fire-running"), where drummers, dragons and demons cavort in the streets. Meanwhile, teams of *castellers* – "castle-makers" – pile person upon person to see who can construct the highest tower.

Chronology

c230 BC > Carthaginians found the settlement of "Barcino", probably on the heights of Montjuïc.

218–201 BC > Romans expel Carthaginians from Iberian peninsula in Second Punic War. Roman Barcino is established around today's Barri Gòtic.

304 AD > Santa Eulàlia – the city's patron saint – is martyred by Romans for refusing to renounce Christianity.

c350 AD > Roman city walls are built, as threat of invasion grows.

415 > Visigoths sweep across Spain and establish temporary capital in Barcino (later "Barcelona").

711 > Moorish conquest of Spain. Barcelona eventually forced to surrender (719).

801 > Barcelona retaken by Louis the Pious, son of Charlemagne. Frankish counties of Catalunya become a buffer zone, known as the Spanish Marches.

878 > Guifré el Pelós (Wilfred the Hairy) declared first Count of Barcelona, founding a dynastic line that was to rule until 1410.

985 > Moorish sacking of city. Sant Pau del Camp – the city's oldest surviving church – built after this date.

1137 > Dynastic union of Catalunya and Aragón established.

1213–76 > Reign of Jaume I, "the Conqueror", expansion of empire and beginning of Catalan golden age.

1282–1387 > Barcelona at the centre of an aggressively mercantile Mediterranean empire. Successive rulers construct most of Barcelona's best-known Gothic buildings.

1348 > The Black Death strikes, killing half of Barcelona's population.

1391 > Pogrom against the city's Jewish population.

1410 > Death of Martí el Humà (Martin the Humane), last of Catalan count-kings. Beginning of the end of Catalan influence in the Mediterranean.

1469 > Marriage of Ferdinand of Aragón and Isabel of Castile.

1479 > Ferdinand succeeds to Catalan-Aragón crown, and Catalunya's fortunes decline. Inquisition introduced to Barcelona, leading to forced flight of the Jews.

1493 > Christopher Columbus received in Barcelona after his triumphant return from New World. The shifting of trade routes away from Mediterranean and across Atlantic further impoverishes the city.

1516 > Spanish crown passes to Habsburgs and Madrid is established as capital of Spanish empire.

1640–52 > The uprising known as the "Wars of the Reapers" declares Catalunya an independent republic. Barcelona is besieged and eventually surrenders to the Spanish army.

1714 > After War of Spanish Succession, throne passes to Bourbons. Barcelona subdued on September 11 (now Catalan National Day); Ciutadella fortress built, Catalan language banned and parliament abolished.

1755 > Barceloneta district laid out – gridded layout is an early example of urban planning.

1778 > Steady increase in trade; Barcelona's economy improves.

1814 > After Peninsular War (1808–14), French finally driven out, with Barcelona the last city to fall.

1859 > Old city walls demolished and Eixample district built to accommodate growing population.

1882 > Work begins on Sagrada Família; Antoni Gaudí takes charge two years later.

1888 > Universal Exhibition held at Parc de la Ciutadella. *Modernista* architects start to make their mark.

1893 > First stirrings of anarchist unrest. Liceu opera house bombed.

1901 > Pablo Picasso's first public exhibition held at Els Quatre Gats tavern.

1909 > Setmana Trágica (Tragic Week) of rioting. Many churches destroyed.

1922 > Parc Güell opens to the public.

1926 > Antoni Gaudí is run over by a tram; Barcelona stops en masse for his funeral.

1929 > International Exhibition held at Montjuïc.

1936–39 > Spanish Civil War. Barcelona at the heart of Republican cause, with George Orwell and other volunteers arriving to fight. City eventually falls to Nationalists on January 26, 1939.

1939–75 > Spain under Franco. Generalitat president Lluís Companys executed and Catalan language banned. Emigration encouraged from south to dilute Catalan identity. Franco dies in 1975.

1977 > First democratic Spanish elections for 40 years.

1978–80 > Generalitat re-established and Statute of Autonomy approved. Conservative nationalist government elected.

1992 > Olympics held in Barcelona. Rebuilding projects transform Montjuïc and the waterfront.

1995 > MACBA (contemporary art museum) opens, and signals the regeneration of El Raval district.

2004 > Diagonal Mar hosts Universal Forum of Cultures, heralding the transformation of the Poble Nou district.

2006 > New statute of autonomy agreed with Spain.

2008 > Montjuïc castle symbolically handed over from state to city, to become a peace museum.

2009 > FC Barcelona are European football champions for the third time (and complete the first Spanish "treble" of league title, national cup and European cup)

Catalan

In Barcelona, Catalan (Català) has more or less taken over from Castilian (Castellano) Spanish as the language on street signs and maps. On paper it looks like a cross between French and Spanish and is generally easy to read if you know those two. Few visitors realize how important Catalan is to those who speak it: never commit the error of calling it a dialect. Despite the preponderance of the Catalan language you'll get by perfectly well in Spanish as long as you're aware of the use of Catalan in timetables, on menus, and so on. However you'll generally get a good reception if you at least try communicating in the local language.

Pronunciation

Don't be tempted to use the few rules of Spanish pronunciation you may know – in particular the soft Spanish Z and C don't apply, so unlike in the rest of Spain, the city is not Barthelona but Barcelona, as in English.

a as in hat if stressed, as in alone when unstressed.

e varies, but usually as in get.

i as in police.

ig sounds like the "tch" in the English scratch; lleig (ugly) is pronounced "yeah-tch".

o a round, full sound, when stressed, otherwise like a soft U sound.

u somewhere between the U of put and rule.

ç sounds like an English S; plaça is pronounced "plassa".

c followed by an E or I is soft; otherwise hard.

g followed by E or I is like the "zh" in Zhivago; otherwise hard.

h is always silent.

j as in the French "Jean".

l.l is best pronounced (for foreigners) as a single L sound; but for Catalan speakers it has two distinct L sounds.

ll sounds like an English Y or LY, like the "yuh" sound in million.

n as in English, though before F or V it sometimes sounds like an M.

ny corresponds to the Castilian Ñ.

qu before E or I sounds like K; before A or O, or if the U has an umlaut (Ü), sounds like KWE, as in quit.

r is rolled, but only at the start of a word; at the end it's often silent.

t is pronounced as in English, though sometimes it sounds like a D; as in viatge or dotze.

v at the start of a word sounds like B; in all other positions it's a soft F sound.

w is pronounced like a B/V.

x is like SH or CH in most words, though in some, like exit, it sounds like an X.

z is like the English Z in zoo.

Words and phrases
BASICS

Yes, No, OK	Si, No, Val
Please, Thank you	Si us plau, Gràcies
Hello, Goodbye	Hola, Adéu
Good morning	Bon dia
Good afternoon /night	Bona tarde/nit
See you later	Fins després
Sorry	Ho sento
Excuse me	Perdoni
I (don't) understand	(No) Ho entenc
Do you speak English?	Parleu anglès?
Where? When?	Dónde? Cuando?
What? How much?	Què? Quant?
Here, There	Aquí, Allí/Allá
This, That	Això, Allò
Open, Closed	Obert, Tancat
With, Without	Amb, Sense
Good, Bad	Bo(na), Dolent(a)
Big, Small	Gran, Petit(a)
Cheap, Expensive	Barat(a), Car(a)
I want	Vull (pronounced "vwee")
I'd like	Voldria
Do you know?	Vostès saben?
I don't know	No sé
There is (Is there?)	Hi ha(?)
What's that?	Què és això?
Do you have...?	Té...?
Today, Tomorrow	Avui, Demà

ACCOMMODATION

Do you have a room?	Té alguna habitació?
...with two beds/ double bed	...amb dos llits/ llit per dues persones
...with shower/bath	...amb dutxa/bany
It's for one person (two people)	Per a una persona (dues persones)
For one night (one week)	Per una nit (una setmana)
It's fine, how much is it?	Esta bé, quant és?
Don't you have anything cheaper?	En té de més bon preu?

DIRECTIONS AND TRANSPORT

How do I get to...?	Per anar a...?
Left, Right	A la dreta, A l'esquerra
Straight on	Tot recte
Where is...?	On és...?
...the bus station	...l'estació de autobuses
...the train station	...l'estació
...the nearest bank	...el banc més a prop
...the post office	...l'oficina de correus
...the toilet	...la toaleta
Where does the bus to...leave from?	De on surt el autobús a...?
Is this the train for Barcelona?	Aquest tren va a Barcelona?
I'd like a (return) ticket to...	Voldria un bitllet (d'anar i tornar) a...
What time does it leave (arrive in)?	A quina hora surt (arriba a)?

NUMBERS

1	un(a)
2	dos (dues)
3	tres
4	quatre
5	cinc
6	sis
7	set
8	vuit
9	nou
10	deu
11	onze
12	dotze
13	tretze
14	catorze
15	quinze
16	setze
17	disset
18	divuit
19	dinou
20	vint
21	vint-i-un
30	trenta
40	quaranta
50	cinquanta
60	seixanta
70	setanta
80	vuitanta
90	novanta
100	cent
101	cent un
200	dos-cents (dues-centes)
500	cinc-cents
1000	mil

DAYS OF THE WEEK

Monday	dilluns
Tuesday	dimarts
Wednesday	dimecres
Thursday	dijous
Friday	divendres
Saturday	dissabte
Sunday	diumenge

MONTHS OF THE YEAR

January	Gener
February	Febrer
March	Març
April	Abril
May	Maig
June	Juny
July	Juliol
August	Agost
September	Setembre
October	Octobre
November	Novembre
December	Desembre

Menu reader

BASIC WORDS

Esmorzar	To have breakfast
Dinar	To have lunch
Sopar	To have dinner
Ganivet	Knife
Forquilla	Fork
Cullera	Spoon
Taula	Table
Ampolla	Bottle
Got	Glass
Carta	Menu
Sopa	Soup
Amanida	Salad
Entremesos	Hors d'oeuvres
Truita	Omelette
Entrepà	Sandwich
Torrades	Toast
Tapes	Tapas
Mantega	Butter
Ous	Eggs
Pa	Bread
Olives	Olives
Oli	Oil
Vinagre	Vinegar
Sal	Salt
Pebre	Pepper
Sucre	Sugar
El compte	The bill
Sóc vegetarià/ vegetariana	I'm a vegetarian

COOKING TERMS

Assortit	Assorted
Al forn	Baked
A la brasa	Char-grilled
Fresc	Fresh
Fregit	Fried
A la romana	Fried in batter
All i oli	Garlic mayonnaise
A la plantxa	Grilled
En escabetx	Pickled
Rostit	Roast
Salsa	Sauce
Saltat	Sautéed
Remenat	Scrambled
Del temps	Seasonal
Fumat	Smoked
A l'ast	Spit-roasted
Al vapor	Steamed
Guisat	Stewed
Farcit	Stuffed

FISH AND SEAFOOD/PEIX I MARISC

Anxoves/Seitons	Anchovies
Calamarsets	Baby squid
Orada	Bream
Cloïses	Clams
Cranc	Crab
Sípia	Cuttlefish
Lluç	Hake
Llagosta	Lobster
Rap	Monkfish
Musclos	Mussels
Pop	Octopus
Gambes	Prawns
Navalles	Razor clams
Salmó	Salmon
Bacallà	Salt cod
Sardines	Sardines
Llobarro	Sea bass
Llenguado	Sole
Calamars	Squid
Peix espasa	Swordfish
Tonyina	Tuna

MEAT AND POULTRY/CARN I AVIRAM

Bou	Beef
Embotits	Charcuterie
Pollastre	Chicken
Xoriço	Chorizo sausage
Pernil serrà	Cured ham
Llonganissa	Cured pork sausage
Costelles	Cutlets/chops
Ànec	Duck
Pernil dolç	Ham
Xai/Be	Lamb
Fetge	Liver
Llom	Loin of pork
Mandonguilles	Meatballs
Porc	Pork
Conill	Rabbit
Salsitxes	Sausages
Cargols	Snails
Bistec	Steak
Llengua	Tongue
Vedella	Veal

VEGETABLES/VERDURES I LLEGUMS

Carxofes	Artichokes
Albergínia	Aubergine/eggplant
Faves	Broad/lima beans
Carbassó	Courgette/zucchini
All	Garlic
Mongetes	Haricot beans
Llenties	Lentils
Xampinyons	Mushrooms
Cebes	Onions
Patates	Potatoes
Espinacs	Spinach
Tomàquets	Tomatoes
Bolets	Wild mushrooms

FRUIT/FRUITA

Poma	Apple
Plàtan	Banana
Raïm	Grapes
Meló	Melon
Taronja	Orange
Pera	Pear
Maduixes	Strawberries

DESSERTS/POSTRES

Pastís	Cake
Formatge	Cheese
Flam	Crème caramel
Gelat	Ice cream
Arròs amb llet	Rice pudding
Tarta	Tart
Yogur	Yoghurt

DRINKS

Cervesa	Beer
Vi	Wine
Xampan/cava	Champagne
Cafè amb llet	Large white coffee
Cafè tallat	Small white coffee
Descafeïnat	Decaf
Te	Tea
Xocolata	Drinking chocolate
Granissat	Crushed ice drink
Llet	Milk
Orxata	Tiger nut drink
Aigua	Water
Aigua mineral	Mineral water
Zumo	Juice

CATALAN SPECIALITIES

Amanida Catalana Salad served with sliced meats (sometimes cheese)

Arròs a banda Rice with seafood, the rice served separately

Arròs a la marinera Paella: rice with seafood and saffron

Arròs negre "Black rice", cooked in squid ink

Bacallà a la llauna Salt cod baked with garlic, tomato and paprika

Botifarra (amb mongetes) Grilled Catalan pork sausage (with stewed haricot beans)

Calçots Large char-grilled spring onions

Canelons Cannelloni, baked pasta with ground meat and béchamel sauce

Conill all i oli Rabbit with garlic mayonnaise

Crema Catalana Crème caramel, with caramelized sugar topping

Escalivada Grilled aubergine/eggplant, pepper/capsicum and onion

Espinacs a la Catalana Spinach cooked with raisins and pine nuts

Esqueixada Salad of salt cod with peppers/capsicums, tomatoes, onions and olives

Estofat de vedella Veal stew

Faves a la Catalana Stewed broad beans, with bacon and botifarra

Fideuà Short, thin noodles (the width of vermicelli) served with seafood

Fuet Catalan salami

Llenties guisades Stewed lentils

Mel i mató Curd cheese and honey

Pa amb tomàquet Bread (often grilled), rubbed with tomato, garlic and olive oil

Pollastre al cava Chicken with cava sauce

Pollastre amb gambes Chicken with prawns

Postres de músic Cake of dried fruit and nuts

Salsa Romesco Spicy sauce (with chillis, nuts, tomato and wine), often served with grilled fish

Samfaina Ratatouille-like stew (onions, peppers/capsicum, aubergine/eggplant, tomato), served with salt cod or chicken

Sarsuela Fish and shellfish stew

Sípia amb mandonguilles Cuttlefish with meatballs

Suquet de peix Fish and potato casserole

Xató Mixed salad of olives, salt cod, preserved tuna, anchovies and onions

PUBLISHING INFORMATION

This first edition published January 2011 by **Rough Guides Ltd**

80 Strand, London WC2R 0RL

11, Community Centre, Panchsheel Park, New Delhi 110017, India

Distributed by the Penguin Group

Penguin Books Ltd, 80 Strand, London WC2R 0RL

Penguin Group (USA) 375 Hudson Street, NY 10014, USA

Penguin Group (Australia) 250 Camberwell Road, Camberwell, Victoria 3124, Australia

Penguin Group (NZ) 67 Apollo Drive, Mairangi Bay, Auckland 1310, New Zealand

Rough Guides is represented in Canada by

Tourmaline Editions Inc., 662 King Street West, Suite 304, Toronto, Ontario, M5V 1M7

Typeset in Minion and Din to an original design by Henry Iles and Dan May.

Printed and bound in China

© Jules Brown, 2011

Maps © Rough Guides

192pp includes index

A catalogue record for this book is available from the British Library

ISBN 978-1-84836-600-8

The publishers and authors have done their best to ensure the accuracy and currency of all the information in **Pocket Rough Guide Barcelona**, however, they can accept no responsibility for any loss, injury, or inconvenience sustained by any traveller as a result of information or advice contained in the guide.

1 3 5 7 9 8 6 4 2

MIX
Paper from
responsible sources
FSC™ C018179
www.fsc.org

ROUGH GUIDES CREDITS

Text editor: Lara Kavanagh

Layout: Sachin Tanwar

Photography: Roger d'Olivere Mapp, Chris Christoforou, Tim Kavenagh

Cartography: Ed Wright

Picture editor: Nicole Newman

Proofreader: Susannah Wight

Production: Rebecca Short

Cover design: Nicole Newman, Daniel May and Chloë Roberts

THE AUTHORS

Jules Brown first visited Barcelona in 1985. Apart from this book he has also written half a dozen other Rough Guides, and contributed as researcher and editor of many others. But he's beginning to think he's left it too late to play for Huddersfield Town.

HELP US UPDATE

We've gone to a lot of effort to ensure that the first edition of **Pocket Rough Guide Barcelona** is accurate and up-to-date. However, things change – places get "discovered", opening hours are notoriously fickle, restaurants and rooms raise prices or lower standards. If you feel we've got it wrong or left something out, we'd like to know, and if you can remember the address, the price, the hours, the phone number, so much the better.

Please send your comments with the subject line "**Pocket Rough Guide Barcelona Update**" to Ⓔ mail@roughguides.com. We'll credit all contributions and send a copy of the next edition (or any other Rough Guide if you prefer) for the very best emails.

Find more travel information, connect with fellow travellers and book your trip on Ⓦ www .roughguides.com

PHOTO CREDITS

All images © Rough Guides except the following:

Front cover Pinnacle, Sagrada Família Ⓛ Look-Foto/photolibrary

Back cover Museu diArt de Catalunya © Chris Christoforou/Rough Guides

p.25 Bar Inopia © Sergio Espinel/Courtesy of Bar Inopia

p.46 Museu d'Història de Barcelona © Ramon Manent/Corbis

p.112 Casa Calvet © Courtesy of Casa Calvet

p.122 Sculpture in Joan Miró park © Sandro Vannini/Corbis

p.146 Torre de Collserola, Tibidabo © Pere Sanz/iStock

p.148 Montserrat mountain © Shurkva/iStock

p.149 Monastery building, Montserrat © Chris Farrugia/iStock

p.154 Sitges © lillisphotography/iStock

Index

Maps are marked in **bold**.

185

INDEX

OVER 300 DESTINATIONS

Andorra The Pyrenees, Pyrenees & Andorra Map, Spain

Antigua The Caribbean

Argentina Argentina, Argentina Map, Buenos Aires, South America on a Budget

Australia Australia, Australia Map, East Coast Australia, Melbourne, Sydney, Tasmania

Austria Austria, Europe on a Budget, Vienna

Bahamas The Caribbean

Barbados The Caribbean

Belgium Belgium & Luxembourg, Brussels, Brussels Map, Europe on a Budget

Belize Belize, Central America on a Budget, Guatemala & Belize Map

Benin West Africa

Bolivia Bolivia, South America on a Budget

Brazil Brazil, Rio, South America on a Budget

Brunei Malaysia, Singapore & Brunei [1 title], Southeast Asia on a Budget

Bulgaria Bulgaria, Europe on a Budget

Burkina Faso West Africa

Cambodia Cambodia, Southeast Asia on a Budget, Vietnam, Laos & Cambodia Map [1 Map]

Cameroon West Africa

Canada Canada, Toronto, Vancouver

Cape Verde West Africa

Caribbean The Caribbean

Chile Chile, Chile Map, South America on a Budget

China Beijing, China, Hong Kong & Macau, Shanghai

Colombia South America on a Budget

Costa Rica Central America on a Budget, Costa Rica, Costa Rica & Panama Map

Croatia Croatia, Croatia Map, Europe on a Budget

Cuba Cuba, Cuba Map, The Caribbean, Havana

Cyprus Cyprus, Cyprus Map

Czech Republic The Czech Republic, Europe on a Budget, Prague, Prague POCKET, Prague Map

Denmark Copenhagen, Denmark, Europe on a Budget, Scandinavia

Dominican Republic Dominican Republic, The Caribbean

Ecuador Ecuador, South America on a Budget

Egypt Cairo & The Pyramids, Egypt, Egypt Map

El Salvador Central America on a Budget

England Accessible Britain, Britain, Camping, The Cotswolds & Oxford, Devon & Cornwall, Dorset, Hampshire & The Isle of Wight [1 title], England, Europe on a Budget, The Lake District, London, London POCKET, London Map, London Mini Guide, Walks In London & Southeast England, Yorkshire

Estonia The Baltic States, Europe on a Budget

Fiji Fiji

Finland Europe on a Budget, Finland, Scandinavia

France Brittany & Normandy, Corsica, Corsica Map, The Dordogne & the Lot, Europe on a Budget, France, France Map, Languedoc & Roussillon, Paris, Paris POCKET, Paris Map, Paris Mini Guide, Provence & the Côte d'Azur, Pyrenees & Andorra Map

French Guiana South America on a Budget

Gambia The Gambia, West Africa

Germany Berlin, Berlin Map, Europe on a Budget, Germany, Germany Map

Ghana West Africa

Gibraltar Spain

Greece Athens POCKET, Athens Map, Crete, Crete Map, Europe on a Budget, Greece, Greece Map, Greek Islands, Ionian Islands

Guatemala Central America on a Budget, Guatemala, Guatemala & Belize Map

Guinea West Africa

Guinea-Bissau West Africa

Guyana South America on a Budget

Holland see Netherlands

Honduras Central America on a Budget

Hungary Budapest, Europe on a Budget, Hungary

Iceland Iceland, Iceland Map

India Goa, India, India Map, Kerala, Rajasthan, Delhi & Agra [1 title], South India, South India Map

Indonesia Bali & Lombok, Southeast Asia on a Budget

Ireland Dublin Map, Europe on a Budget, Ireland, Ireland Map

Israel Jerusalem

Italy Europe on a Budget, Florence & Siena Map, Florence & the best of Tuscany, Italy, Italy Map, The Italian Lakes, Naples & the Amalfi Coast, Rome, Rome POCKET, Sardinia, Sicily, Sicily Map, Tuscany & Umbria, Tuscany Map, Venice, Venice POCKET, Venice Map

Jamaica Jamaica, The Caribbean

Japan Japan, Tokyo

Jordan Jordan

Kenya Kenya, Kenya Map

Korea Korea, Seoul

Laos Laos, Southeast Asia on a Budget, Vietnam, Laos & Cambodia Map [1 Map]

Latvia The Baltic States, Europe on a Budget

Lesotho South Africa, Lesotho & Swaziland [1 title]

Download or buy from all good bookstores or roughguides.com

Lithuania The Baltic States, Europe on a Budget

Luxembourg Belgium & Luxembourg, Europe on a Budget

Malaysia Malaysia Map, Malaysia, Singapore & Brunei [1 title], Southeast Asia on a Budget

Mali West Africa

Mauritania West Africa

Mexico Baja California, Mexico, Mexico Map, Yucatán, Yucatán Peninsula Map

Monaco France, Provence & the Côte d'Azur

Montenegro Montenegro

Morocco Europe on a Budget, Marrakesh Map, Morocco, Morocco Map,

Nepal Nepal

Netherlands Amsterdam, Amsterdam POCKET, Amsterdam Map, Europe on a Budget, The Netherlands

New Zealand New Zealand, New Zealand Map

Nicaragua Central America on a Budget

Niger West Africa

Nigeria West Africa

Norway Europe on a Budget, Norway, Scandinavia

Panama Central America on a Budget, Costa Rica & Panama Map, Panama

Paraguay South America on a Budget

Peru Peru, Peru Map, South America on a Budget

Philippines The Philippines, Southeast Asia on a Budget,

Poland Europe on a Budget, Poland

Portugal The Algarve Map, Europe on a Budget, Lisbon POCKET, Lisbon Map, Portugal, Portugal Map, Spain & Portugal Map

Puerto Rico The Caribbean, Puerto Rico

Romania Europe on a Budget, Romania

Russia Europe on a Budget, Moscow, St Petersburg

St Lucia The Caribbean

Scotland Accessible Britain, Britain, Camping, Europe on a Budget, Scotland, Scottish Highlands & Islands

Senegal West Africa

Serbia Montenegro, Europe on a Budget

Sierra Leone West Africa

Singapore Malaysia, Singapore & Brunei [1 title], Singapore, Southeast Asia on a Budget

Slovakia Czech & Slovak Republics, Europe on a Budget

Slovenia Europe on a Budget, Slovenia

South Africa Cape Town & the Garden Route, South Africa, Lesotho & Swaziland [1 title], South Africa Map

Spain Andalucía, Andalucía Map, Barcelona, Barcelona POCKET, Barcelona Map, Europe on a Budget, Madrid Map, Mallorca & Menorca, Mallorca Map, The Pyrenees, Pyrenees & Andorra Map, Spain, Spain & Portugal Map

Sri Lanka Sri Lanka, Sri Lanka Map

Suriname South America on a Budget

Swaziland South Africa, Lesotho & Swaziland [1 title]

Sweden Europe on a Budget, Scandinavia, Sweden

Switzerland Europe on a Budget, Switzerland

Taiwan Taiwan

Tanzania Kenya & Northern Tanzania Map, Tanzania, Zanzibar

Thailand Bangkok, Southeast Asia on a Budget, Thailand, Thailand Map, Thailand Beaches & Islands

Togo West Africa

Trinidad & Tobago The Caribbean, Trinidad & Tobago

Tunisia Tunisia, Tunisia Map

Turkey Europe on a Budget, Istanbul, Turkey, Turkey Map

Turks and Caicos Islands The Caribbean

United Arab Emirates Dubai, Dubai & UAE Map

United Kingdom Accessible Britain, Britain, The Cotswolds & Oxford, Devon & Cornwall, England, Europe on a Budget, The Lake District, London, London POCKET, London Map, London Mini Guide, Scotland, Scottish Highlands & Islands, Wales, Walks In London & Southeast England, Yorkshire

USA Boston, California, California Map, Chicago, Colorado, Florida, Florida Map, The Grand Canyon, Hawaii, Las Vegas, Los Angeles Map, Los Angeles and Southern California, Miami & South Florida, New England, New England Map, New Orleans & Cajun Country, New York City, New York City POCKET, New York City Map, New York City Mini Guide, Oregon & Washington, San Francisco, San Francisco Map, Seattle, Southwest USA, USA, Washington DC, Yellowstone & the Grand Tetons National Park, Yosemite National Park

Uruguay South America on a Budget

US Virgin Islands The Caribbean

Venezuela South America on a Budget

Vietnam Southeast Asia on a Budget, Vietnam, Vietnam, Laos & Cambodia Map [1 Map]

Wales Britain, Camping, Europe on a Budget, Wales

World Coverage Clean Breaks, Earthbound, First Time Africa, First Time Around the World, First Time Asia, First Time Europe, First Time Latin America, Great Escapes, Make the Most of Your Time in Britain, Make the Most of Your Time on Earth, Make the Most of Your Time on Earth (compact edition), Travel with Babies & Young Children, Ultimate Adventures

Start your journey at www.roughguides.com